INFORMATION TECHNOLOGY AND EDUCATIONAL MANAGEMENT IN THE KNOWLEDGE SOCIETY

IFIP – The International Federation for Information Processing

IFIP was founded in 1960 under the auspices of UNESCO, following the First World Computer Congress held in Paris the previous year. An umbrella organization for societies working in information processing, IFIP's aim is two-fold: to support information processing within its member countries and to encourage technology transfer to developing nations. As its mission statement clearly states,

> *IFIP's mission is to be the leading, truly international, apolitical organization which encourages and assists in the development, exploitation and application of information technology for the benefit of all people.*

IFIP is a non-profitmaking organization, run almost solely by 2500 volunteers. It operates through a number of technical committees, which organize events and publications. IFIP's events range from an international congress to local seminars, but the most important are:

- The IFIP World Computer Congress, held every second year;
- Open conferences;
- Working conferences.

The flagship event is the IFIP World Computer Congress, at which both invited and contributed papers are presented. Contributed papers are rigorously refereed and the rejection rate is high.

As with the Congress, participation in the open conferences is open to all and papers may be invited or submitted. Again, submitted papers are stringently refereed.

The working conferences are structured differently. They are usually run by a working group and attendance is small and by invitation only. Their purpose is to create an atmosphere conducive to innovation and development. Refereeing is less rigorous and papers are subjected to extensive group discussion.

Publications arising from IFIP events vary. The papers presented at the IFIP World Computer Congress and at open conferences are published as conference proceedings, while the results of the working conferences are often published as collections of selected and edited papers.

Any national society whose primary activity is in information may apply to become a full member of IFIP, although full membership is restricted to one society per country. Full members are entitled to vote at the annual General Assembly, National societies preferring a less committed involvement may apply for associate or corresponding membership. Associate members enjoy the same benefits as full members, but without voting rights. Corresponding members are not represented in IFIP bodies. Affiliated membership is open to non-national societies, and individual and honorary membership schemes are also offered.

INFORMATION TECHNOLOGY AND EDUCATIONAL MANAGEMENT IN THE KNOWLEDGE SOCIETY

IFIP TC3 WG3.7, 6th International Working Conference on Information Technology in Educational Management (ITEM)
July 11–15, 2004, Las Palmas de Gran Canaria, Spain

Edited by

Arthur Tatnall
Victoria University
Australia

Javier Osorio
Campus Universitario de Tafira
Spain

Adrie Visscher
University of Twente
The Netherlands

Springer

Library of Congress Cataloging-in-Publication Data

A C.I.P. Catalogue record for this book is available from the Library of Congress.

Information Technology and Educational Management in the Knowledge Society/ Edited by Arthur Tatnall, Javier Osorio, Adrie Visscher

p.cm. (The International Federation for Information Processing)

ISBN: (HB) 0-387-24044-6 / (eB00K) 0-387-24045-4 Printed on acid-free paper.

Printed in the United States of America.

9 8 7 6 5 4 3 2 1 SPIN 11365372 (HC) / 11365402 (eBook)
springeronline.com

TABLE OF CONTENTS

ITEM Focus Group Reports

Preface

The Gran Canaria (Las Palmas) ITEM conference was a special one as it was exactly ten years since the first ITEM conference (although we did not then use that acronym) was held. In 1994 Ben-Zion Barta and Yaffa Gev from the Ministry of Education in Israel were aware of the growing need to share information, and managed to obtain funding to organize a conference on the utilization of information technology for the administration and management of schools. Scientists, system developers, implementers and others active in this area travelled to Jerusalem where these practitioners and experts from around the globe were brought together for the first time to share their knowledge.

The paper presentations and workshops were so successful that it was decided to organize an ITEM conference every two years. (Yaffa Gev invented the ITEM acronym which stands for Information Technology in Educational Management.) Since Jerusalem, these conferences have been held respectively in Hong Kong (1996), Maine (USA, 1998), Auckland (New Zealand, 2000), and in Helsinki (2002). The next conference will be held in Hamamatsu in Japan in 2006.

Quite a few people who attended the Jerusalem conference are still active in ITEM and also attended the Las Palmas conference. Since 1994 we have also welcomed several new ITEM members, and some delegates attended an ITEM conference in Las Palmas for the first time.

The conferences have engendered a spirit of co-operation amongst people around the world: they have resulted in papers and special issues for scientific journals, obtained research funding, carried out research projects and organized research fellowships. As a group we successfully applied in 1996 for the establishment of IFIP (International Federation for Information Processing) Working Group 3.7 to promote the effective and efficient use of information technology for the management of educational institutions in all respects. (For more information, please refer to http://ifip-item.hkbu.edu.hk). International co-operation and exchange of information on the state of the art of the research, development, and implementation of ITEM will help us to achieve this overall goal.

This book is the result of an international call for papers addressing the challenges faced by the information technology and educational management (ITEM) field in a society where knowledge management is becoming a major issue both in educational and business systems. As a result a number of papers were received. Each paper was peer reviewed by two acknowledged ITEM specialists who provided useful feedback to authors of accepted papers. These papers were presented at an International Working Conference in Grand Canaria, and were subject to discussion and criticism. After the conference a selection was made of papers for inclusion in this book, and the authors were give the opportunity to modify their work according to feedback obtained at the conference. This publication is the end result of this process.

The papers in this book fall broadly into five main categories: School-based educational issues regarding ITEM; case studies regarding ITEM use in schools; issues relating to ITEM in higher education; research, technology and business issues; and reports of the focus group meetings held at the conference.

The first group of papers is concerned with ITEM issues in schools. The first paper by Len Newton questions the adequacies of school ITEM systems in meeting the needs of teachers and pupils in relation to assessment for learning purposes, and suggests further challenges for the design and development of these systems for handling useful assessment information. Newton notes that in addition to administrative data, we need information to inform pedagogical processes including data that will embrace pupils' learning skills. Ian Selwood follows with a paper reporting on the findings of a baseline study on Primary School Teachers' use of ICT for administration and management in England. He notes that even though primary teachers are generally positive about ICT and its ability to support their administrative and management duties, the findings point to low levels of use of ICT for administration and management. Chris O'Mahony then reports on a survey of ICT access, ability and use conducted among 25 schools in England and Wales in 2002/03. The survey results indicated that access to ICT resources was high both at school and at home, and staff reported overall satisfaction with their ICT abilities across core applications, whilst calling for more training in 'advanced' applications. The next paper, by Connie Fulmer, discusses accountability in distance-learning programs in the US. She points out that accountability is a complex process in any organizational learning experience, particularly in distance-learning environments. The paper describes online-accountability innovations used in distance-learning programs and how these online tools help students provide evidence of their readiness for educational-leadership positions. Alex Fung and Jenilyn Ledesma then describe an interactive, web-based, real-time platform for delivery of teaching and learning in Hong Kong when classes were suspended during the SARS outbreak in 2003. Finally in this group of papers, Chris Thorn discusses systemic reform efforts in the US in relation to data-based decision making and decision support systems. He describes the latest generation of collaborative systems that support knowledge exchange and expertise location services and argues that the human capacity to evaluate programs, curricula, and other reform efforts has not kept pace with technological developments.

In the next group of papers several authors describe specific school-based examples of ITEM systems. Greg Baker describes some of the issues involved in developing an integrated information system that contributes to the management of an Australian independent school. He demonstrates that it is possible and feasible to develop an information system that meets both the needs of staff and is customized for the users' requirements. Ronald Bisaso and Adrie Visscher then outline an exploratory study on the usage of computerised school information systems in the administration and management of the biggest secondary schools in Uganda. Omponoye Kereteletse and Ian Selwood next describe a study that evaluated system usage of the computerised information system implemented by the Ministry of Education in Botswana.

University ITEM systems are then the subject of a set of papers. Geoff Sandy and Bill Davey begin by considering issues of data quality for ITEM systems used in higher education decision making. Jacques Bulchand and Jorge Rodríguez then outline the process that the University of Las Palmas de Gran Canaria went through in planning, building and implementing a new ITEM system. In the paper they describe a methodology composed of nine steps that involves the whole university community and not just IS/ICT technicians. In the next paper Bill Davey and Arthur Tatnall argue for university ITEM systems that provide useful information to teaching academics as well as to university administrators, and lament the lack of such system in most universities. Lucía Melián, Víctor Padrón and Tomás Espino next consider issues of quality management in virtual universities.

The next papers cover a wide range of issues relating to research, technology and business issues. To begin, a paper by Mikko Ruohonen looks at knowledge networks for educational management and lessons that might be learned from industry. Toshio Okamoto and Mizue Kayama next propose and discuss functionality required for collaborative learning and introduce a platform for a collaborative learning environment called RAPSODY-EX (REX) that they have developed. A paper from Jose Diaz follows describing a strategic project for an information society in the Spanish Region of Extremadura. An aspect of this project was development of GNU/LinEx and associated Free Software, and the paper elaborates the advantages of this Free Software. In similar vein, Pedro Baquero, Alfredo Santana, Ignacio Zubiria and Manuel Prieto then outline a global solution that covers the ICT infrastructure necessities of an educational community in the Canary Islands. This consists of a basic technological architecture of: Individualized Networks of Schools, the Integrated Broadband Network and the Management System. This study has been framed inside MEDUSA project. In the last paper, Arthur Tatnall explores ITEM as an innovation and argues for research, framed by innovation theory, into why some schools, regions and countries adopt ITEM more fully and in different ways than others.

The final papers report on the discussions that took place in the focus groups that met during the conference. Firstly Arthur Tatnall and Bill Davey describe the discussions of a group that was considering future directions in item research. Connie Fulmer next details the discussions of the second group on issues in the management of distance and lifelong learning.

We hope and trust that these papers will prove interesting and useful to other researchers and to educators with an interest in Information Technology in Educational Management.

Javier Osorio
Adrie Visscher
Arthur Tatnall

Data, Information and Questions of Pupil Progress

Food for Thought, Challenges for ICT

Leonard R. Newton
School of Education, University of Nottingham UK.
Len.Newton@nottingham.ac.uk

Abstract: Developments in management information systems (MIS) have been well suited to the collation, storage and dissemination of summative assessment data and have reached a point where data can now be used for comparative purposes at national, local and individual pupil levels. Trends in assessment in English secondary schools have focused primarily on its use for purposes of monitoring and accountability. Recently, there has been a resurgence in interest in using assessment data formatively to improve teaching and learning: this poses challenges to designers and users of MIS. This paper considers literature in educational assessment, and current trends and rhetoric in assessment practices and purposes, to identify the changing needs of potential users of MIS for learning purposes. The adequacies of MIS in meeting the needs of teachers and pupils in the context of assessment for learning purposes are then considered. From this discussion further challenges for the design and development of MIS for handling useful assessment information are identified.

Key words: Assessment, data, learning.

1 INTRODUCTION AND BACKGROUND

Advances in management information systems (MIS) in recent years now mean that many schools are 'data rich'. In particular, there have been significant developments in MISs to support the administration of schools in the context of increasing school management autonomy. A large-scale study of the use of one MIS in English schools showed that the predominantly used MIS had positive effects in some key aspects of school administration (Visscher et al. 2003). But Visscher et al. also reflected on the dominance of MIS usage for 'clerical' activities rather than strategic uses; they argued for the need to find ways to promote more strategic use of MIS to support policy making (Visscher et al. 2003, p 364). Conceptions of the educational uses of MIS have also begun to embrace their potential use in the classroom, but this is problematic (Newton and Visscher 2003).

The dominance of administrative uses of MIS in English schools is arguably a reflection of developments in information technology and the concomitant raised awareness, in software designers and users, of the potential of these technological advances to fulfil certain administrative functions. But it is also a reflection of contexts in which MISs have evolved where localised management has driven schools to find ways of using ICT to support administration. Therefore developments in MIS software and its use can be viewed as largely needs-led.

In the contemporary context, there is a strong focus on raising educational standards and so it is appropriate to ask what MISs can do to support this endeavour, which, after all, is the core purpose of educational institutions. In the rhetoric of the so-called 'standards debate' it is all too easy to become focused on whole-school data and notions of school performance at the possible expense of recognising that performance data represent the achievements of individual pupils and their teachers. Raising educational standards means raising the attainment of the individual pupils who are the members of classes, cohorts and whole-school pupil populations. For teachers, the contribution that they make to raise educational standards is based upon their work with the individuals and groups of pupils they teach. For this reason a key question in the use of MIS to support teachers' work is whether (and how) the data made available through these systems can be used to support teachers' decisions about teaching and learning, and how MISs might be developed to manage new kinds of useful data. Thus the link between pupil performance data and pedagogy needs to be established by exploring how data can be used *as information* to support the teaching-learning process.

2 DATA, DATA EVERYWHERE…

The approaches to assessment that have been adopted in recent years in English schools have focused primarily on monitoring pupils' attainment in core national curriculum subjects. The outcomes of these assessment practices have provided summative data on pupils' attainment against so-called 'level descriptors' in these subjects. Prior to the inception of the national curriculum in England and Wales, there had been many years' work on projects that had explored and developed the use of assessment information for the purpose of directly supporting learning (Black and

Wiliam, 2003). These developments necessarily placed high value on teachers' knowledge of their pupils' progress and conceptualised aspects of the assessment process as instrumental in fostering pupils' learning. Despite initially embracing the principles of these so-called 'formative' assessment practices and the role of teachers in the assessment process, successive UK governments, in the 1980s and 1990s, allowed these aspects of assessment to fade (Black and Wiliam ibid.). So, for a significant period of time, the assessment agenda in England and Wales has been driven by the need to serve the purposes of monitoring and accountability, rather than the use of assessment for learning purposes. However, recently there has been a resurgence of interest in the role of assessment for learning purposes, especially in middle years education during key stage 3 (ages 11 to 14 years). I will return to this issue later in the discussion.

In English schools, the use of data is seen as providing a powerful means of raising pupil achievement and driving forward the agenda to achieve 'World Class' education. For example, it has been suggested that *'regular enquiry and the use of data to inform teaching and learning'* are key features of school leadership to support high levels of achievement (Specialist Schools Trust 2003a, page 5). Moreover, in the English state school system, the use over many years of statutory Standard Attainment Tests or 'SATs' at the end of key stages of education (at ages 7, 11 and 14 years) means that there is an increasing mass of data on pupil performance. Of course, information technology provides a valuable means of storing and interrogating this information, and communicating it more widely. Notably, developments in technology have led at least one influential educational body in England to articulate a vision of "*Teachers using ICT as an aid to manage pupils' learning, every pupil with an individual education plan, accessible to pupils and parents on line.*" (Technology Colleges Trust, 2000 p31). The availability of individual performance data signals its potential to support a more individualised approach to teaching but the nature of any relationships between performance data and the selection and implementation of learning and teaching approaches need to be examined.

Since the late 1980s successive UK governments have supported the establishment of schools designated with specialist status, including 'Technology College status' where there is an expectation of strong emphases on the use of ICT to support teaching and pupil learning. The achievements of specialist schools have proved to be influential in educational policy. The current UK government has signalled its intention to extend the network of specialist schools in England, albeit in a reformed system (DfES 2003) and ICT figures prominently in these plans. One ambition is that ICT will help schools to develop *'more individualised learning and assessment programmes for every child'* (ibid. p47). This is further evidence of the contemporary focus on individual pupil progress and the role of ICT, and ways need to be found to enable teachers to respond to this drive.

In a recent lecture, the UK Secretary of State for Education and Skills described a data management initiative known 'Pupil Achievement Tracker' or 'PAT' system and its potential to provide individualised and comparative pupil performance data (Specialist Schools Trust, 2003b). This development has become possible since, in England, pupils have been allocated unique reference numbers that allow their progress to be tracked through the education system. It is argued that pupils' performance on national tests at key stage 2 (taken at age 11 years) are strong predictors of their future performance. Thus developments in the management of assessment data in England mean that data is now available at the international, national, school, group and individual levels. With the PAT system, it is envisaged that teachers will be able to use comparative data to identify under-performing pupils and to better tailor their teaching to the needs of individual pupils. However, the question remains of what precisely is the relationship between data and individualised pupil action planning? To indicate to a pupil that they have achieved level 5 in a key stage 3 test and that their target grade should be level 7 tells the pupil nothing of how to reach the target grade.

3 DATA RICH BUT INFORMATION POOR?

Performance data collected from SATs is just one source of data currently available in English secondary schools. There is by no means universal agreement that the SAT system provides a reliable or valid means of assessing pupil progress. Indeed, in 2003, the devolved government in Wales launched a review of testing and league tables to explore whether they should be abandoned in favour of teacher assessment in key stage 2 (age 11 and key stage 3 (age 14). In its final report (Daugherty, 2004) there is a recommendation that tests at the end of key stage 3 should be phased out over time. Nevertheless, national testing using SATs has remained a cornerstone of successive governments' monitoring and accountability measures and there are even proposals to extend testing at age fourteen in England.

Improvements in whole school attainment are predicated upon the achievements and improvements of individual pupils, as revealed through the instruments used for assessment purposes. Taken together, there is now a wealth of data available to schools and teachers on their pupils' current performance and indications of their future potential. There is a genuine sense in which schools can be viewed as data rich. However, data only becomes *information* when it is interpreted for a particular purpose. It is legitimate to ask the question of whether data of particular kinds is universally suited to a range of interpretations. In the context of assessment, it has been argued that summative data may too coarsely grained or ill-timed to support meaningful interpretations for the purposes of guiding individual pupils' learning (Wiliam and Black, 1996).

3.1 On Assessment and Learning

Improving pupils' performance is about developing their knowledge, understanding and skills in a range of subject disciplines. It is about pupils developing their skills as learners and their understandings about how they think and learn. A key question therefore, is how the wealth of available data can be used as information to support teachers (and pupils) in making progress in these areas. The focus of teacher and pupil action needs to be directed towards using information to enlighten and develop the processes of teaching and learning in meaningful ways. In the argument presented here, it is suggested that this link is not currently well made and there is considerable ambiguity in the relationships between data, information and the needs of teachers and learners.

4 KNOWING THAT AND KNOWING HOW

Contemporary ideas about learning have been heavily influenced by constructivist and social constructivist psychology. These perspectives put pupils at the centre in learning situations; thus in structuring learning activities for pupils, a key step is to determine what the pupils already know and understand about the topic to be learned. In constructivist teaching approaches, it is necessary to make learners' prior ideas (and misconceptions) explicit, so that these can be used as the basis for building new understandings that move the learner on. Teachers use a range of strategies to probe and elicit pupils' understanding. These approaches are essentially used for diagnostic purposes in order to help the teacher understand the starting points of pupils in a group and to design learning experiences that will take account of these and address progress. Assessment can itself be viewed as a cyclic process (Wiliam and Black, 1996) within the constructivist paradigm of elicitation, interpretation and action. Feedback to the learner from the interpretation of data needs to 'close the gap' between what is already known and understood, and the desired knowledge and understanding (Wiliam and Black, 1996 p543).

It is interesting to note that the introduction of the national curriculum in England and Wales in the late nineteen eighties has been described by Black and Wiliam (2003, p625) as beginning the "*decline of the development in formative assessment*" practices; so that by 1995, as Black and Wiliam put it: "*nothing was left of the advances made in the previous decades*" (ibid., p626). Against this background, where assessment for summative purposes has dominated the agenda, it is perhaps paradoxical that 'assessment for learning' has become one of the central themes in contemporary English secondary education, in particular during middle years education at Key Stage 3 (age 11-14 years). The supremacy of summative assessment has brought with it an undue focus on 'ends' as opposed to the means by which these ends are achieved. It is possible that current interest in how the processes of assessment can link to learning represents a shift in policy.

Assessment for learning (AfL) requires clarity about what is to be learned and the use of carefully framed targets that will enable pupils to move towards achieving the learning goals. However, evidence from the English Office for Standards in Education (Ofsted), quoted by the Specialist Schools Trust, (2003b p15) indicates that less that 40% of schools are 'good or better at using assessment data to inform teaching and learning practice and school improvement policies'.

Diagnostic assessment is recognised as a feature of good assessment practice (Ofsted 2003a p86). At its best, this assessment information can be used formatively, leading to targets for pupil action. There is a significant body of literature on assessment but of particular importance in the UK and elsewhere, has been the work of Black and Wiliam (1998) on formative assessment. In formative assessment, pupils can be viewed as partners in the assessment process. Its value for learning lies in the understanding that pupils gain through the process of assessment. Pupils learn what they need to do in order to improve their knowledge, understanding and skill. But it is about more than pupils being able to understand just what they need to do; it can also concern how to achieve it. Thus effective formative assessment practices help move pupils forward both in terms of learning content and learning skills.

A related issue in pupils' learning skills, is that 'thinking skills' are intended to be embedded in national curriculum subjects in England and Wales. Space does not permit a detailed discussion of this dimension to pupil learning but in addition to providing explicit opportunities to develop these skills an important feature of the teaching approach (as with other constructivist approaches to learning) is to help pupils to gain metacognitive insights into the processes involved in a range of thinking skills and practice in their application in new contexts.

5 ASSESSMENT FOR LEARNING

As we have seen, assessment *for* learning (AfL) is different from assessment *of* learning in that its focus is closely linked to the processes of classroom learning. At the core of AfL is pupils' understanding of the purposes of the learning, their current understanding in relation to what is to be learned and of how to achieve this new learning (Assessment Reform Group, ARG 1999). In order to develop AfL strategies in classrooms, teachers need to develop a repertoire of approaches in their teaching that serve to contextualise expected learning outcomes and to elicit pupils' current understanding through active approaches that engage them and encourage them to take responsibility for their learning (ARG, 2002). In England there is a range of support material available to teachers to help identify effective teacher behaviours to foster assessment for learning (Qualifications and Curriculum Authority QCA, 2003). Not all these teacher behaviours are obviously or directly supported by management information systems, yet if the potential of ICT to support teachers' work and pupil learning is to be realised, thought needs to be given as to how the capabilities of ICT and the contemporary needs of teachers to handle assessment information can be usefully aligned.

6 GOOD PRACTICE IN ASSESSMENT: IMPLICATIONS FOR MIS

Recent reports from the Ofsted have identified features of good assessment practice from a group of case study schools (Ofsted 2003b). Of particular interest to the present discussion are the following points:

- Emphasis on the use of baseline data to monitor and review individual pupils' progress and to set targets
- A holistic approach to monitoring and support that involves subject and pastoral concerns, and encompasses attitudinal and developmental matters.
- Use of efficient and accessible information systems to reduce the burden on teachers.

It is broadly accepted that there is scope for improvement in assessment practices that support learning. It is clearly the hope of politicians and others in England that the best practices of formative assessment will be more widely implemented in schools and that pupils will benefit as a result. However the present use of MIS for management of data appears to support this goal in only limited ways.

Many English schools currently make use of the assessment management tools of MIS to handle summative assessment data. In addition, the government has developed software tools to support diagnosis and analysis of summative data. For example, the PAT system described above and the 'Online autumn package' which provides data on national curriculum statutory assessment. In addition, the QCA has developed software to enable teachers and school managers to carry out diagnostic analysis of statutory and optional tests.

Current management information systems provide efficient ways of managing data in the form of summative test and grade scores. As summative measures of attainment, these scores represent relatively coarse-grained data. In a narrow sense there is scope for summative assessment information made available through current MISs to be used formatively, for example in providing information about current achievement and in using this to set target minimum grades for pupils to work towards. But coarse-grained information is of limited use in relation to the operational processes that will help pupils to secure the target grade; nor is it particularly helpful to the teacher in the nuanced adjustments required in teaching approach. Moreover, the kind of information that supports assessment for learning reflects something of the social and behavioural aspects of learning as well as knowledge and understanding. In broad terms, information derived for formative assessment purposes needs to focus more on the strategies and actions required of learners for improving their performance. It also needs to relate closely to the context of subject knowledge, understanding and skills to be learned. This kind of information is much more finely grained than summative test scores and may require different conceptions of the features and functionality of an MIS if the power of ICT is to be harnessed to support teachers in the classroom.

6.1 Challenges to MIS Designers

So key challenges for MIS to support learning remain. What are the useful alignments between pedagogy, standards based curricula and assessment? Standards based curricula and assessment can be usefully aligned to provide summative assessment data. However, pedagogy is concerned with the processes of teaching and learning and these are only partly informed by summative information. We need information of other kinds to inform pedagogical processes including data that will embrace pupils' learning skills. Systems are needed that will enable qualitative data to be recorded and managed for developmental purposes. There are questions here about ownership of and access to such data that need to be addressed. It would be valuable for teachers and pupils to make use of a shared repository of information for the purposes of negotiated personal action planning to support pupils' progress. Such systems are already in use in higher education where students are expected to take significant responsibility for managing their own learning. It could be possible to use similar systems with pupils in ways that support their fuller involvement in the assessment process and this would also support key principles of AfL including helping pupils to develop there skills in self-appraisal (ARG, 2002).

Can the social dimensions of teaching and learning be reconciled with data? At the level of day to day classroom interaction, it is not easy to conceive of how MIS can directly support the teaching-learning dynamic. Nevertheless periodic reviews with pupils where their achievements and approaches to learning are foci of discussion could provide opportunities to embrace further principles of AfL and ICT can provide a means of recording and sharing this information. Performance data are partial reflections of these dimensions but they are viewed through the prism of the assessment instruments that generate test and grade scores. Can such data be used to drive AfL without the risk of 'the backwash effect' of teaching to the test? To achieve this it will be necessary to break the link between formative assessment processes and statutory assessment requirements if MIS are to be used to support use of qualitative data for learning.

So, what other kinds of data would be useful to teachers? Assessment for learning focuses on individuals' achievements as well as attainment. Can useful systems be designed to provide achievement data for individual pupils to reflect their progress towards attainment targets taking account of their different starting points? Can target banks be developed that are closely aligned to curriculum statements that reflect attainment goals? Can learning skills be identified and used as a stimulus for discussion with pupils about next steps towards learning goals? Can target systems be developed that take account of affective as well as cognitive domains? Can systems be designed that enable pupils to take ownership of their progress by recording and managing target setting processes?

In each of these areas it is possible to think of ways in which ICT could be used to achieve these goals. But a key issue rests in the functionality and usability of any software developed for these purposes and whether its usefulness outweighs any overheads in its use and management. By finding answers to these questions, it is possible that MIS may reach a new level of usefulness to teachers in managing pupils' learning and improving their progress.

7 REFERENCES

Assessment Reform Group (ARG) (1999) Assessment for Learning: Beyond the Black Box (University of Cambridge School of Education, 1999). Available at http://www.assessment-reform-group.org.uk/AssessInsides.pdf [accessed January 21st 2004]

Assessment Reform Group (ARG) (2002) assessment for Learning 10 Principles. Available at http://www.assessment-reform-group.org.uk/principles.html [accessed January 21st 2004]

Black, P. and Wiliam, D. (1998) Inside the Black Box: Raising Standards Through Classroom Assessment. King's College London School of Education. http://www.kcl.ac.uk/depsta/education/publications/blackbox.html [accessed 20/11/2003]

Black, P., and Wiliam, D. (2003). 'In Praise of Educational Research': formative assessment. British Educational Research Journal, 29(5), 623-637.

Daugherty (2004) Learning Pathways Through Statutory Assessment: Key Stages 2 and 3. Daugherty Assessment Review Group Final Report. Available at http://www.learning.wales.gov.uk/pdfs/daugherty/daughety-final-report-e.pdf [accessed July 2004]

DfES (2003) A New Specialist System: Transforming Secondary Education, London: DfES [ISBN 1841858951]

Newton, L R and Visscher (2003) 'Management Systems in the Classroom.' In Selwood, I.D., Fung, A.C.W. and O'Mahony, C. D. Management of Education in the Information Age- The Role of ICT. Dordrecht: Kluwer Academic Publishers [ISBN 1402074301]

Ofsted (2003a) Handbook for inspecting secondary schools, London: Ofsted [HMI 1360]

Ofsted (2003b). Good assessment in secondary schools: Office for Standards in Education (OFSTED).

Qualification and Curriculum Authority (QCA) (2003) Characteristics of AfL. Available at http://www.qca.org.uk/printable.html?url=/ages3-14/afl/296.htm&title=Characteristices of AfL [accessed 19 January 2004]

Specialist Schools Trust (2003a) World Class Education London: Specialist Schools Trust [ISBN 1873882734]

Specialist Schools Trust (2003b) Pupil-centred learning: using data to improve performance, London: Specialist Schools Trust [ISBN 1873882807]

Technology Colleges Trust (2000) Best Practice in Technology Colleges – a guide to school improvement, London: TC Trust [ISBN 1873882513]

Visscher A., Wild P., Smith D. and Newton L. (2003) Evaluation of the implementation, use and effects of a computerised management information system in English secondary schools. British Journal of Educational Technology, June, vol. 34, no. 3, pp. 357-366(10)

Wiliam, D., and Black, P. (1996). Meanings and Consequences: a basis for distinguishing formative and summative functions of assessment? British Educational Research Journal, 22(5), 537-548.

Primary School Teachers' Use of ICT for Administration and Management

Ian Selwood
The University of Birmingham, School of Education, Edgbaston, Birmingham, UK
I.D.Selwood@Bham.AC.UK

Abstract: This paper reports on the findings of the baseline study "*ICT Test Bed Project*" in England as they relate to Primary School Teachers' use of ICT for administration and management. Data is presented that illustrates primary teachers' attitudes towards ICT and its use for administration and management; their access to ICT and satisfaction with this; their views on training and the type of training they have received; and their use of ICT for administration and management including frequency of use, and factors that influence their use. Even though primary teachers are generally positive about ICT and its ability to support their administrative and management duties, the findings point to low levels of use of ICT for administration and management. Reasons for this lack of use relate to lack of quality training and the availability of time and quality ICT resources.

Key words: ICT, Primary Teachers, Administration, Management, Workload.

1 INTRODUCTION

The publication "*Information and communications technology in UK schools: An independent enquiry*" by the Stevenson Committee (1997) highlighted not only the potential uses of ICT in UK schools but concluded that the state of ICT in UK schools was primitive and not improving and that it should be a national priority to increase the use of ICT in schools. Since 1997 there have been several government initiatives in the UK to encourage the use of ICT in schools, notably the implementation of the National Grid for Learning (NGfL) (DfEE, 1997); the lottery funded (New Opportunities Fund (NOF)) scheme to provide ICT training or re-training for all 500,000 practising teachers and school librarians (TTA, 1998); and Curriculum Online (DfES, 2002). The "*ICT Test Bed Project*" (DfES, 2003) is one of the UK governments' latest ICT initiatives and combines large-scale investments in ICT hardware, software and support, with a commitment to professional development and collaboration between participating schools and colleges, over a four-year period. The emphasis of the project is placed upon: "Using ICT to:

- Raise standards and performance, concentrating in particular on school improvement and raising the quality of teaching and learning.
- Enable more effective leadership and management in schools.
- Help teachers to concentrate their time on core task of teaching.
- Enable more effective collaboration between schools and with their local colleges.
- Provide wider learning opportunities to pupils, their families and the wider community in a home environment." (DfES, 2003)

To enable progress to be monitored, a baseline study of the 28 schools involved in the project (5 secondary, 1 special school and 22 primary schools) was undertaken by a team from The University of Birmingham led by Professor Hywel Thomas. The schools in the "Test Bed Project" were chosen by the DfES after LEAs had submitted details of clusters of schools that they felt could work effectively together, to allow the exploration of the potential of ICT to support greater collaboration between schools.

The baseline study took place between 18th October and 6th November 2002 when all of the "Test Bed Schools" were visited, and all teaching and support staff completed a very comprehensive questionnaire, which achieved a response rate of 91%. Additionally, during the school visits a cross-section of staff (Headteacher, member of Senior Management team, middle manager, class teachers and teaching assistants) were interviewed. A great deal of the data collected relates to the use of ICT in supporting teaching and learning. However, this paper presents only the data that relates to primary teachers' use of ICT for administrative and management purposes. Research on teacher workloads is extensive but there is relatively little on the role ICT can play in reducing teacher workloads (Becta, 2003), and there is also very little research on the use of ITEM by classroom teachers (Selwood, Smith and Wishart, 2001). The results presented in this paper may, in some small way, redress this situation by illustrating the current position in English Primary Schools.

2 RESULTS

2.1 Primary Teachers' Views on the Use of ICT

Table 1. Primary teachers' views on the use of ICT

	VS.Dis[1]	S.Dis	Dis	Agree	S.Agree	V.S.Agree
I find it easy to use ICT	2%	5%	27%	39%	19%	8%
Working with ICT makes me nervous	17%	14%	36%	26%	6%	2%
ICT makes work less enjoyable	16%	25%	47%	11%	2%	0%
Working with ICT is boring	24%	25%	46%	5%	0%	0%
ICT makes school work more enjoyable	0%	1%	20%	57%	13%	9%
Using ICT will reduce my workload	1%	4%	28%	50%	11%	6%
Using ICT makes me more productive	1%	2%	26%	58%	8%	5%
I work better when I work with ICT	2%	5%	47%	34%	7%	5%
ICT is used effectively by my school to manage resources	2%	5%	41%	43%	5%	5%
ICT is used effectively by my school in decision making	2%	6%	54%	33%	5%	1%

Attitudes towards ICT are important if its potential is to be utilised. Table 1 shows the opinions of primary teachers with respect to their use of ICT and the use of ICT in their schools. Confidence in using ICT is relatively high with about two thirds of teachers agreeing with the statement 'I find it easy to use ICT' and this corresponds with one-third agreeing with the statement that ICT can make them nervous. Only 13% of teachers felt ICT made work less enjoyable and 5% that working with ICT was boring. Whereas 79% felt ICT made work more enjoyable. With respect to primary teachers' views on the effect of ICT on workload, over two-thirds felt that ICT will reduce their workload and 71% that ICT made them more productive. However, only 46% felt that they actually worked better when they work with ICT. This apparent contradiction may relate to primary teachers' perception that they need more training (see 2.4). The final two rows of Table 1 differ from the others in that they show primary teachers perceptions of how the school uses ICT rather than how they personally use ICT. Just over half (53%) felt that ICT was used effectively by their school to manage resources, but only 39% felt that ICT was used effectively by their school in decision making.

[1] In all tables VS.Dis=Very Strongly Disagree, S.Dis=Strongly Disagree, Dis=Disagree, S.Agree=Strongly Agree, VS.Agree=Very Strongly Agree

2.2 Access to ICT

If teachers are to use ICT for administration and management then access to quality hardware and software are important factors. It is also apparent that with the very limited non-contact time that primary teachers have in the UK, that access to ICT outside of their school is also an important factor. Teachers were therefore asked about where they could access computers; their satisfaction with the quality of the hardware and software in their school; and what provision their schools made in supporting their access to ICT in their homes.

2.2.1 Where can primary teachers use a computer?

Table 2. Places where primary teachers can use a computer

	0	1	2	3	4	5	6
This School	2%	0%	0%	0%	2%	29%	68%
Another School	58%	6%	19%	1%	2%	11%	4%
Other Work Place	67%	8%	13%	1%	2%	8%	2%
Home	4%	9%	0%	0%	4%	8%	76%
Public Library	45%	2%	2%	2%	26%	14%	10%
Internet Café	54%	3%	6%	5%	9%	9%	14%
Community Centre	70%	12%	4%	1%	6%	5%	2%

Table 3. Key to Table 2

0	No response	1	There is no computer here
2	I am not allowed to use a computer here	3	There is a computer here, but it costs too much for me to use it
4	There is a computer here but it is usually too busy	5	I can usually use a computer here
6	I can use a computer here whenever I want		

Analysing the places where teachers can readily access computers it is apparent that the main place of use "whenever they want" or where they can "usually" get access is at home (84%) and at school (97%). Use of computers at other locations is relatively rare with the public library being the next highest and scoring only 24%. However with the high levels of access at school and at home, lack of use in other locations is not surprising.

2.2.2 Primary teachers' satisfaction with hardware and software at school

Sixty-nine percent of primary teachers, either agreed, strongly agreed or very strongly agreed that the school's computers were suitable to their needs.

With reference to other hardware and software the number of positive responses were lower 59% and 54% respectively. However, in relation to this paper these responses may be somewhat misleading as they may relate to the suitability of hardware and software for supporting teaching and learning, as the context of this question was not specified. On the other hand, it could be argued that, if the hardware and software is not suitable for teaching and learning this will add to teachers' workload.

Table 4. Primary teachers' satisfaction with hardware and software at school

	VS.Dis	S.Dis	Dis	Agree	S.Agree	V.S.Agree
The computers in school are suitable to my needs	5%	6%	20%	54%	9%	6%
The other hardware (e.g. printers, scanners) is suitable to my needs	5%	9%	29%	46%	9%	4%
The software in school is suitable to my needs	5%	9%	32%	45%	5%	4%

2.2.3 Schools' ICT hardware and software for use at home

Table 5. Schools' ICT hardware and software for use at home

	Agreeing
The school provides me with a laptop for use at home	40%
The school provides me with a desktop computer for use at home	0%
The school provides me with additional computer hardware for use at home (e.g. printer, scanner or digital camera)	5%
The school provides licensed software for use at home	12%
The school pays internet charges at home	0%
I can access school e-mail at home	37%
I can access my school computer and transfer files electronically to my home computer	8%
I can access the school website and staff resources from home	21%

In 2.2.1, it was reported that there was high access to computers at home. However, across all primary schools, responses to the statements in this section show limited levels of school-supported access to ICT hardware and software at home. The highest level of support was 40% of primary teachers having access at home to a laptop computer provided by the school, though according to interviews the laptop was often shared by two or more teachers. Provision of a desktop computer, for use at home, across all schools was negligible. Similarly, there was very limited home provision of other hardware and licensed software. No teachers reported assistance in meeting the costs of home Internet use. Only 8% of primary teachers could transfer files electronically between school and home and only 21% could "access the school website and staff resources from home". However, 37% of primary teachers reported the ability to access school e-mail from home.

In the open-ended questions at the end of the questionnaire, primary teachers commonly raised the issue that they needed better access to hardware and software, and that the hardware and software needs to be fit for use.

2.3 Primary Teachers' Knowledge/Confidence in ICT

Table 6. Primary teachers' knowledge/confidence in ICT

	I've never used this	I need more training to learn the basics	I need to improve my skills	I have most of the skills I need	My skills are sufficient for my needs	I am good enough to teach this to others
Word processor	0%	4%	15%	16%	26%	39%
Database	9%	17%	32%	18%	17%	7%
Spreadsheet	15%	15%	29%	17%	13%	11%
Presentation software	23%	16%	29%	11%	11%	11%
Desktop publishing	22%	17%	27%	15%	10%	10%
Administration and management software	42%	17%	22%	10%	6%	2%
School intranet	27%	10%	18%	20%	14%	12%
Search the internet / WWW	2%	7%	16%	22%	21%	32%
Create web pages	56%	16%	16%	5%	4%	4%
Internet discussion boards or chat rooms	51%	8%	16%	11%	9%	5%
E-mail	6%	9%	15%	17%	26%	27%
Peripheral hardware e.g. scanner, printer	6%	15%	24%	20%	23%	12%
Personal digital assistant (PDA)	80%	6%	8%	2%	2%	0%
Video conferencing	80%	10%	9%	1%	0%	0%
Authoring own multimedia or web resources	77%	10%	9%	3%	1%	1%

In commenting on this section an initial benchmark of the percentage of teachers who respond positively to any of the three statements 'I have most of the skills I need', 'My skills are sufficient for my needs' and 'I am good enough to teach this to others' is used. Across all primary schools, four applications attract agreement from 50% or more: word processing (81%), the Internet (75%), e-mail (70%) and peripheral hardware (55%). Furthermore, an examination of Table 6 reveals that more than 20% of primary teachers responded that 'I've never used this' for 9 of the 15 items.

2.4 Training in ICT

2.4.1 Primary teachers' views on training

Table 7. Primary teachers' views on training

	VS.Dis	S.Dis	Dis	Agree	S.Agree	V.S.Agree
I have improved my ICT skills in the last 12 months	0%	2%	7%	53%	26%	12%
The training I have received in using ICT in the last 12 months has been good	10%	9%	28%	39%	10%	4%
I do not need to learn to use ICT	34%	23%	39%	3%	1%	0%

The great majority (91%) of primary teachers felt that they had improved their ICT skills in the 12 months prior to completing the questionnaire. However, their opinions on the quality of the training they had received over the same period was less positive with only just over half (54%) agreeing that the training was good. Nonetheless, 96% disagreed with the statement "I do not need to learn to use ICT", implying they wanted further training.

2.5 Types of Training

It should be noted that more than one response is possible to each of the statements in Table 8, although in practice, few teachers made multiple entries. The low level of what might be termed formal training as compared with 'no training' and 'help from a friend or colleague', other than a school ICT expert, is worrying. In summary, for 14 of the 15 items, 20% or more of teachers report having received no training or help; for 7 of these items, 50% or more teachers report having received no training or help. Examining the items where primary teachers report the higher levels of more formal training only two (word processing at 64% and spreadsheets at 50%) were identified by 50 per cent or more teachers. Databases (48%), Internet (43%) and e-mail (34%) were the next highest.

Table 8. Types of training

	No training or help	Help from a friend or colleague	Help from a school ICT expert	An ICT course taught by your school ICT expert	An ICT course taught by an expert outside school	Part of a nationally recognised qualification
Word processor	17%	32%	11%	6%	29%	18%
Database	34%	23%	9%	4%	20%	15%
Spreadsheet	36%	18%	8%	4%	22%	16%
Presentation Software	48%	20%	6%	3%	14%	8%
DTP	56%	20%	4%	3%	11%	4%
Administration and management software	68%	10%	5%	2%	12%	3%
School intranet	46%	17%	18%	6%	9%	0%
Search the internet	20%	39%	12%	9%	17%	5%
Create web pages	75%	7%	2%	2%	10%	1%
Internet discussion boards or chat rooms	77%	13%	2%	1%	4%	1%
E-mail	26%	42%	11%	8%	12%	3%
Peripheral hardware	35%	42%	12%	4%	5%	2%
Personal digital assistant (PDA)	97%	1%	1%	0%	1%	0%
Video conferencing	87%	2%	1%	0%	4%	0%
Authoring own multimedia or web resources	84%	2%	1%	0%	6%	0%

The interviews revealed that thcre is a need for more training and time to practice what has been learned in formal training sessions. However, NOF ICT training is generally regarded as having been ineffective overall, but four of the twenty-two primary schools reported positive experiences of NOF training. LEA training was generally regarded as effective, but there were some comments regarding variability in quality and responsiveness to needs. In-house formal training is a strong feature of ICT training, and it is generally regarded as very effective. However, the interviews supported the questionnaire data that primary schools rely a lot on in-house self-taught approaches based on learning by doing the job supported by manuals. This is a response to necessity and while it meets an immediate need staff are concerned that this approach can only do so much and that opportunities for learning could be lost.

At the end of the questionnaire open-ended questions were asked regarding issues that most concerned respondents regarding their use of ICT, and they were also asked to give examples of what they needed to further develop their role through use of ICT. In response to both questions, the most common response was need for more and better training for staff and need for time to practice what they have learnt. Primary teachers also felt there was a need to improve use of ICT in administration and management of teaching and learning e.g. access to and analysis of pupil progress data

2.6 Use of ICT

2.6.1 Frequency of use of ICT for management and administration

Table 9. Frequency of use of ICT for management and administration

	Don't use	Less than once a month	At least once a month	At least once a week	1-2 hours a day	More than 2 hours a day
Word processor	22%	10%	12%	35%	17%	4%
Database	60%	19%	10%	7%	2%	1%
Spreadsheet	59%	19%	11%	9%	1%	1%
Presentation software	81%	11%	6%	2%	0%	0%
Desktop publishing	75%	12%	6%	7%	0%	0%
Administration and management software	68%	11%	6%	8%	6%	2%
School intranet	71%	7%	5%	12%	3%	2%
Search the internet	60%	8%	11%	14%	6%	2%
Create Web Pages	98%	1%	0%	1%	0%	0%
Internet discussion board or chat room	98%	1%	1%	0%	0%	0%
E-mail	69%	9%	6%	9%	6%	1%
Personal digital assistant (PDA)	97%	1%	0%	1%	1%	1%
Peripheral hardware	46%	8%	9%	25%	11%	1%
Video conferencing	100%	0%	0%	0%	0%	0%
Authoring own multimedia or web resources	99%	0%	0%	0%	0%	0%

Frequency of use of ICT for management and administration, as revealed by the responses in this section of the questionnaire, were generally low. Taking use of once a week or more, only three categories achieved more than a 20% response - word processing (56%), searching the Internet (22%) and the use of peripherals (37%). Furthermore, 13 of 15 areas of use were reported as not being used by 59% or more of primary teachers. Presenting the data in terms of more modest levels of use, 10 out of the 15 categories were used for management or administration purposes, by 20% or more of teachers in primary schools.

2.6.2 Ways in which primary teachers use ICT to support their work

Table 10. Ways in which primary teachers use ICT to support their work

	Use
Resource/material preparation	77%
Lesson Planning	71%
Report writing	64%
Curriculum planning	64%
As a lesson resource (e.g. web site)	60%
Timetabling	47%
School policy development	43%
Reprographics/photocopying	43%
Presentations/demonstrations	38%
Monitoring pupil progress	35%
Marking and Assessment	33%
Record Keeping (e.g. database entry)	31%
Special Educational Needs Coordination (SENCO)	31%
Development planning	31%
Exam entries and results	28%
Records of achievement	26%
Extra curricular activities	23%
Registration	20%
Staff appraisal/supervision or mentoring	18%
Monitoring attendance	17%
On-line communities	17%
Financial records	14%
Continuing professional development/training	12%
Budgeting	12%
Partnership links (contact outside the school)	11%
Pupil contact (e.g. E-mail/intranet)	8%
Staff contact (e.g. arranging meetings through E-mail/intranet)	8%
On-line purchasing of services and/or goods	6%
Parent/Carer contact (e.g. E-mail)	3%

Five items were selected by half or more of the primary teachers: preparation of resources (77%), lesson planning (71%), report writing (64%), curriculum planning (64%) and as a lesson resource (60%). A further 7 items were selected by more than 30% of teachers: record keeping (e.g. database entry) (31%), special educational needs coordination (SENCO) (31%), development planning (31%), marking and assessment (33%), monitoring pupil progress (35%), presentations/demonstrations (38%), school policy development (43%), reprographics/photocopying (43%), and timetabling (47%). It was expected that the use of ICT for financial management and administration would not be used widely as these applications tend to be used by a few senior managers in schools, and this was the case. However, the use of ICT for electronic communications was noted as being very low, with only 8% of primary teachers reporting use of email for contacting pupils or other staff, and 3% for parent or carer contact.

The interview data tends to support data gathered by the questionnaire, with the most frequently mentioned examples of the use of ITEM being: planning for teaching and learning; monitoring student progress and assessment; report writing and production of lists. Interviewees were also asked to give examples of the benefits of using ICT for management and administration and the most common responses were: more efficient and effective management of work because documents can be updated, edited and shared more easily; more efficient and effective handling of data; access to data improved; quality of data and how it can be used is improved; reduction of workload; and improved presentation and quality of work.

2.6.3 Factors that might encourage greater use of ICT

Table 11. Factors that might encourage greater use of ICT

	VS.Dis	S.Dis	Dis	Agree	S.Agree	V.S.Agree
Easier access to a computer at home	8%	3%	22%	25%	13%	29%
Cheaper training	2%	2%	26%	39%	16%	17%
Free training	2%	1%	10%	32%	18%	37%
Training classes at school / work	2%	1%	5%	33%	23%	36%
If I had more spare time	2%	0%	5%	21%	27%	44%
If I was released from work to train	1%	0%	2%	19%	28%	50%
Cheaper computers and free software	1%	0%	16%	25%	25%	34%
Free computers or software	1%	0%	9%	20%	22%	48%
Cheaper internet access	2%	0%	8%	25%	25%	40%
Free internet access	2%	0%	6%	17%	19%	56%

It is apparent from the results discussed earlier, that primary teachers are in general positive about the use of ICT to support their administration and management. However, it is also apparent that such use is limited. When asked what factors might encourage them to use ICT more the results shown in Table 11 were obtained. Primary schools teachers' responses to all the options presented to them in this question show high levels of agreement with a range from 67% to 97%. Only two items score lower than 80% and these were easier access at home (67%) and cheaper training (72%). The highest scoring item was a wish to be 'released from work for training', which attracted 97 per cent agreement.

3 CONCLUSION

The results of this baseline study clearly show that primary teachers are positive about the value of ICT in supporting their administrative and management duties. However, when primary teachers' actual use of ICT for administration and management is analysed, the levels of use are quite low. Primary teachers appeared to be aware of the potential of ICT to reduce their workload and improve the quality of their work but also recognise their need further training, which they are keen to undertake. It is apparent that primary teachers have very little non-contact time in English primary schools, and if they are to make greater use of ICT for administration and management either more non-contact time is essential or they need better and cheaper communications between home and school, or both. Furthermore, concerns over access to quality ICT equipment appears to be a real and major issue.

4 REFERENCES

Becta, (2003). *What the research says about ICT and reducing teacher workloads*. Coventry: Becta. www.becta.org.uk/research/ictrn

Department for Education and Employment. (1997). *Connecting the learning society: National Grid for Learning* (Government Consultation Paper). London: DfEE.

Department for Education and Skills. (2002). *Curriculum Onli*ne. London: DfES. www.dfes.gov.uk/curriculumonline

Department for Education and Skills. (2003). *ICT Test Bed Project*. London: DfES. www.dfes.gov.uk/ictinschools/ict_active/subject.cfm?articleid=474

Selwood, I., Smith, D., Wishart, J., (2001). Supporting UK teachers through the National Grid for Learning in Nolan, P., Fung, A.C.W., & Brown, M.A. (Eds), *Pathways to Institutional Improvement with Information Technology in Educational Management*. p 159-171. Boston: Kluwer.

Stevenson Committee. (1997). *Information and communications technology in UK schools: An independent enquiry* (The Stevenson Report). London: Pearson. [http://www.rubble.ultralab.anglia.ac.uk/stevenson/ contents.html]

Teacher Training Agency. (1998). *New Opportunities Fund. The use of ICT in subject teaching lottery-funded training. Expected outcomes*. London: DfEE.

5 ACKNOWLEDGEMENTS

The research described in this paper was led by Professor H Thomas and undertaken by G Butt, T Fielding, J Foster, H Gunter, A Lance, R Lock, L Potts, R Pilkington, S Powers, S Rayner, D Rutherford, I Selwood and A Soares.

Reaping ITEM Benefits

A Link Between Staff ICT Access, Ability and Use

Christopher O'Mahony
Saint Ignatius' College, Riverview, Sydney, Australia
COMahony@riverview.nsw.edu.au

Abstract: This paper reports on a survey of ICT Access, Ability and Use conducted among 25 schools in England and Wales in 2002/03. The survey concentrated on school staff, and sought to investigate links between four key areas: (a) access to ICT both in and outside school; (b) perceived and desired ICT ability of staff; (c) use of ICT both in and outside school; and (d) issues which inhibit increased use of ICT in teaching, learning and administration. Survey results indicated that access to ICT resources was high for this sample, both at school and at home. Furthermore, staff reported overall satisfaction with their ICT abilities across core applications, whilst calling for more training in 'advanced' applications. Despite these confident results regarding Access and Ability, staff reported wide variability in actual Use of ICT. Results drawn from the survey are contrasted with comparable studies from the UK and overseas, with a view to assisting schools to reap the benefits of e-learning innovations.

Key words: School information systems, Professional Development, Educational Management, information technology.

1 INTRODUCTION

A number of commentators have highlighted concerns regarding the implementation of ICT policies for staff in schools. These concerns revolve around issues relating to staff access to ICT resources, staff ICT training, and the encouragement of staff ICT confidence and competence. Conventional wisdom suggests that high access to ICT and high ability with ICT must lead to high use of ICT. That is, "ICT Access + ICT Ability = ICT Use". It is unclear in the literature, however, how these variables may be linked, if at all.

A pilot study conducted in late 2001 at one school (O'Mahony 2002) suggested certain trends:

- Home access to ICT, including Internet and email, was high.
- Staff confidence with a number of ICT applications was strong, and staff were seeking to advance their skills.
- Classroom use of ICT was variable.
- The key inhibitors to using ICT in the classroom were time, training and resources.

The pilot study had a sample population of some 100 staff members. It was clear that a wider study would help to either corroborate these findings, or suggest alternative trends. The main research questions for the 2002/03 study were as follows:

- What are the current levels of access to ICT resources among school staff?
- What are the current levels of ability with ICT among school staff?
- What are the current levels of use of ICT resources among school staff?
- What are the main barriers to increasing the use of ICT in teaching, learning and administration?
- What links can be perceived between ICT Access, Ability and Use?

In late 2002, the British Educational Communications and Technology Agency (Becta) sponsored research to seek answers to the areas noted above. The research had two main phases: Survey and Scholarship. Both phases were conducted concurrently between October 2002 and March 2003. A questionnaire was developed in August and September 2002, and administered in October 2002. The target population were 2800 staff members drawn from the 3,500 staff employed in the 25 schools operated by the Girls' Day School Trust (GDST). In total, 1366 responses were received, analysed between November 2002 and March 2003.

At the same time, an extensive review of the literature was conducted, investigating links between key research dimensions. The two phases of the research programme were complementary. The scholarship phase helped to inform questionnaire construction and survey design. Similarly, results of the survey were compared with benchmarks drawn from the literature.

Results indicated that although access to ICT resources was high, staff throughout the Trust could improve their integration of ICT use in teaching, learning and administration. High levels of access to ICT resources were reported, well above national averages (Watson 2001, DfES 2000). Despite concentrations of ICT use, however, and some exciting initiatives both locally and centrally, the majority of staff used these resources less frequently than anticipated. The level of ICT training was perceived as insufficient to meet needs, the main criticism being a lack of time available for training, given the range of commitments in which staff are involved.

Outcomes of the survey included practical areas for consideration, including training programmes, home-school network links and carefully targeted ICT resourcing. Although much had been invested, the challenge was to reap the return on that investment more fully.

2 THEORETICAL BACKGROUND AND CONTEXT

2.1 ICT Access

The general domain regarding ICT in schools has gathered significant research momentum in recent years (Stevenson 1997, Research Machines 2000, National Statistics 2002). One area of debate concerning ICT in schools is a recognition that high levels of access are required to achieve a 'critical mass' of user confidence and ability. Since the publication of documents such as the Stevenson Report (1997), schools have experienced large-scale funding of infrastructure and equipment, especially in connection with the National Grid for Learning (DfES 2001).

Case studies reflecting successful computer integration have all shown such schools to be provided with excellent facilities, technical backup and financial resources (Mumtaz 2000). Other writers express reservations that access to ICT, on its own, will provide positive educational outcomes (Cuban 2000). High level of access to ICT resources is an important goal, but is itself a means to a greater end. Within the literature concerning ICT access, therefore, are frequent links with ICT use and ICT ability. Government agencies in particular seek to quantify return on investment, and seek to collect qualitative evidence of ICT effectiveness in schools (Becta 2000, Becta 2001a, Becta 2001b, NGfL 2001, DfES 2002).

National Statistics (DfES 2002) report, in a study based on data collected in early 2002, that 85% of teachers had access to home computers. There is growing evidence that higher ratios of home access have a positive effect on ICT ability and use. For instance, the major Impact2 study (NGfL 2002b) reports that "Having a computer at home has a significant impact on teachers' ICT capability."

2.2 ICT Ability

It is generally acknowledged in the literature that getting ICT professional development 'right' is very difficult to achieve (Mumtaz 2000, Selwood et al. 2000, Visscher & Brandhorst 2001, McDougall & Squires 1997). At the same time, despite the difficulties, there is also recognition that there are critical links between staff ICT ability and staff ICT use, and staff ICT ability and student ICT ability (Kennewell et al. 2000, Russell et al. 2000, NGfL 2002c).

2.3 ICT Use

A number of factors influence staff ICT use. The survey reported here looked closely at relationships between ICT Access, ICT Ability, ICT Use and ICT Inhibitors to use. These factors, and others, can be discerned in the literature. Mumtaz (2000), in her review of this area, highlights both positive and negative factors affecting ICT use. Positive factors include "...collegiality among computer-using teachers at their school, school support for consequential computer activities, resources for school development, smaller class sizes and more formal computer training." (Mumtaz 2000). Technical support and senior management commitment are other recurring themes (NGfL 2002d).

Another theme apparent in the literature is the attitudes of staff. National Statistics notes that 76% of teachers felt confident using ICT in the curriculum (National Statistics 2002). However, "Schools can only go so far to encourage ICT use - actual take-up depends largely on teachers' personal feelings, skills and attitudes to IT in general." (Mumtaz 2000). This is corroborated by Hruskocy et al. (2000), Kirkman (2000), and Yee (2000).

2.4 ICT Inhibitors

Although reports concerning improvements in ICT Access and ICT confidence are encouraging, such improvements appear to be patchy across phases, subject areas and geographical location. A number of inhibitors to ICT use are evident in the literature, which appear to be cross-phase, cross-department and geographically independent. Foremost among these inhibitors are the following:

- Lack of time (NGfL 2002a, NGfL 2002b, Mumtaz 2000, Kirkman 2000).
- Lack of training (Kirkman 2000, Mumtaz 2000).
- Lack of senior management support (Kennewell et al. 2000, NGfL 2002a, NGfL 2002b, Passey 2002).
- Lack of technical support (Sheingold & Hadley 1990, NGfL 2002c, NGfL 2002d, Yee 2000).
- Lack of a genuinely supportive culture (Sheingold & Hadley 1990, Kennewell et al. 2000, Mumtaz 2000).
- Lack of teacher confidence and motivation (Kirkman 2000, NGfL 2001, NGfL 2002a, NGfL 2002b).
- Lack of ICT resources (Sheingold & Hadley 1990, Mumtaz 2000).

In summary, the literature is rich in both qualitative and quantitative studies concerning the four dimensions under investigation in this survey. Although these four dimensions frequently appear, however, there are few studies that attempt to quantify the relationships between them. In this context, a quantitative study of the relationship between ICT Access, ICT Ability, ICT Use and ICT Inhibitors would appear timely.

2.5 Contextual Background

The Girls' Day School Trust has been operating since 1872, and is the largest group of independent schools in the UK. Twelve of the schools are based in London, and another thirteen are in regional centres. GDST schools have about 20,000 students on roll at any one time. Around 3500 staff are employed in GDST schools, of which 2800 were targeted in this study.

In 1995, the Trust made a commitment to ICT in its schools. At that time, it embarked on a policy which included a strong investment in ICT infrastructure, including LANs in each school and a Wide Area Network connecting all Trust sites, investments in software and hardware, staff training and ICT management mechanisms. A rollout of ISDN connections was completed in 1997, providing data communications links between schools and Trust Office, as well as access to Trust-wide email services and to the Internet. Local Area Networks in individual schools progressed simultaneously, funded centrally. To make effective use of this infrastructure, the Trust set aside funding on a per capita basis for each school, designed to cover purchasing of PCs and other peripherals, software licences, consumables, staff training and ongoing maintenance.

An important element of the Trust's initiative was the establishment of IS management posts in each school. Historically, like many other schools, the Trust had relied on enthusiastic teaching staff to provide technical ICT support. As the initiative developed and ICT became more complex and more pervasive, the Trust recognised the need for full-time technical support. By 1998, all Trust schools had either an Information Systems Manager or Network Manager and at least one ICT technician. This followed on from the establishment of a central support team who have provided high-level technical support and R&D, as well as assisting in setting policies and strategy, monitoring targets and technical progress in schools throughout the initiative.

Major internal audits of the Trust's ICT initiative in 1997, 1998 and 2001 (conducted by the Education, Finance, and ICT Managers) provided useful steering mechanisms. These audits helped to establish key elements of the Trust's ICT policies, including:

- Agreement on a common network infrastructure.

- Agreement on a common MIS solution, including the strategic use of assessment data.
- Agreement on the need for an annual ICT strategic planning process.
- Agreement on specific targets for ICT competence among both staff and students.
- Agreement on both central and local strategies designed to meet those targets.

Within and between Trust schools, there is a growing recognition throughout their communities (Staff, students, parents, and the like) that:

- Information and communication is swiftly becoming the 'nervous system', or the bloodstream of the school.
- ICT increasingly enables this flow of information and communication.
- ICT is the current fulcrum of radical change in education.
- ICT is an integral part of learning, both as content and medium, and is essential to the management of teaching and administration of the school.

In this context, the Trust was keen to explore links between the key research variables. In liaison with the Heads of each school, approval was given to approach staff for the purposes of this investigation.

3 METHODOLOGY

Both Scholarship and Survey phases occurred concurrently. An extensive literature review was undertaken before, during and after the survey instrument was administered. Results drawn from sources such as National Statistics, DfES, Becta, BESA, Fischer Family Trust, relevant academic journals and conference proceedings in this field were used to provide benchmarks for the survey phase. As responses were analysed, these benchmarks were used to contextualise and validate the results.

In the Survey Phase, a survey instrument was administered across 25 schools in September 2002. The survey investigated the four dimensions previously stated. Research questions drew on the work of previous research (McDougall & Squires 1997, Cox et al. 1999, Mumtaz 2000, O'Mahony 2000, O'Mahony 2002). The primary focus of the survey was its practical element. It was designed to provide swift feedback into ICT strategic planning exercises. In this sense, the study had a strong Action Research dimension (Baskerville & Wood-Harper 1996, Klein & Myers 1999).

Completed survey forms were collated in October 2002, and results were analysed from November 2002 to February 2003, according to strata such as School, Region, Age, Phase (Primary, Secondary) and Department. Data were analysed to explore relationships between dependent and independent variables.

4 RESULTS

4.1 ICT Access

Respondents were asked about their access to ICT at home. Results are shown below in Table 1, categorised by age group.

Home Access to computers	**<25**	**25-34**	**35-44**	**45-54**	**>54**	**TOTAL**	**%**
TOTAL	31	222	290	522	224	1302	95%
Percent	100%	93%	95%	99%	94%	95%	
Home Access to Internet							
TOTAL	28	193	262	454	190	1127	83%
Percent	90%	81%	86%	86%	79%	83%	
Home Access to email							
TOTAL	24	188	260	449	189	1110	82%
Percent	77%	79%	85%	49%	79%	82%	

Table 1: Home access to ICT

Respondents were asked to evaluate their access within school to computers, Internet and email, using a scale of 1 to 4, where 1 = Very difficult, and 4 = Very easy. The following table (Table 2) shows school access to ICT broken down by age and phase:

Stratum	# Responses	Computer Access	Internet Access	Email Access
<25	31	3.58	3.19	3.35
25-34	247	3.44	3.32	3.20
35-44	305	3.43	3.20	3.25
45-54	530	3.37	3.13	3.16
>54	239	3.27	3.11	3.09
All Primary	377	3.46	3.04	3.12
All Secondary	989	3.36	3.18	3.18
TRUST AVERAGE	1366	3.39	3.18	3.18

Table 2: Work Access to ICT (Where 1 = Very difficult, and 4 = Very easy)

4.2 ICT Ability

In Question 19 of the questionnaire, staff were asked to self-assess their current ability with a selection of applications. In Question 20, they were asked to nominate their desired level of ability with the same selection of applications. To determine 'training priorities', the differential between 'current' and 'desired' was calculated for each application. These priorities were calculated for primary and secondary phases, and are shown in Table 3:

Priority	Trust-Wide Application	Primary Application	Secondary Application
1	Digital Whiteboards	Powerpoint	Powerpoint
2	Powerpoint	Digital Whiteboards	Digital Whiteboards
3	Microsoft Publisher	Microsoft Publisher	Microsoft Publisher
4	Web Design	Web Design	Data Projectors
5	Data Projectors	Microsoft Access	Microsoft Access
6	Microsoft Access	Microsoft Excel	Web Design
7	Microsoft Excel	Data Projectors	Microsoft Excel
8	Web Searching	Web Searching	Web Searching
9	Email	Email	Email
10	Microsoft Word	Microsoft Word	Microsoft Word

Table 3: ICT Training Priorities

As can be seen from Table 3, most GDST staff expressed confidence in their ability with core applications such as word processing, email and Internet searching. The main priorities perceived by GDST staff were for training in presentation-based applications (hardware and software), the clear implication being that they recognised genuine benefit for teaching and learning from these skills.

4.3 ICT Use

The following table (Table 4) summarises staff responses regarding Use of ICT. These figures are broken down by age strata, and are expressed in terms of average hours per week.

	<25	25-34	35-44	45-54	>54	AVG
Home Computer						
For Home	2.68	1.95	1.98	1.88	2.42	2.02
For School	3.13	3.27	3.10	3.31	2.87	3.16
Home Internet						
For Home	1.99	1.51	1.25	1.32	0.97	1.29

For School	0.86	0.77	0.75	0.80	0.43	0.72
Home Email						
For Home	1.11	0.89	0.86	0.90	0.93	0.90
For School	0.15	0.21	0.21	0.35	0.17	0.26
At work						
Work Computer	5.98	3.94	6.64	4.74	4.61	5.03
Work Internet	1.09	1.02	0.83	0.82	0.59	0.82
Work Email	0.99	0.92	1.21	1.00	1.12	1.06
In Class						
Class Computer	0.48	1.34	1.44	1.37	1.18	1.31
Class Internet	0.18	0.36	0.28	0.28	0.21	0.28
Class Email	0.03	0.02	0.01	0.07	0.01	0.04

Table 4: Staff ICT Use (Average hours per week)

4.4 ICT Barriers

Staff were asked to rank a set of ten items in response to the question "What's holding you back?" These items were ranked on a scale of 1 to 10, where 1 = biggest problem, and 10 = least problem. The following table (Table 5) ranks these inhibitors across strata:

	Whole sample	Primary	Secondary	<25	25-34	35-44	45-54	>54
Time	1	1	1	1	1	1	1	1
Quantity of ICT Training	2	2	2	2	2	2	2	2
Quantity of Classroom ICT resources	3	4	3	4	3	3	3	4
Quantity of ICT Support	4	3	5	8	5	4	4	3
Quantity of Staff ICT Resources	5	8	4	=5	4	6	5	7
Quality of Classroom ICT Resources	6	6	6	=5	6	5	6	5
Quality of ICT Training	7	5	7	3	7	7	7	6
Quality of Staff ICT Resources	8	9	8	7	8	8	8	9
Quality of ICT Support	9	7	9	9	9	9	9	8
Willingness	10	10	10	10	10	10	10	10

Table 5: ICT Barriers to Use (1=biggest problem, 10 = least problem)

Analysing the above table provides a rich indicator for ICT strategic planning. The 'top five' inhibitors were those perceived by a significant proportion of respondents as needing addressing.

- Across the entire sample, TIME was seen as the biggest barrier to the use of ICT.
- The amount of ICT training (Quantity) was perceived as a significant barrier to the use of ICT.
- Other barriers tended to focus on the level of resourcing (Quantity), rather than the quality of those resources.

4.5 Correlating the Results

The main research hypothesis sought to test the notion that "ICT Access + ICT Ability = ICT Use". A number of different correlations were tested across the sample. Results show that generally staff will use ICT more when they have greater access. More specifically, the results show that ability, rather than access, is a stronger predictor of ICT use. There appear to be a large number of staff who have reasonable access to ICT both at home and at school, but at the same time demonstrate low ICT use. These staff will clearly need to be the focus for subsequent ICT initiatives.

In the under 25 age group, ability is related to ICT use far more than for other age groups. This suggests that age may influence ICT use and ICT ability. Younger staff also demonstrate greater ICT access, particularly at home. One possible explanation may be that people under 30 who have used computers since being students themselves have greater ICT confidence, and therefore demonstrate greater ICT use. Conversely, the staff to target are therefore those over 30 who have indicated low ICT ability. ICT training initiatives should target those who are uncomfortable using ICT.

Correlation coefficients were calculated for all variables, and were tested at the 0.005 level of validity (Attwood et al. 2000). That is, there is a less than 0.5% chance that these correlations are purely by chance. The coefficients were found to be significant, thus the null hypothesis - "Access + Ability <> Use" must be rejected.

5 CONCLUSIONS

The main research questions for this study were as follows:

- What are the current levels of access to ICT resources among school staff?
- What are the current levels of ability with ICT among school staff?

- What are the current levels of use of ICT resources among school staff?
- What are the main barriers to increasing the use of ICT in teaching, learning and administration?
- What links can be perceived between ICT Access, Ability and Use?

5.1 ICT Access

Both at home and at work, respondents reported high levels of access to computers, including Internet and email access. Arising from this finding, it is recommended that school managers target their funding and resources on that diminishing number of staff without access. Furthermore, the finding suggested that strategies such as a global staff laptop programme were not warranted. Rather, concentrating funding on the development of remote-access technologies, such as Extranets, Virtual Private Networks and Virtual Learning Environments would help school managers to reap the benefits of this high level of access.

5.2 ICT Ability

In terms of ability, it was found that most staff perceived that they had a core competence in ICT applications, and were seeking to extend their abilities to a higher level. This finding confirmed the results of other internal reviews into investment in training strategies such as ECDL. In order to make best use of this core competence and extend it, school managers should consider the development of a central ICT staff training function. Such a role could centrally monitor and coordinate staff training in ITEM as well as exemplary ICT for teaching and learning.

5.3 ICT Use

Within the sample under investigation, staff reported relatively high use of ICT resources at home and outside of classes. Within classes, however, wide variability of ICT use was reported (between 0 and 11 hours per week, depending on departmental area). As noted above, the development of remote access technologies may well encourage the transfer of staff ICT use from home to school. It is further recommended that school managers target individual departmental areas to encourage classroom use of ICT. This should be closely linked to externally mandated curriculum outcomes as well as internal curriculum targets.

5.4 Barriers to ICT Use

The study highlighted some barriers confronting staff as they seek to integrate ICT use more fully in their teaching, learning and administration. Chief among these were lack of time, amount of support staff, and the amount and quality of ICT training. To a lesser extent, but still worthy of comment, many staff reported that both the quantity and quality of staff ICT resources was a significant issue. These issues present serious challenges for school managers. Suggestions for overcoming these barriers include:

- Celebrate existing successful strategies for enabling staff sufficient time to assimilate new learning technologies.
- Continue to seek further innovative models for staff ICT training.
- Revisit both the job and person specification of ICT support personnel, as well as the quantity of ICT support provision in individual schools.
- Set specific targets within individual school IT strategic plans for delivering resources, time and support for staff, as well as clearly-defined targets for evidence of ICT use in teaching, learning and administration.

5.5 Correlations between variables

There is a positive correlation between (ICT Access + ICT Ability) and ICT Use (0.54)

This correlation is most pronounced among staff under 35 years old: (0.67)

Work Access is seen as a stronger predictor of ICT Use than Home Access: (0.3383 vs 0.2118)

These correlations are significant at the 0.005 level (Attwood et al. 2000)

6 IN CONCLUSION

This research sought to answer questions regarding ICT Access, ICT Ability and ICT Use among a large sample of UK school staff. On the one hand, there are some encouraging results, suggesting that core issues regarding access to ICT resources and core competence with ICT are being addressed. This is the result both of interventionist policies by the GDST, as well as the influence of external factors outside the control of the Trust.

On the other hand, challenges exist. Despite an underlying willingness to move forward with ICT Ability and ICT Use, staff feel constrained by issues such as lack of available time, and a lack of relevant training. Like other schools and school authorities, the GDST is also constantly faced with other challenges, such as sustainability, security, cost management, technical support management and change management.

The future for ICT in the Girls' Day School Trust looks exciting, as it considers the way forward with evolving technologies such as VLEs and MLEs, integrated management systems, videoconferencing and the like. By maintaining their agility in an ever-changing ICT landscape, staff of the GDST are well-placed to respond positively to these evolving technologies, and truly 'reap ITEM benefits.'

7 BIBLIOGRAPHY

Attwood, G., Dyer, G., and Skipworth, G., (2000), *Statistics 3.* Oxford: Heinemann.

Baskerville, R.L., Wood-Harper, T., (1996), "A critical perspective on action research as a method for information systems research", *Journal of Information Technology,* 1996, 11, pp235-246.

BECTA (2000), *Connecting Schools, Networking People: ICT planning, purchasing and good practice for the national Grid for Learning*, Coventry: British Educational Communications and Technology Agency.

BECTA (2001a), *Primary Schools of the Future - Achieving today. A report to the DfEE by Becta*, Coventry: British Educational Communications and Technology Agency.

BECTA (2001b), *The Secondary School of the Future. A preliminary report to the DfEE by Becta*, Coventry: British Educational Communications and Technology Agency.

Cox, M., Preston, C. and Cox, K (1999), *What factors support or prevent teachers from using ICT in their classrooms?* Paper presented at the British Educational Research Association Annual Conference, University of Sussex, Brighton, November 1999.

Cuban, L. (2000), *Oversold and Underused: Computers in the Classroom.* Cambridge, MA: Harvard University Press.

DfES (2000). *Information Management Strategy for Schools and LEAS.* http://www.dfee.gov.uk/ims/summary.brief.shtm. DfEE. London

DfES (2001), *ICT Access and Use: Report on the Benchmark Survey*, DfES Research Report No 252. London: Department for Education and Skills.

DfES (2002), *Transforming the way we learn: a vision of the future of ICT in schools*, London: Department for Education and Skills.

Hruskocy, C., Cennamo, K.S., Ertmer, P.A., Johnson, T., (2000) "Creating a community of technology users: students become technology experts for teachers and peers", *Journal of Technology and Teacher Education*, Vol 8, pp69-84

Kirkman, C., (2000), "A model for the effective management of information and communications technology development in schools derived from six contrasting case studies", *Journal of IT for Teacher Education* (JITTE), V 9, No 1, 2000.

Kennewell, S., Parkinson, J., and Tanner, H., (2000), *Developing the ICT-capable School.* London: Routledge Falmer.

Klein, H.K., & Myers, M.D., (1999), "A set of principles for conducting and evaluating interpretive field studies in information systems", in *MISQ*, Vol 23, No 1, March 1999, pp 67-93.

McDougall, A., and Squires, D., (1997), "A framework for reviewing teacher professional development programmes in information technology", *Journal of Information Technology for Teacher Education*, 6, 2, 1997.

Mumtaz, S (2000), "Factors affecting teachers use of information and communications technology: a review of the literature", *Journal of Information Technology for Teacher Education*, 9, 3, 2000.

NGfL (2001), *Impact2: Emerging findings from the evaluation of the impact of information and communications technologies on pupil attainment.* ICT in School Research and Evaluation Series - No 1. Annesley: DfES.

NGfL (2002a), *Impact2: The impact of information and communication technologies on pupil learning and attainment.* ICT in School Research and Evaluation Series - No 7. Annesley: DfES.

NGfL (2002b), *Impact2: Learning at home and school: Case Studies.* ICT in School Research and Evaluation Series - No 8. Annesley: DfES.

NGfL (2002c), *NGfL Pathfinders: Second report on the roll-out of the NGfL programme in ten Pathfinder LEAs.* ICT in School Research and Evaluation Series - No 10. Annesley: DfES.

NGfL (2002d), *NGfL Pathfinders: Final report on the roll-out of the NGfL programme in ten Pathfinder LEAs.* ICT in School Research and Evaluation Series - No 11. Annesley: DfES.

National Statistics (2002). www.dfes.gov.uk/statistics/db/sbu/ b0360/sb07-2002.pdf

O'Mahony, C.D., (2000), *The evolution and evaluation of information systems in NSW Secondary schools in the 1990s: the impact of values on information systems.* PhD Thesis (unpublished): Sydney: Macquarie University.

O'Mahony, C.D. (2002), *Managing ICT Access and Training for Educators: A Case Study*, Proceedings: Information Technology for Educational Management (ITEM2002 conference), Helsinki (Forthcoming).

Passey, D., (2002), *ICT and School Management: A review of Selected Literature.* Unpublished Research Report: Lancaster University, Department of Educational Research.

Research Machines PLC (2000) *The RM G7 (8) Report 2000 comparing ICT provision in Schools*, Abingdon: RMplc.

Russell, G., Finger, G., Russell, N., (2000), "Information technology skills of Australian teachers: implications for teacher education", *Journal of IT for Teacher Education* (JITTE), V 9, No 2, 2000.

Selwood, I.D., Smith, D., & Wisehart, J. (2000), "Supporting teachers through the National Grid for Learning", in Nolan, C.J.P., Fung, A.C.W. & Brown, M.A. (2000), *Pathways to institutional improvement with information technology in educational management.* Boston: Kluwer.

Sheingold, K., & Hadley, M., (1990), *Accomplished teachers: integrating computers into classroom practice*, New York: Centre for Technology in Education.

Stevenson, R., (1997), *Information and Communications Technology in UK Schools: an independent inquiry* (The Stevenson Report).

Visscher, A.J. & Brandhorst, E.M. (2001), How should School Managers be Trained for Managerial School Information System Usage? In *Pathways to Institutional Improvement with Information Technology in Educational Management.* Edited by Nolan, C.J.P., Fung, A.C.W., & Brown, M.A. Kluwer for IFIP. London

Watson, G (2001), "Models of information technology teacher professional development that engage with teachers' hearts and minds", *Journal of IT for Teacher Education (JITTE)*, 10, 1-2, 2001.

Yee, D.L., (2000), "Images of school principals' information and communications technology leadership", *Journal of IT for Teacher Education* (JITTE), V 9, No 3, 2000.

Managing Accountability Innovations in Distance-Learning Programs

Connie L. Fulmer
University of Colorado at Denver, USA
Connie.Fulmer@cudenver.edu

Abstract: Accountability is a complex process in any organizational learning experience and even more so in distance-learning environments. Some of the complications include issues of measuring performance, using authentic assessments, meeting performance-based standards, and integrating all with distance-learning technologies. This paper describes online-accountability innovations used in distance-learning programs and how these online tools help students provide evidence of their readiness for educational-leadership positions.

Key words: Accountability, self-assessment, project-based learning, reflective-justification rubric, professional-growth charts.

1 INTRODUCTION

Colorado led the nation (USA) in the adoption of performance-based standards for preparing both principals and superintendents. The Interstate Leadership Licensure Consortium (ISLLC) standards quickly followed and were adopted in whole or part by forty-four of the fifty states. In addition, the Technology Standards for School Administrators (TSSA) were adopted by a consortium of organizations and provide further direction for leadership preparation. More recently, the Educational Leadership Constituent Council and the National Council for Accreditation of Teacher Education (ELCC-NCATE) adopted program performance standards set forth by the National Policy Board for Educational Administration (NPBEA, 2002) and used them to accredit both schools and colleges of education and individual program areas. The ALPS program faculty, like many others, found themselves facing multiple sets of standards. As a result, our redesigned program meets the following sets of standards: (a) Colorado Principal/Administrator licensure standards, (b) ELCC-NCATE program standards, and (c) Technology Standards for School Administrators.

The Administrative Leadership and Policy Studies (ALPS) faculty responded to issues related to accountability, performance-assessment standards, and distance-learning technologies (Baker, 2003; Hutchins, 2003; Howell, Williams, & Lindsday, 2003) by designing online accountability tools for managing assessment 'of learning' and 'for learning' (Stiggins, 2001; Chappius, Stiggins, Arter, & Chappius, 2003) in an online principal-licensure program.

Baker (2003) provided a framework with twenty-six elements for the design and evaluation of Internet–based, distance-learning courses. We focused on seven of these elements listed below:

Practice – provide online activities that require students to practice the skills necessary to achieve the desired behavior and provide a feedback mechanism to correct student mistakes during practice activities.

Variety – create a variety of learning experiences (and distance learning tools) to enhance student learning.

Outcomes – match distance learning tools and the required outcomes.

Integration – create activities that include skill development that would be related to a variety of contexts and other subjects/fields.

Baseline evaluation – use self-assessment tools to determine a baseline for growth comparison.

Successive evaluations – have students repeat self-assessments during the program.

Appropriate evaluation type – ensure that the skills and knowledge necessary to successfully complete the evaluations representative of the skills and knowledge necessary to achieve the intended behavior.

Chappuis, Stiggins, Arter, and Chapppius (2003, p. 35) provided our faculty with the concept of assessment 'for' instruction. These authors claim that assessment 'for' instruction is far more than was intended through a formative assessment process. We adopted the following elements of assessment for learning:

Understanding and articulating *in advance of teaching* the achievement targets that their students are to hit.

Informing their students about those learning goals *in terms that students understand* form the very beginning.

Engaging students in regular self-assessment with standards held constant so they can watch themselves grow over time and thus learn to become in charge of their own success.

Making sure that students understand how the achievement targets that they strive to hit now relate to those that will come after.

2 ONLINE-ACCOUNTABILITY TOOLS

Accountability tools used in the distance-learning program include: (a) online project-based learning, (b) performance-based standards; (c) self assessments (d) a reflective-justification rubric, (e) professional-growth charts, and (f) the scurry matrix. These tools are used in programs that require both face-to-face and online experiences (hybrid programs) but were developed specifically for the distance-learning cohort. Each of these online tools is described below.

2.1 Project-Based Learning

As standards were first introduced in Colorado the ALPS faculty responded by transforming their course-based program into four eight-credit learning domains. With the addition of performance assessments and the opportunity provided by the online program to *stretch* projects over four semesters, instructional teams moved to project-based learning. The projects crossed traditional course and semester boundaries and provided an organizing structure for our principal-licensure program. These projects are vehicles for transforming learning experiences for cohort students and faculty. They provide opportunities for both student and program assessment and facilitate optimal integration of traditional curriculum, real-world assignments of principals in the field, and the requirements placed on programs by various sets of performance-assessment standards and accrediting bodies..

A description of these projects is beyond the scope of this paper but a partial list can provide an overview of the type of work students tackle during their four-semester-long program: (a) a knowledge-base journal, (b) mission-vision project, (c) culture study, (d) legal audit (e), instructional-leadership work sample, (f) school improvement planning, and (h) a leadership resume. Each online project is presented to students complete with rationale, description, guiding questions, relevant literature, learning activities, required work products, and a detailed process for writing up the project in artifact format.

The artifact format requires three components or sections: (a) a cover page, (b) a reflective justification, and (c) any work products produced during the learning experience. Project-based learning is the first online accountability tool and provides students and faculty with authentic learning experiences upon which to build both personal and professional knowledge of the field of leadership.

2.2 Performance-Based Standards

Students in our online programs must present evidence that they have met the Colorado Principal/Administrator licensure standards. These standards are organized into eleven categories: (a) foundations for learning, (b) contextual understanding, (c) planning and organizing contextual understanding, (d) content knowledge instruction, (e) individualization of instruction, (f) management and evaluation of instruction, (g) supervision of personnel, (h) supervision of student conduct, (i) resources, (j) school safety and maintenance, (k) parent and community involvement. Each of these categories has a set of associated standards. Electronic versions of these standards are provided to support student work. The first instance was a copy in PDF format. The second was a file set up to print on the front and back of name-card stock. Once printed separated, these name cards become a deck of performance standards for students to sort into piles related to specific program projects. The third file was in word format so students could cut and paste individual standards into the artifact product.

2.3 Self Assessments

Using principles of assessment (Stiggins, 2001; Chappius, Stiggins, Arter, & Chappius, 2003) and effective online delivery (Baker, 2003; Hutchins, 2003) faculty designed a complete set of online assessment tools for each set of standards. These electronic forms were linked to online learning environments and students were able to complete these self-assessments four times during the course of their program.

Data collected included student name, cohort instance, survey instance, and for each standard and standard element the level of understanding as well as evidence supporting the selected level reported by the student. Four levels of understanding/evidence (little evidence, some evidence, conceptual evidence, and performance evidence) were constructed based on the ELCC-NCATE requirements and are described in the reflective justification rubric section of this paper. If students selected either conceptual evidence (level three) or performance evidence (level four) to describe their level of understanding, they were required to provide a description of that experience or a reference to a particular portfolio artifact in a text box option on the online survey.

These self-assessments tools served both purposes of assessment '*of*' and '*for*' learning (Stiggins, 2001; Chappius, Stiggins, Arter, & Chappius, 2003). These assessments are used by faculty to determine the learning needs of the students before finalizing learning projects for the group or customizing projects for specific partnership districts. Students use self-assessment results to document their learning progress on the growth charts describe below. At the end of the program, students were able to determine which standards they had mastered and which standards required further attention. These unmet standards became targets for professional growth and were listed in students' professional-growth plans.

2.4 Reflective-Justification Rubric

The reflective-justification rubric in Table 1 is an online tool used by students and faculty to evaluate student performance. The rubric outlines four levels of performance evidence. Students use the rubric to construct their reflection justifications, one of the three components of the artifacts students must produce. Faculty members use the rubric to evaluate online submissions of student work. Students are expected to write their reflective-justification at level three or four. Artifacts are returned to students until each standard referenced meets these minimum levels. Each of these levels is described below.

2.4.1 Evidence Level One

Initially, when students begin to address standards they reference the standard and allude to its importance. They may say that professional development strategies were important for a principal to use with the staff. However, in this statement there is no evidence that the student knows anything about professional development. No standard was referenced and no authors or work was cited. Many students have level one reflective justification instances in their earliest work in the program.

2.4.2 Evidence Level Two

As students begin to integrate literature, research, and concepts with school contexts they are able to provide some evidence by citing authors and referencing a standard. A student might write that DuFour and Eaker (1998) know how to create professional learning communities and that when they become a principal they will build a learning community. Such a statement fall shorts of evidence of conceptual understanding. Missing are the six characteristics of a professional learning community and the strategies a principal might use to develop such a community. At this level program faculty have little confidence that this student would be able to provide leadership for developing a professional learning community. Level two work would be returned to the student for additional work.

Table 1. Reflective-Justification Rubric

CAPABILITY	CAPABILITY is defined as the application of knowledge and skills to specific problems of practice.
Level Four	**Evidence of Practical Experience:** Student evidence meets all criteria specified at Level Three but also references one or more instances of actual practical experience in a school setting.
UNDERSTANDING	UNDERSTANDING is defined as integrating knowledge to school environments, integrating concepts with practice, and using knowledge and skills in context.
Level Three	**Evidence of Conceptual Experience:** Student evidence includes a description of the context of the school, the conceptual frameworks and understandings used for interpretation, citations of relevant literature, and supported references standards with evidence of knowledge or skills level requirements.
AWARENESS	AWARENESS is defined as acquiring information, concepts, definitions, and procedures.
Level Two	**Some Evidence of Awareness:** Submission includes references to literature and performancc standards without any evidence of student's knowledge or skill level.
Level One	**Little Evidence of Awareness:** Submission did not include references to literature or standards.

2.4.3 Evidence Level Three

To achieve level three on the rubric, student reflections must include the following elements. First, they must describe the context in which their leadership strategies would be implemented. Second, students must reference authors and provide evidence of the models, frameworks, characteristics, or concepts developed by those authors that provide ideas and successful implementation strategies that might be employed by the future principals in the actual practice of leadership. Level three reflections include the use of *'I'* statements. Initially, students may write that '*principals*' (third person reference) should have a particular position on some issue. We typically return this work to students, ask for personal evidence of what each would do in the situation, and request that *'I'* statements be used to communicate their leadership intentions. Reflections written at level three express what each student would do, whose research they would use, and what frameworks and authors would inform their practice. If these elements are present for each standard referenced, students are writing at level three and are rewarded with signatures from instructional-team members. Once artifacts are signed, they are placed into the students' program portfolios.

2.4.4 Evidence Level Four

This evidence level includes all requirements listed for level three but must include evidence of actual performance in a school setting. Many of these standards are met through clinical-practice activities. Students would reference standards, authors, research, models, recommended strategies, results achieved, and would perhaps reflect on the success of these activities or changes they might make on future instance. In our program, level three is the minimum requirement for signature and level four can only be attained through clinical-practice experiences.

2.5 Professional-Growth Charts

As students complete the online self-assessment surveys and use the reflective-justification rubric to measure their learning, they record their progress on the third online tool, professional-growth charts. Figure 1 provides a view of one of the eleven growth charts for standard eight of the Colorado Principal Performance Standards. There are six additional charts for the TSSA standards and six more for the ELCC-NCATE standards. Students enter self-assessment scores into driver cells on these growth charts and the graph lines adjust to represent the scores. Students repeat the self-assessment three more times during the program and record the results on the growth charts. Students save and print these growth charts at the end of the program as work products for an artifact. Standards not achieved are targeted by the students as elements to be addressed in their professional-growth plan.

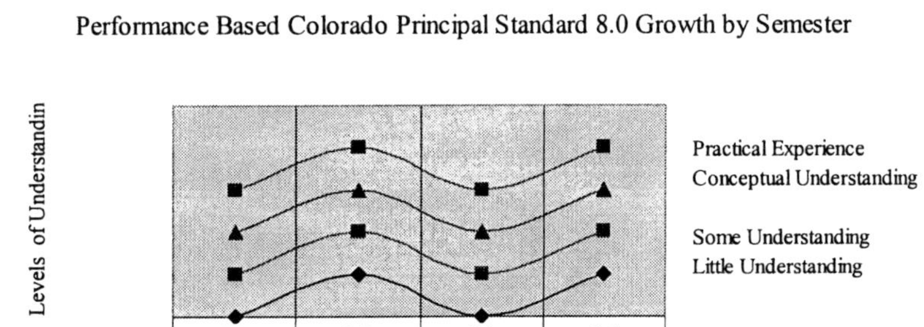

	8.1	8.2	8.3	8.4
1st Semester	0	1	0	1
2nd Semester	1	2	1	2
3rd Semester	2	3	2	3
4th Semester	3	4	3	4

Standard 8.0

Figure 1. Professional growth charts where students record their self assessment scores. The chart illustrates student progress in mastering performance standards by academic semester.

2.6 The Scurry Matrix

The scurry matrix, depicted in Table 2 and inspired by the mouse character in *Who Moved My Cheese* (Johnson & Blanchard, 1998), is another online-accountability tool developed to help students keep track of both standards met and artifacts completed. The matrix guides students as they develop artifacts and demonstrates evidence of their learning. Faculty members use the matrix to assess the scope and sequence of not only student projects rendered in artifact format, but also the extent to which students covered particular standards across artifacts. The matrix provides yet another way to manage accountability in an online leadership program.

3 EFFECTS OF ACCOUNTABILITY INNOVATIONS

The effects of these online innovations are distributed across all of the accountability tools and all levels of stakeholders (students, faculty, and program). The use of the online tools (project-based learning, performance standards, self-assessment surveys, the reflective-justification rubric, growth charts, and the scurry matrix) in the leadership program produced students

Table 2. The Scurry Matrix: Evidence of performance standards mastered by project.

	A[a]	B	C	D	E	F	G	H	I
8.1[b]	✓[c]			✓				✓	
8.2				✓			✓		
8.3	✓		✓			✓			
8.4					✓				✓

[a] Names of specific students artifacts are listed on the matrix.
[b] Specific standards are typed into these areas on the matrix.
[c] Denotes the standard was met in this particular artifact

who were able to think about and write reflective justification evidence at level three and four, demonstrating that they have met state and national performance standards. This practice results in students who have a developed their own personal and professional knowledge base as well as strategies for a variety of contexts in which to demonstrate their leadership capabilities. All of these online-accountability innovations are used in distance-learning leadership cohorts to help students develop and faculty to determine student-readiness levels for important educational leadership positions.

Since implementing these accountability tools, faculty have reported that the transition for students from teacher to leader that traditionally occurred near the end of the program or during their clinical practice experiences was occurring much earlier in the program. With their first artifact, students are asked to report what they would do, what literature or research supported their intended strategies, and how those strategies might be mediated by the context of their particular school during the course of the program. The perceived impact of these accountability tools appear to result in the development of administrator perspective in students during the middle of the second of four semesters rather than at the end of the program or not at all. Prior to the implementation of the online-accountability tools, student work was less focused and evidenced fewer instances and lower levels of intensity of leadership efficacy. Since implementing the online tools, students report that they feel prepared to be principals, are looking forward to their first assignments, and are already considering geographical moves to obtain that first leadership position.

Next steps for ALPS faculty include designing research that will result in not only a thick description of the transition from teacher to leader tracked by the accountability tools but other data that will track self-assessments collected over time, by individual student, and by cohort group. These data will be used to continue to modify projects and learning activities to enhance instances and degree of leadership efficacy in principal candidates.

4 REFERENCES

Baker, R. (2003), A Framework for Design and Evaluation of Internet-Based Distance learning Courses: Phase One – Framework Justification, Design and Evaluation, *Online Journal of Distance Learning Administration, VI*(11). Retrieved September 15, 2003 from http://www.westga.edu/%7Edistance/ojdla/summer62/summer62.html

Chappius, Stephen; Stiggins, Richard; Arter, Judith & Chappius, Jan. (2003) *Assessment FOR Learning: An Action Guide for School Leaders, Assessment Training Institute*, Portland, OR, USA.

DuFour, Richard; Eaker, Robert. (1998) *Professional learning communities at work*, Association for Supervision and Curriculum Development, Alexandria, VA,, USA.

Howell, S.L, Williams, P.B., & Nathan, K. L. (2003) Thirty-Two Trends Affecting Distance Education: An Informed Foundation for Strategic Planning. Online Journal of Distance Learning Administration, VI (III).

Hutchins, H. (2003) Instructional immediacy and the seven principles: Strategies for facilitating online courses, *Online Journal of Distance Learning Administration 2003: VI*(11). http://www.westga.edu/~distance/ojdla/fall63/fall63.htm

Johnson, Spenser and Blanchard, Kenneth. (1998) *Who moved my cheese?*, Putnam, New York, USA.

National Policy Board for Educational Administration (2002). Standards for advanced programs in educational leadership for principals, superintendents, curriculum directors, and supervisors, Author, Arlington, VA, USA.

Stiggins, Richard. (2001) Student-Involved Classroom Assessment (3rd ed.), Merrill, Upper Saddle River, NJ, USA.

Extending the Classroom

The Virtual Integrated Teaching and Learning Environment (VITLE)

Alex C.W. Fung and Jenilyn Ledesma
Faculty of Social Sciences, Hong Kong Baptist University, Hong Kong
alexfung@hkbu.edu.hk

Abstract: This paper reports the case of an interactive, real time platform using web-technology in the delivery of teaching and learning when classes were suspended during the Severe Acute Respiratory Syndrome (SARS) outbreak in April 2003 in Hong Kong. Responding to the suspension of schools during that unprecedented difficult period, the Hong Kong Baptist University offered schools free use of its Internet-based Virtual Integrated Teaching and Learning Environment (VITLE) platform. Teachers and their students were encouraged to adopt e-Learning by continuing their classes on the VITLE platform, and 75 schools registered to use the new technology. This is a specific example of taking advantage of streaming technologies to create a rich, multi-media communication solution for the benefits of the students, teachers and schools.

Key words: VITLE, real-time, synchronous, e-Learning, virtual classroom

1 INTRODUCTION

The past few years have seen an enormous growth in the accessibility of Internet technologies, especially the World Wide Web (WWW). The rise of the Internet as a communication medium continues to transform education, and teachers must now re-think how to conduct their teaching. The widespread availability of high speed Internet connections, such as broadband and digital subscriber lines (DSL), has allowed teachers to make greater use of these technologies. Real-time interactions with audio-video and multimedia features between teachers and students are already possible inside 'virtual classrooms' on the Internet. E-Learning is likely to be pervasive as the technology becomes more widespread and affordable, as this paper illustrates.

Advances in information and communications technology (ICT) have significantly changed the ways students learn, the ways teachers teach, and the means with which both parties access information (Leidner & Jarvenpaa, 1993; Starr, 1997). In a traditional classroom, students learn from the physical delivery of lessons, which to a great extent depends on the teacher. In a virtual classroom, the delivery of lessons depends not only on the teacher but also on the technology used to deliver the teaching materials (Cyrs, 1994). With the increasing use of the virtual environment, technologies have become a critical component affecting teaching and learning effectiveness (Alavi, 1994; Sankar, Ford & Terase, 1997); and students as well as instructors could become free from the time and space constraints of having to be in the same physical room, at the same time (Althaus, 1997; Barnard, 1997).

A more significant way with which the Internet has changed the dynamics of teaching and learning is to make possible direct teaching over distances. With this, a teacher could give instruction to students at any point in time through the Internet without having to meet face-to-face. Although video-conferencing facilities can be used for this purpose, the cost of doing so is prohibitive because both the teachers and students need to invest in the same set of specialized hardware and software. Moreover, the requirement of designated point-to-point connection with video-conferencing excludes the flexibility of access 'anywhere' as with the Internet.

This situation has changed drastically with the latest developments in Internet video-conferencing capabilities (Gale, 1994; Jacobs & Rodgers, 1997; Kaye & Medoff, 1999). With such capabilities, a teacher and her students located in different parts of the world can engage in a virtual class using standard personal computers and very affordable off-the-shelf hardware and software requirements (Porter, 1997; Riel, 2000). Students are no longer subjected to the constraints of geographical barriers in their quest for knowledge. Teachers are no longer restricted by physical distances in their attempt to give personal attention to students.

This paper illustrates the use of the Virtual Integrated Teaching and Learning Environment (VITLE) platform, which incorporates Internet video-conferencing, ICQ, and other interactive multi-media features in virtual classrooms to maintain teaching and learning in Hong Kong when classes were suspended due to the SARS outbreak.

2 BACKGROUND

The outbreak of the severe acute respiratory syndrome in Hong Kong forced kindergartens, primary and secondary schools, and universities to suspend classes in March 2003 – which affected teaching and learning progress significantly. To enable students to continue with the lessons during the class suspension period, the Department of Education Studies (EDUC) and the School Administration and Management System (SAMS) Training and Research Unit of the Hong Kong Baptist University (HKBU) launched the 'Virtual Integrated Teaching and Learning Environment' (VITLE), a free new platform which breakthrough the limitations of physical classrooms during the class suspension period. The idea to launch VITLE was initiated by Dr. Alex Fung, Head of EDUC and Director of SAMS, and was made possible within 48 hours with the support of a number of sponsoring organizations[2] from the business sector. Realizing the impact of such an unprecedented closure of schools on children and their families, the "Classes Suspended but Learning Continues" Initiative was officially launched on 1st April 2003, enabling teachers to interact with their students and to conduct lessons through the web (SCMP, 2003a; 2003b; 2003c). The goal of the Initiative was to provide a territory-wide solution urgently not only to bring the disruption to kids' learning to a minimum, but also to confine them in a safe environment at home away from the danger of the contagious epidemic.

The University developed VITLE as part of its e-learning infrastructure since September 2002, and was due to conduct pilot tests in June 2003. But after the Hong Kong government decided to suspend classes in late March 2003, the need to continue education over the Internet was evident. As an e-learning application, VITLE was made available to all primary and secondary schools the day classes were suspended so that teachers could stay in touch with their students in virtual classrooms while schools were closed. About 75 schools and thousands of students took part in the initiative, which also attracted international attention. As journalist Benny Evangelista wrote in the San Francisco Chronicle on April 21, 2003, "The Hong Kong example may be the first instance in which online learning has been used to replace real classrooms because of a major disruption in the education system." (San Francisco Chronicle, April 21, 2003). Macromedia chairman and chief executive Rob Burgess also said, "We are starting to see more and more examples of the Internet being used as a two-way communications medium, and Hong Kong Baptist University created a live virtual classroom where students were able to see the teacher on the screen literally conduct the class through this difficult time.

[2] The sponsoring organisations included the Hong Kong Daily News, Cellwise Technologies Ltd., Macromedia Hong Kong Ltd., Microsoft HK Ltd., and PowerNet Internet Group.

Knowing that some schools might not be able to run their own virtual classes for students, apart from providing the platform for schools to continue classes, the HKBU also launched the big virtual community education hall "HKBU VITLE Class' for all secondary and tertiary students as well as the general public. The number of registered participants with HKBU VITLE Class surged to 10,000 within the few weeks of operation. VITLE became one of the important communication channels for individual schools with their students during the outbreak of SARS in Hong Kong. For more information about the HKBU VITLE Classes, please visit http://www.ilearn.com.hk.

3 VITLE: ARCHITECTURAL OVERVIEW

The Virtual Integrated Teaching and Learning Environment (VITLE) is a web-based platform providing simultaneously on one screen in real-time mode the following features in support of teaching and learning: Video Broadcast (in three modes: teacher, teaching assistant, student), Interactive Question and Answer, Whiteboard, and Slide Presentation. The teacher can control the activation of the tools / features by clicking icons on the control panel. When a feature is turned OFF (by the teacher) the students will not see that particular function. This virtual environment is designed to model traditional classroom settings so that teachers can adapt to e-Teaching easily. Figure 1 shows the Teacher's View after logging in to a VITLE virtual classroom with a presentation slide loaded.

Basically, VITLE provides an interactive virtual classroom for teachers and students to meet in cyberspace. Each party needs only a multimedia PC (with an optional web-camera) and access to the Internet and hundreds of students can 'enter', i.e., log in to the room with the teacher together at the same time. Inside a VITLE virtual classroom, the student learns in real time:

1. with the teacher explaining over a web-camera;
2. with the slides shown by the teacher (with or without a transparency overlay);
3. with an electronic whiteboard; and
4. through Q&A with the teacher similar to ICQ

Students equipped with a web-camera can also present themselves, as chosen by the teacher, inside the virtual classroom. A Teaching Assistant / Invited Guest Speaker can join in to team teach as well when given access by the teacher. Figure 2 below shows how the screen looks to a student.

Figure 1. A Teacher's View inside the VITLE Virtual Classroom

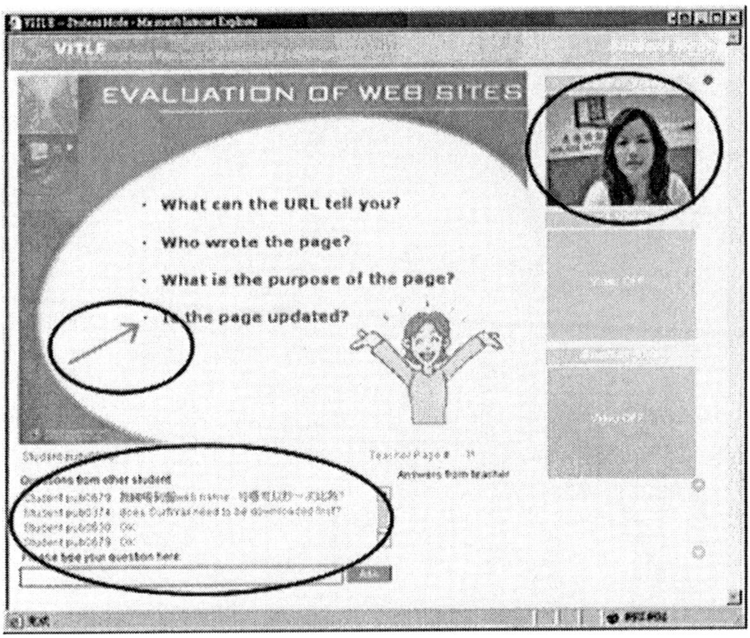

Figure 2. A Student's View inside the VITLE Virtual Classroom

The implementation for VITLE uses the capabilities and ease of use of Macromedia Flash Communication Server MX 1.5 to provide unlimited concurrent access to all users. It comprises a web front-end which serves as an entrance to the platform, provides presentation files management, and is powered by Macromedia ColdFusion MX 1.5. Other Macromedia products used in conjunction included Macromedia Flash MX for connecting users to real-time data exchange server provided by Flash Communication Server (FCS). Multiple users can connect to the same application running on FCS which acts as a communication channel between the connected users. The web front-end is built from Macromedia ColdFusion MX. The operating system is Microsoft Windows 2000 Server with a Microsoft SQL 2000 Server. The hardware consisted of two servers (PIII Xenon 550 x 4, 2GB ECC RAM).

VITLE allows for real-time, synchronous interaction between teachers and students who logon together in virtual classrooms. A teacher who is logged-on to the virtual environment can immediately begin teaching without the need for additional downloads and program installations. Students could watch their teachers (or even other students, if they had web cameras) live. All that was needed for them was a Web camera, a computer with Internet access, and a Macromedia Flash player (free software). As the streaming technology advances, VITLE makes virtual meetings possible anywhere at any time.

4 USER FEEDBACK

User feedback via telephone interview was collected from 9 schools using the VITLE platform. At the user level, both teachers and students perceived the platform to be useful and convenient as they could access it from any computer with access to the Internet. In short, VITLE has provided them access to learning like never before. They also preferred the platform because no special software and hardware equipment are required. However, they found some limitations with the platform. Somc students commented that no 'archives' were available for downloading, so they were unable to view a missed programme. Another comment about the use of this platform was the technology. The sound quality and the video clarity were some of the issues raised. Another limitation was the necessity of converting Power Point slides to Flash files (in swf format). The Whiteboard, which only allows texts and arrows, was also limited. according to the comments received. Transmission delay was also another problem.

At the school level, the principals commented that the platform was relatively easy to use and learn. They also found the stability to be acceptable, and thought the platform could be really interactive particularly during remedial classes or tutorial sessions, or even as a communication channel between staff! They thought it had helped breakthrough the limitation of time and space, and was effective since lessons could also be conducted outside school hours. Because of the audio-visual presentation, lessons were richer and more vivid so helping increase students' concentration span. Self-learning amongst students was also actively promoted as a result of the opportunity provided by VITLE. The principals also mentioned that the platform helped enhanced teacher professionalism and confidence. It also provided them the opportunity to offer subjects beyond the school curriculum by integrating the use of IT. And since they have to prepare the materials before the session, teachers became more well-prepared and organised. Sharing also prevailed amongst the teachers, as they constantly discussed the subject matter.

However, some principals were concerned about the 'presence' of the students, and were unsure whether the students were 'attending' the lessons or not. Principals also perceived the process of converting Power Point files to 'swf' format as an additional workload and burden to teachers who were not computer literate. They also complained about problems with the Question and Answer Tool. For instance, only the teacher can choose which student's question to respond to. Likewise, the teacher also controls which student (and only one at a time) to appear live on screen. The students also had difficulty expressing themselves through written words, and were not fast enough in typing in the questions.

5 SUMMARY

The Severe Acute Respiratory Syndrome (SARS) struck badly in a number of regions in the world in 2003. The contagious and killing disease threatened and seriously interrupted different walks of life. In Hong Kong the SARS outbreak forced the suspension of schools for the whole month of April 2003, which significantly affected the teaching and learning progress of more than a million students. To enable students to continue with lessons during the class suspension period, Hong Kong Baptist University (HKBU) provided an e-learning solution to schools and teachers. Using virtual classrooms accessible on the VITLE platform via the Internet, teachers conducted lessons with students in the safety of their homes. VITLE became one of the important communication channels for individual schools to keep learning going for their students, and was a prime source of e-Learning for the community as well during the SARS crisis in Hong Kong.

VITLE was designed as an emergency alternative for schools to maintain a certain degree of teaching and learning for their students who could not physically attend classes during the SARS period. VITLE has also enabled Hong Kong education community to respond quickly to classroom suspension by providing an online learning community which allowed students to easily 'attend' classes with rich interactive functionality from the comfort of their own homes. The power and potential of using IT in education, especially for e-Learning, has been demonstrated. However, our experience has also sharply reflected the problem of the digital divide – the 'haves' and 'have-nots' – since only students with IT facilities at home and access to the Internet could be benefited. The project has also provided a test-bed for a large number of teachers and students to experiment and reflect upon their ways of teaching and styles of learning. Teaching in a virtual classroom is very different from that within a traditional classroom. What works and what doesn't for effective learning is yet very uncertain. Students' self-learning responsibility is undoubtedly a crucial factor, as they can choose to easily log out from an uninteresting lesson.

Schooling in the traditional sense implies attending classes and learning from the face-to-face delivery of lessons, which requires teachers and learners to be present physically at the same place at the same time. In contrast, VITLE virtual classrooms enable teachers and learners to attend classes in cyberspace, also interacting face-to-face, at the same time, but without having to be together at the same physical location. The VITLE platform is an impressive example of creating a rich, multimedia communications solution for e-Learning in virtual classrooms. This technology leads to different ways of communicating and processing information between teachers and learners, bringing about the potential for new forms of e-Teaching and e-Learning. It can be envisaged that the technology will be extended to applications of virtual rooms in a much broader sense for meetings of different kinds in cyberspace. In the not too distant future, the owning of a private virtual room may become as common as having an email account.

6 THE WAY FORWARD

The past decade has been a time of technological convergence. In the past, audio, video, text and film were different media relatively independent on their own. But now they are made compatible through digitization, which can be woven together into a single presentation (Webster, 1998; Webster & Hackley, 1997). This paper demonstrates the promise of Internet video-conferencing technologies as a means for conducting distance education. The VITLE technology opens up new opportunities for students to study when, where and how they want. It has the potential of enhancing the teaching and learning experience through virtual classrooms. The platform is also a solution in ensuring that the continuity of teaching and learning is not jeopardized in light of any unforeseen crisis. Given the widespread availability of low-cost personal computers, and the widespread use of the Internet, it is plausible that this mode of distance education may partially replace face-to-face teaching sessions. The sessions can also become more stimulating since students can see or hear what is best for them, which in turn leads to a more efficient use of classroom time. More importantly, the benefits of the technological capabilities can potentially extend beyond physical classrooms to larger-scale distance education efforts.

ICT has permeated many aspects of education, and these technologies will continue to impact education in the future. Such technologies can certainly facilitate distance learning and teaching by helping to break geographical barriers. In the 21st century when ICT is likely to play a critical role in enabling effective education, knowledge accumulated on existing and emerging technologies can guide us in terms of what technologies are appropriate under what circumstances. Rather than seeing technology as a solution to an existing problem, it is more fruitful to examine how the collection of ICT may complement each other to open up new and exciting possibilities for educating people.

7 REFERENCES

Alavi, M. (1994). Computer–mediated collaborative learning: An empirical evaluation. *MIS Quarterly, 18(2),* 159 – 174.

Althaus, S. (1997). Computer-mediated communication in the university classroom: An experiment in on-line discussions. *Communication Education, 46,* 158 – 174.

Barnard, J. (1997). The World Wide Web and higher education: The promise of virtual universities and online libraries. *Education Technology, 37(3),* 30 – 35.

Cyrs, T.E. (1994). *Essential skills for college teaching.* Las Cruces, NM: New Mexico State University.

Gale, S. (1994). Desktop video conferencing: Technical advances and evaluation issues. In: Stephen A.R. Scrivener (Ed.), *Computer-supported cooperative work: The multimedia and networking paradigm.* Aldershot, England: Avebury Technical.

Jacobs, G., & Rodgers, C. (1997). Remote teaching with digital video: A trans-national experience. *British Journal of Educational Technology, 28(4),* 292 – 304.

Kaye, B., & Medoff, N. (1999). The world wide web: A mass communication perspective. Mountain View, CA: Mayfield.

Leidner, D.E., & Jarvenpaa, S.L. (1993). The information age confronts education: Case studies on electronic classrooms. *Information Systems Research, 4(1),* 24 – 54.

Porter, L.R. (1997). Creating the virtual classroom: Distance learning with the Internet. New York, NY: John Wiley.

Riel, M. (2000). The future of technology and education: Where are we heading? In D.M. Watson & T. Downes (Eds.), *Communications and networking in education.* Boston, MA: Kluwer Academic Press, pp. 9 – 24.

San Francisco Chronicle (2003). SARS crisis shows value of Internet education. Online platforms mean lessons can continue while schools are closed. April 21, 2003 (San Francisco Chronicle).

Sankar, C.S., Ford, F.N., & Terase, N. (1997). Impact of video conferencing in teaching an introductory MIS course. *Journal of Educational Technology Systems, 26(1),* 67 – 85.

SCMP (2003a). Classes suspended but learning continues: HKBU helps to breakthrough class suspension with VITLE. March 31, 2003 (South China Morning Post).

SCMP (2003b). Technology keeps classes open for more than 60 Hong Kong schools April 18, 2003 (South China Morning Post).

SCMP (2003c). e-Learning brings classrooms to Hong Kong students. May 3, 2003 (South China Morning Post).

Starr, R.M. (1997). Delivering instruction on the World Wide Web: Overview and basic design practices. *Educational Technology, 37(3),* 7 – 15.

Webster, J. (1998). Desktop video conferencing: Experiences of complete users, wary users, and non-users. *MIS Quarterly, 22(3),* 257 – 286.

Webster, J., & Hackley, P. (1997). Teaching effectiveness in technology-mediated distance learning. *Academy of Management Journal, 40(5),* 1282 – 1309.

Systemic Reform Efforts in the U.S.

Role of Information Technology in Fostering Collaboration within New Partnerships

Christopher A. Thorn
University of Wisconsin-Madison – Wisconsin Center for Education Research
cathorn@wisc.edu

Abstract: While data-based decision making and decision support systems are making inroads into educational management, the human capacity to evaluate programs, curricula, and other reform efforts has not kept pace. The latest generation of collaborative systems that support knowledge exchange and expertise location services hold great promise for building communities around these issues and supporting emerging research capacity in schools and districts.

Key words: Collaboration, knowledge management systems, school reform.

1 INTRODUCTION

Much of the work being done on the roll of information technology in improving school performance is in the area of data-based or data-driven decision making. The rising importance of standardized test results in national-, state-, and local-level accountability has led to a new interest in using individual level data generated for external reporting to guide local improvement efforts. The concept of school and district *report cards* has been taken to the next level in many places with interactive web sites that allow external viewers to examine the performance of subgroups and different accountability metrics. Data warehouse efforts within districts are attempts to put more instructionally relevant data into the hands of decision makers at all levels.

What these efforts often neglect to acknowledge is that we already had a pretty good idea of which groups are suffering from performance deficits. Improvement efforts have been the focus of many years of professional development and curriculum reform. The U.S. National Science Foundation has initiated a program area that combines lessons learned from a decade of systemic reform initiatives and from recent advances in research-based teaching materials for K-12 education in STEM (Science, Technology, Engineering, and Math). This new program is called Math and Science Partnerships and is intended to help bridge the gaps between state of the art research in STEM, leading education schools, and districts willing to adopt high-strength curricula and changes in teaching practices directed at closing the achievement gap between white and minority (particularly African American) students.

2 RESEARCH AGENDA

The research effort here is focused on the question of what support is needed to build human capacity to use student and staff outcome data. Early efforts to support data-based decision making were founded on a philosophy that could be summed up as "build it, and they will come". While there is little argument that school data systems were inadequate to support good decision making based on performance measures (for student or staff), the creation of these systems did not imbue decision makers with skills they did not possess. This approach also did nothing to address the need to build social networks around evidence to promote the diffusion and use of successful strategies. This gap has led my research and development work in the direction of examining the role of collaborative (primarily web-based) technologies in providing the social space to build these communities and the related skills.

The program I will be describing as a backdrop for this paper is the System-wide Change for All Learners and Educators [SCALE]. The SCALE partnership is made up of two universities and four school districts. First, there are two large university research centers – the Wisconsin Center for Education Research [WCER], University of Wisconsin-Madison and the Learning Research and Development Center [LRDC], University of Pittsburgh. Both of these partners bring different strengths to the partnership. WCER connects the partnership to the $600 million a year research base at UW-Madison - including leading centers for materials science, genetics, computers science, mathematics, and engineering. The LRDC has a outreach arm (the Institute for Learning [IfL]) that provides high-level technical assistance to 12 medium and large school districts across the country. Its approach, known as disciplinary literacy, is a holistic approach to teaching reform and related governance structures that is closely tied to the research base at the LRDC. This university partnership is supporting the development of new immersion curricula units in STEM subject areas that has as its goal the opportunity for each student to have one or more experiences each year doing authentic, hands on science. The SCALE partnership at the district level is made of two large districts – Los Angeles Unified School District and Denver Public Schools – and two medium-sized districts – Madison Metropolitan School District and Providence School District.

There are several key differences in this new round of funded projects that makes this partnership different from previous systemic reform efforts. First, SCALE is not trying to create new teacher training and teacher professional development relationships with these districts. The IfL already has existing, strong ties to each district. Each district has already bought into the professional development strategies of the IfL and is working with local coordinators to adapt the IfL approach to local district standards and organizational structures.

Second, UW-Madison is home to a number of large research efforts that have at least a decade of experience developing K-12 materials as a part of their STEM research efforts. Madison also has ties to similar projects at other large research universities and can act as a clearing house for similar work from other research teams.

Finally, the National Science Foundation has with its most recent round of large grants ($35 million for five years), operationalized a new organizational model for research coordination. In the past, grants would have been made at this amount or less. Any university coordination or interaction with more than one or two districts would have gone through relevant program officers at the National Science Foundation. The MSP program recognizes that coordination and cooperation at this level cannot be accomplished with the NSF program officers as the bottleneck for information flow. In a sense, the NSF has delegated part of its management authority to the partnership. In fact, the governing agreement for the partnership is not a traditional contract. It is called a cooperative agreement and is negotiated after the award is made. The negotiation process both allowed the NSF officials to help refine the goals and gave the partners a clearer picture of what the metrics of success would be.

3 A CASE STUDY OF SYSTEM IMPLEMENTATION

The primary study in the project is a case study of the implementation of an enterprise-level knowledge management and expertise discovery system across the leadership level of this partnership. As I said at the outset, there is a strong focus – particularly at the district level – on the use of achievement data (both high stakes outcome data and interim measures) to track the performance of states, districts, schools, teachers, and children. From the perspective of SCALE, this approach is clearly important. The partners must be able to evaluate the effectiveness of the interventions and both intermediate test scores and high stakes results will provide much of the key data for that work. However, there is a larger and more challenging problem on the other side of the partnership. The university units, school district offices, and funders do not share a single security environment and lack the tools necessary to support the complex interactions that would be necessary for them to achieve their goals. At this point, it is important to consider the characteristics of the partners from the point of view of their traditional strengths and ways of doing business.

The SCALE partnership is made up of two distinctly different groups. The organizational characteristics of these groups suggest that different forms of interaction will be differentially effective and that incentives for engagement will have to reflect each member's particular needs. In the case of the R&D units – WCER and LRDC – the two units are engaged in research into the basic elements of educational sciences. We also see both groups using that research expertise to gain a competitive advantage in the market of ideas (academic press, recruitment of faculty, getting research grants, etc.). There are areas in which two centers compete directly in the same markets (NSF funding for math or systemic reform research) and areas in which we have very little overlapping interest such as the IfL's teacher professional development programs and its presence in districts.

The second cluster of organizations is the districts. The literature on collaboration would codify them more in the role of core customer in a close supply-chain relationship. The districts actually have little in common since they serve different markets and in no way compete with one another. There are no strong, near-term links that tie these organizations to one another – aside from growing concerns about persistent gaps in test scores by race/ethnicity. The long-term prospect of leveraging of successful models may hold some appeal, but many districts find replication within their own districts to be enough of a challenge.

3.1 Characteristics of Successful Cooperative Ventures

In earlier (Thorn 1995) work, I have argued that successful collaboratives have to focus first on defining the overlapping interest that members share. One of the ways this condition is met in SCALE is the agreement on the common problems – high dropout rates, low test scores in math and science in urban districts, and widening performance gaps between whites and other ethnic/racial groups. This agreement on the challenge provides a shared sense of threatened core values – equal education for all, issues of competitiveness and success as a nation of large portions of the population are undereducated, social and economic decay of urban centers are a few of the core concerns shared by all members. This act of defining shared values and concerns both creates a social place for engaging in the partnership's work and says to everyone involved that other efforts by the members that do not fit with this common interest are not on the table for discussion.

The other important finding from this research was a short list of characteristics of successful consortia. First, there had to be a small leadership group that engaged in what is often called *unconditional giving* or (in economic terms) the commitment of resources beyond a level that appears rational for short- to mid-term calculations. Second, there had to be formal, transparent agreements about methods for the organization of work in the collaborative space. This included training around meeting management, conflict resolution, etc. This creation of a common working culture was a key factor in helping members from different organizations to be effective and productive after a short time. Members of one particularly successful consortium described the importance of *knowing* how to interact with others on his team and *knowing* they would all be interacting based on accepted norms and procedures. This certainty kept conflict to a minimum and helped to keep meetings short and productive. This contrast to the practices of their home organizations (computer and semiconductor firms) was quite striking for many members.

The creation of complex consortia of research units and school districts will require new workflows for creating curriculum and teacher training materials. It will require new tools for coordinating geographically-distributed teams from different organizations. These new groupings will transcend traditional hierarchical relationships within each partner and will have no mechanisms for controlling the work of individual members. Rather, these new teams must be collaborative communities that focus on shared goals and that are motivated by those goals.

At the same time, each of the individual members of the collaborative will also be creating new teams within their respective organizations that will be directly responsible to leadership. These teams will likely cross existing organizational boundaries (discipline, sub-district, roles) and will need additional support for their work, since traditional supports would be based on the needs of their operational units and not reflect the needs of a new organization form.

3.2 A Comparison of Two Research-Based Systems

What this problem space calls for is a set of collaboration tools that support group work and knowledge management in several forms. First, loose confederations of collaborators that are engaged in problem definition and in creating new communities will need tools that allow for the creation of new affinity groups. One of the problems encountered by teams of scientists as they begin coordination with science education and other teacher education professionals is that neither group has clear understanding of who should be working with whom. Tools such as the Fraunhofer Institute's Basic Support for Cooperative Work [BSCW] provide shared folders, discussion lists, tasks, and calendars for geographically-distributed teams.

An important aspect that is often overlooked, however, is its approach to creating groups. BSCW supports the traditional method of forming groups in IT systems. One can create predefined groups as a manager and invite all appropriate members to join. This group is typically assigned to a particular, pre-defined directory structure. Another option, however, is for individual users to invite others to their own work spaces to collaborate on smaller tasks. This identification of and support for local affinity groups is a powerful addition to collaborative technologies and enables partnerships that coalesce and flourish outside of traditional hierarchies.

This feature is a key difference between BSCW and many other collaborative environments that are only extensions/virtualizations of existing hierarchies. One of the strengths of BSCW in this area is a philosophy of making membership in the environment explicit and searchable. Openness is a default setting. While this design approach makes collaboration across teams within the same organization much easier, it also makes more complex forms of organization and the ability to hide groups that need protection from oversight or some form of anonymity very difficult to support. Sophisticated security models and support for complex organizational forms exist at the other end of the tool spectrum. This emerging need for enterprise-scale collaborative tools encouraged me to start a new research initiative to find and implement a collaborative environment designed around complex partnerships. This effort identified Intraspect[1] as a leader in the field.

4 FINDINGS

While the initial research focused on BSCW, the ongoing work is focused on the creation of collaborative work and presentation spaces in our new Intraspect environment. We are now nine months into an implementation of this high-level collaboration, knowledge discovery, and expertise location system. My team is in the midst of documenting the affordances of the system for different forms of university-district-school partnerships. The preliminary finding show identify four different features that seem to be necessary to support the ongoing work across the different managerial levels of the partnership as well as vital to the work of dispersed teams working on particular curricular areas.

4.1 Secure Space for Risk Taking is Vital in Districts with Low Trust between Groups

Teachers or building leaders taking advantage of new high strength curricula or other professionally challenging endeavors may see student outcomes decline in the first year of implementation. In a high stakes environment, this can be seen as risky behavior. Participants need a safe space to collaborate that cannot be observed by others above them in the school or district hierarchy. At the same time, district leaders need to be able to provide political and other social support to teams at a distance – perhaps in a school climate that is not open to change. The ability to create a secure *ad hoc* space for collaboration can also free participants from some of the challenges of hierarchy.

4.2 Building Ties to Experts (and Expert Knowledge)

Intraspect and other KM systems can be seen as repositories for complex collections and may capture tacit knowledge in the form of email exchanges and other informal data types. One aspect of KM support in which Intraspect excels is the area of expertise identification. The metadata architecture and search engine preferences the association of individual with search terms. This makes it trivially easy to locate people associated with artifacts, concepts, or groups. When one searches, named users are always associated visually with all hits to make location easier. The search logic also preferences individuals in the system who are the owners of documents that contain the search terms. Multiple hits in documents introduced into the system by an individual will usually put the user in the top 10 hits. This linkage between artifacts and human expertise is a feature that SCALE is using explicitly to foster connections and knowledge exchange between groups.

4.3 Building Custom Spaces for Work and Presentation

This complex partnership has multiple dimensions of membership – organization, knowledge domain, level in the hierarchy, etc. The *work* of any individual member will differ based on their role in any grouping of actors. In the case of district leaders, they have asked for presentation spaces that display current and planned activities that will be taking place in their district as well as staff and student outcomes from past events. Disciplinary teams, on the other hand, want work spaces in which they can exchange and edit documents and manage complex workflows. Research and evaluation teams want workspaces organized around the projects deliverables. The object oriented design of the Intraspect system allows for the rapid development of custom spaces that explicitly support these different configurations and needs. No district- or university-centric system could provide these services. This enterprise/supply chain problem space requires specialized tools to address the challenges faced by the SCALE partnership.

4.4 Object Oriented Design for Customization

As noted above, object oriented technology has proven to be a crucial element of this implementation. The complexity of this research and development project with its tight links to school districts and their reform efforts means that we have many users who have multiple group memberships and may serve in multiple roles across those groups. Tools to support complex organizational models must respect this reality and provide quick and easy access to information and work spaces based on complex memberships.

5 CONCLUSION

The jury is still out on the effectiveness of the SCALE partnership. What seems clear, however, is the importance of providing collaborative support to university-district-school partnerships that allow for secure access to expertise and custom spaces. The National Science Foundation has reviewed the progress to date and is working with my group to explore extending our Intraspect environment to include members at the foundation. They have identified the lack of a collaborative environment as one of the biggest barriers they face in helping these large research projects deliver on their stated goals.

6 REFERENCES

Thorn, C. (1995). State Involvement in the Semiconductor Industry: The Role and Importance of Consortia. *Benevolent conspiracies: the role of enabling technologies in the welfare of nations : the cases of SDI, SEMATECH, and EUREKA*. H. Willke, C. P. Krück and C. Thorn. New York, Walter de Gruyter.

1 Recently renamed Vignette Business Collaboration Server after the firm was purchased by Vignette Corporation in December 2003.

Developing an Integrated School Information System

Greg Baker
Scotch College, Melbourne, Australia
Greg.Baker@scotch.vic.edu.au

Abstract: This paper describes some of the issues in developing an integrated school information system that contributes to the management of a school. The system is based on an SQL relational database with a browser-based interface for all queries and transactions. The use of a standard interface makes it easy for end-users to navigate what is, in fact, a complex system. The user input and self-service provisions are important aspects of this system. This paper demonstrates that it is possible and feasible to develop an information system in a school that meets the needs of staff and is customized for the users' requirements.

Key words: Educational management, school information system, integrated school system, information infrastructure.

1 INTRODUCTION

Pauline Wilson walks into her first class for the day at Scotch College. She carries her lightweight notebook computer that is already started and connected securely to the school's wireless network. She calls her class list up on the notebook screen, quickly marks the absentees and then clicks the Update button. The results are immediately stored on the school's information system and are available to all those with authority to access it. Within minutes, accurate attendance records have been completed for all 1,850 students in the school. Students taking music instrumental lessons have been flagged, as have those going on an excursion to the Art Gallery.

Earlier in the day, the schools' rowing crews finished their early morning training on the river and the students have headed to the pavilion for breakfast. As they walk in the door, they pass their student cards under a barcode reader to record their attendance at breakfast. At the end of breakfast, the teacher in charge authorizes a batch account to be processed and the charge for breakfast will be added to the student's next fee account.

2 INFORMATION NEEDS

Each school is different and has different information needs. Centrally designed systems can meet *most* of a school's needs *most* of the time, but not always. At Scotch College an information system that meets the needs of all the staff has been developed. As those needs change, so does the system. Functions are developed in response to requests from staff. In some cases, needs are anticipated and catered for.

2.1 Goals of the System

The goals of the system are to provide:

- Accurate, up-to-date data.
- An interface that staff find easy to use.
- Access from a variety of locations – at a desk, in a classroom, on the school oval, at home.
- Differing access rights to the data depending upon need.
- Designed so that it is integrated across the school
- Self-service access to reports.

3 INFORMATION SYSTEMS AT SCOTCH COLLEGE

A computer-based information system was first considered at Scotch College in 1978. An initial definition of the information system was prepared by the then Director of Computing and the Records Sub-committee of the school (Graham, 1978). The document was "... an attempt to define the records and information systems at Scotch College ... and to give an accurate and valid picture of our information system." (Graham, 1978).

At that time, the primary source of information about current and past students was known as the "Blue Card". The blue card was, in fact, a blue card that was regularly added to by members of staff. The blue card became the definitive document that recorded a student's progress through the school. In the early 1990's the blue cards were all transferred to microfiche and they remain a primary source of historical data for the school.

At that time also, "... a file of names and addresses of people associated with the school was kept on the Melbourne Stock Exchange System. These records were the responsibility of the school's alumni group – the Old Scotch Collegians' Association (OSCA). This file was to form the basis of the school's information system.

The original coding specifications indicate that the school's initial decision was to develop the system using Cobol. However, when it came to time to carry out the development, the database chosen for use was DEC's Relation Database (DEC Rdb) and the programming language was VAX BASIC (Graham, 1985). A relational database model was chosen for the reasons that have subsequently become standard textbook criteria including:

- Minimization of duplication of data.
- Elimination of modification anomalies.
- Ease of data retrieval (Kroenke, 1983).
- Data consistency and accuracy.
- Multi level integrity (Hernandez, 2003).

With the increase in processing power available, the relational model has proven to be most useful in this context.

3.1 The First System

The first system was developed internally and put into production in the early 1980s. The hardware used was a DEC VAX 11/750 using DEC Rdb, VAX BASIC and a fourth generation programming language called Datatrieve. The operating system was DEC's VMS. The system was a menu driven one with different access levels provided for different staff. Terminals were provided for all key staff and all teaching staff had access to the information system. Over a period of some 15 years, the system was enhanced, supported and maintained internally. During that period, the school had essentially *one* database that served the needs of the key constituents including:

- Staff.
- Admissions.
- Alumni (OSCA).
- Fund raising (development).

A key benefit of the system was that an address update in one area of the school was immediately reflected throughout the system and available to all authorized users.

3.2 A New System

In 1996, Aspect Computing was engaged to advise on a replacement for the above system. The key reasons for considering a change were:

- The need to "… record and track relationships between students and school community members; and
- The need to furnish the Development Office with appropriate tools to assist in fund raising." (Firkin, 1997).

Associated with changed needs were changes in the computer industry that affected the choice of tools and platform. In particular:

- DEC Computer Company divested many of its software tools to Oracle, including DEC Rdb.
- DEC itself was taken over by Compaq Computer Company, which was later absorbed into Hewlett Packard.

The first system was built using exclusively DEC tools – hardware, software including operating system and development tools, as well as support. The nature of the industry thus accelerated the need for change. At the same time, came an urgent need from within the school to develop a system that enabled the electronic recording of attendances. Figure 1 below shows the strategy used in terms of hardware, software and tools.

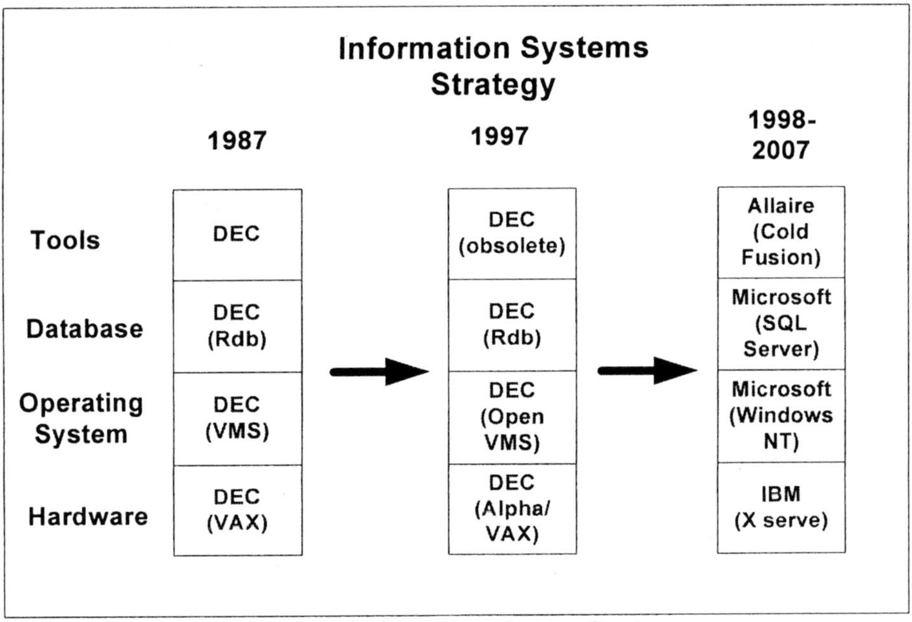

Figure 1: Information System Strategy

Other key reasons for developing the system internally included:

- No single externally produced software package met the school's needs.
- The school's needs continually change and there was a need to respond to those changes in a timely manner.

- The need for it to be supported on more than one platform (i.e. Microsoft Windows and Apple Macintosh).

At the time, most of the software packages that could be purchased 'off the shelf' were not Web-enabled.

3.3 Designing a New System

A consultant from Aspect Computing assisted in the initial scope of the project (Aspect Computing, 1997). Key requirements of the project were to:

- Convert the existing school administration system to the new system with at least the same functionality.
- To have minimal impact on running of the school.
- To improve response times.
- To ensure that there was a standard user interface that was acceptable to users.
- To add new, required functionality to the system.

A new logical data model was created and the existing database was mapped into this new model. As noted by Tatnall and Davey (2001), the involvement of users is a key component of the success of a school system. Key users were consulted at each stage and helped specify the outcomes. Each of the various menu items was developed in response to a request from a member of staff – both teaching and non teaching. During 1998 the data structures were defined, created and brought across to the new system. The data transfer was successful.

The first new application developed was to track student attendances. This was done in about five working days and the first version was put into use at the start of 1999. The decision to use Allaire's Cold Fusion as a rapid application development environment was taken after advice from a Gartner Group consultant at Gartner's Annual IT Expo in 1998. That decision has proved successful but had some impact on staffing that is referred to later.

4 AN INTEGRATED SYSTEM

The system was designed to ensure that it was integrated across a range of levels and functions within the organisation. The system can track a person from birth to death and beyond. The system is centred on a *person* as the key entity. A person has many different attributes as he or she interacts with different facets of the school. A person can be:

- A future student
- A current student
- A past student

- A future parent
- A current parent
- A past parent
- A future member of staff
- A current member of staff
- A past member of staff.

A person can have a number of those attributes at the one time (eg. a past student and a future parent). The previous system had used different entities for a person – eg. a student was one entity and his parents were different entities with different attributes.

Once the person is created on the system, he or she may never be deleted. (The only deletions from the system are those future enrolees to the school and their parents who never actually come to the school and have no other association with the school.) At the time of writing, there were more than 60,000 people on the system.

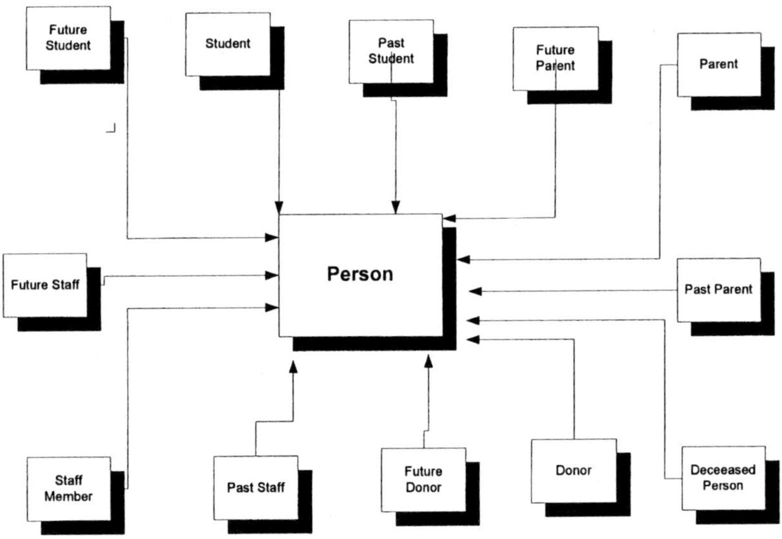

Figure 2: A person can have many different attributes.

4.1 Relational Database

The back-end system is a relational database made up of some 90 different tables. It would be nice to claim that it is fully normalized but, in the words of the database manager (Leon Seremelis), "It's pretty good". The relational database structure minimizes the duplication of data and makes it relatively simple to update that data.The data storage, retrieval and querying is carried out using stored procedures in Microsoft SQL Server. The Cold Fusion pages generate queries that have been created by users. That is, the users can often decide on the type of data required.

4.2 Updating Addresses

One of the key challenges is to keep address and contact details up-to-date and accurate. Address changes come from a variety of structures within the organization: The can come from:

- Teachers
- Reception
- Admissions
- Alumni
- Fund raising.

The following assumptions are made about addresses:

- Each person can have three addresses:
    - Home
    - Postal
    - Business
- A number of people can have the same address.

When an address is updated, the user is given the choice to make the change for:

- That person only, or
- The other persons at that address.

The system automatically shows all the other people who have the same address. Once the address is changed, it is immediately reflected throughout the system. For example, a parent's address change is immediately reflected in information looked at through the student view of the system.

5 BROWSER-BASED

An important aspect of the system is to make it easy for staff to use. A decision was made very early in the development process that user access would be via a browser-based system.

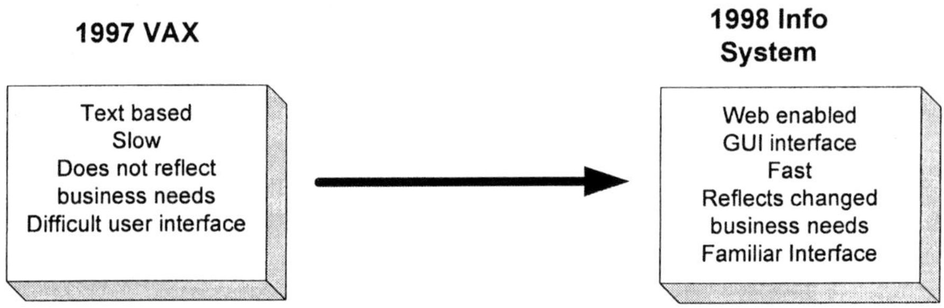

Figure 3 Moving from a text based system to web based system.

The standard browser used is Internet Explorer – an interface that all staff had become familiar with in using the Internet. One of the design goals was to make the system easy to use and easy to navigate. A browser-based system at the front-end poses some challenges in developing transaction-based databases in that interactions are stateless until a transaction is committed. The system that has been developed uses Microsoft SQL Server as the back-end database and Macromedia Cold Fusion as middle ware to provide the browser front-end.

The client or staff computer makes an HTML request that is sent to the Cold Fusion Server. This translates it into an SQL query that is forwarded to the SQL Server. The data is returned to the Cold Fusion Server and then presented in the browser to the user. Staff are able to access a wide range of data that is of use and to download appropriate data for mail merge or personal use.

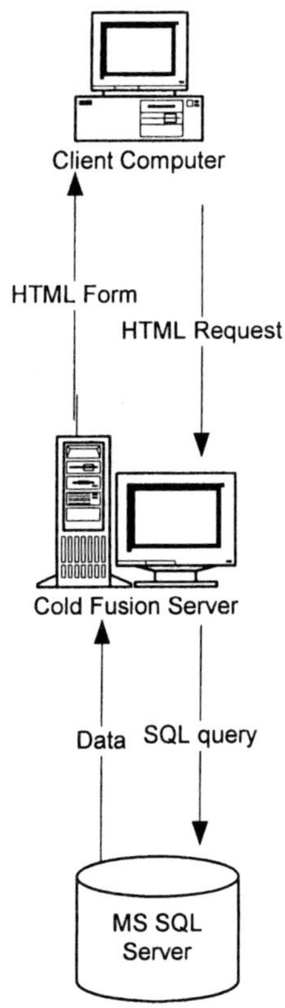

Figure 4 Microsoft SQL Server and Cold Fusion

6 MODULES AVAILABLE

The following are the key modules available:

- Student
  - Classes
  - Sports
  - Activities

  - Learning difficulties
  - Reporting
- Teachers
  - Classes
  - Excursions
  - Trips
- Attendance
- People
- Accounts
- Bookroom
- Alumni
- Fund Raising
- Enrolments
- Personnel

The following modules are planned for future development:

- Music School
- Swap shop
- Sporting Team Management

The modules and functionality are developed in response to requests from staff – both teachers and non teachers.

7 ACCESSIBLE ANYWHERE

The data is accessible throughout the school campus for all staff. Each member of the teaching staff is provided with a notebook computer and an Ethernet connection at his or her desk. That connection provides access to the administrative network.

There are some 32 wireless access points throughout the campus providing access to the student network. Using a Cisco VPN Concentrator, staff can securely access the administration network and check class rolls and access all the information normally available at their desks. The Cisco VPN software includes a personal firewall on each staff member's notebook computer. At home, staff can access the information via the school's portal page using the Internet. Users are authenticated via the firewall and SSL encryption is used of queries and transactions.

The system is available to *all* staff, anywhere in the school. Access rights vary according to need. A limited number of staff are able to update information. Again, this is based on the member of staff's needs.

8 SELF-SERVICE ACCESS TO REPORTS

The provision of self-service access is of key importance in giving control to the users. Typically, the user provides the criteria for selection and the query is processed by the system. A range of files can be downloaded for use on the staff members' computer. In particular, class lists, sporting lists etc can be downloaded.

Communication with students and/or parents can be done by email – classes or other groups can be emailed from within the system. Immediately a class is changed for any reason, the email list dynamically changes. The need to alter groups in a Microsoft Exchange server is not required. Staff can download files based on their selections to be used in mail merge documents. A large range of standard merge fields is provided and these can be used in documents and mailing labels. Templates are provided for the mailing labels.

One of the outcomes of this process is that staff are not reliant on centrally produced reports or documents but are able to generate these themselves *when* they need them.

9 SYSTEMS INTEGRATION

There are, of course, other database systems operating within the school. These are being integrated into the architecture of the system so that updates between systems are made when required. One such example is the development of the school's timetable. Timetabling is a complex and specialized function. Rather than re-inventing the wheel, a timetabling package is used. In this case, student data is sent to the timetable package, student choices are entered into that package and a timetable is created. The timetable data is then sent back to the main information system. The timing of this is at the discretion of the person in charge of the timetable (i.e. in the hands of the key user).

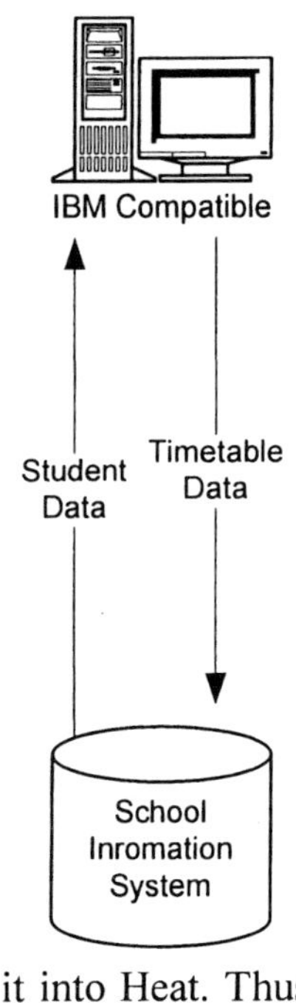

Figure 5: School Information and Timetable System.

A second example of system integration is help desk software called Heat from Front Range. This is also SQL based and a help desk call looks up the data about users on the Scotch Information System and pulls it into Heat. Thus, user data is maintained in one source, the SIS, but help desk functionality remains in Heat. Systems integration is a key issue for the future as we investigate further on line services and individual portal interfaces for staff, student, parents and alumni.

10 USER INTERFACE

The user interface is designed to:

- Make it intuitive for users to find information.
- Provide links to relevant information.
- Make it easy to carry out every day tasks.
- Be consistent.

Figure 6: Information about a student

Figure 6 shows part of the user interface. The following are important parts of the design:

- Menus across the top as hyperlinks.
- Menus at the left, also as hyperlinks.
- Query window – student number etc.

The result of the query is in the right side of the window (partially shown in figure 6).

In Figure 7 it can be seen that a range of information is available by clicking on the hyperlinks. This is typical of the system – a vast amount of information available for all those who need to access it.

However, as the system has grown the menus have become somewhat clumsy in places and a new design is being implemented. Figure 8 shows a first version of that design that will be tested with users before implementation.

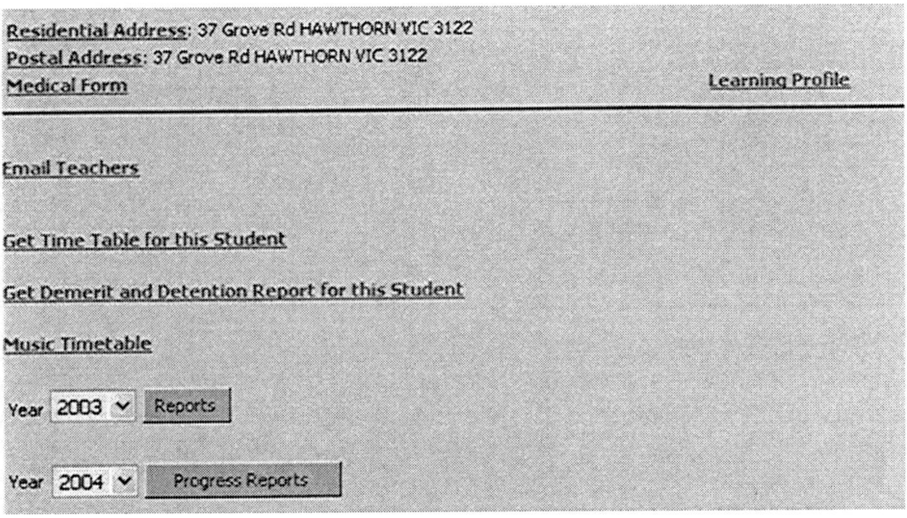

Figure 7: Further information about a student

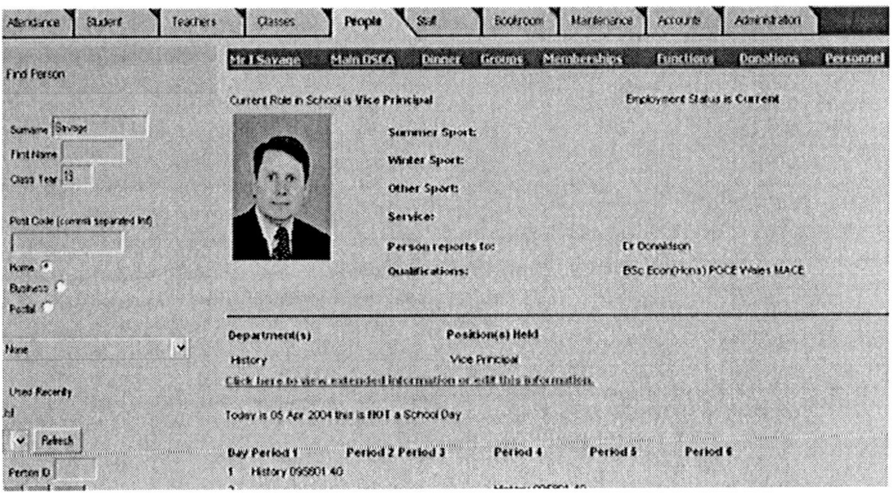

Figure:8 A new interface

11 BUILDING LINKS WITHIN THE COMMUNITY

The next key steps are to build links with the school community. The system currently provides personalized access for staff members, based on their login details and their position within the school.

The future involves development of the web interface and providing access to both students and parents when and where they need it. These groups can expect to have access to secure, personalised access:

- Student reports.
- Forthcoming events.
- Sporting activities and teams.
- Sports results.
- Activity sign-on.
- Fee account status, approval and payment.

The challenge is to ensure that these functions are:

- Developed using agreed standards.
- Communication is secure and encrypted.
- Integrated with specialized systems provided by third parties.

12 CONCLUSION

This system was one of the first, if not the first, school administration packages developed in Australia using only a web front end for all users. This provides users with a familiar, intuitive interface that is easy to navigate. The user self-service provisions give control to users over *what* they need and *when* they want it. The system meets the needs of an individual school but could be developed to meet the needs of a wider range of schools.

The future integration into homes provides an exciting school/home interface that will improve communication and help the school to better meet the needs of its students and parents.

13 REFERENCES

Aspect Computing, (1997). "Scotch College Administration System Scope Issue 1.0", 10 December 1997, internal publication.

Baker, G. M. (1997). "Information System Strategy", November 1997, internal document.

Firkin, H. (1997). "Scotch College School Administration System Proposal Issue 1.0", Aspect Computing Pty Ltd, 31 October 1997.

Graham, J. D. and the Records Sub-committee of Scotch College (1998), "Definition of the Information System of Scotch College, Melbourne", 1978, internal publication.

Graham, J.D. (1985) – in conversations from the mid 1980s.
Hernandez, M. J. (2003) "Database Design for Mere Mortals", 2nd ed, Addison-Wesley, USA
Kroenke, D. (1983). "Database Processing 2nd edition", Science Research Associates, USA.
Rees, M, White, A, White, B, (2001). "Designing Web Interfaces", Prentice Hall, USA.
Tatnall, A. and Davey, B. (2001). Open ITEM Systems are Good ITEM Systems. *Institutional Improvement through Information Technology in Educational Management.* Nolan, P. Dordrecht, The Netherlands, Kluwer Academic Publishers: 59-69.

Computerised School Information Systems Usage in an Emerging Country - Uganda

Ronald Bisaso and Adrie Visscher
Department of Educational Organisation and Management
Faculty of Behavioural Sciences, University of Twente, The Netherlands

Abstract: This paper describes an exploratory study on the usage of computerised school information systems (CISs) in the administration and management of the biggest secondary schools in Uganda. The field of information technology in educational management (ITEM) has been mostly confined to the developed countries that its potential in the developing countries in regard to its usage and implications on the schools that use it has not been studied (Bisaso, 2003). The literature reveals that developing countries are lagging behind in the use of CISs partly because of the resource constraints in skilled expertise, finance, and computer equipment (Visscher, 2001). But this magnitude of inferiority in school administrative computing has not been proven hence this study. The results of this exploratory study reveal that the CISs in Uganda are mainly used for clerical purposes while managerial usage by school managers is very limited. Relevant factors relating to the effective use of the CISs are identified. Users are generally positive on the effects of CISs use. It is concluded that wider and better CIS usage would be promoted by carefully designed user training grounded on a thorough analysis of the needs of the user group. Moreover, the support of the systems administrator is considered vital as a catalyst of CIS usage. A comparative summary with earlier studies in the developed countries is made.

Key words: Computerised school information systems (CISs), information technology in educational management (ITEM), school processes, management of schools.

1 INTRODUCTION

Information technology in educational administration and management (ITEM) of secondary schools in developing countries in general and Uganda in particular is a relatively new field that not only needs in-depth study on system utilisation in schools but also on effects on the school processes and maybe outcomes. This is a concept that needs to be systematically embraced and studied in its genesis or initiation so as to come up with an advanced design of a CIS for schools in Uganda. Moreover, this can be a starting point for further research on ITEM in other developing countries providing a concrete generalisation. Uganda in the last 6 years has had a dramatic rise in the numbers of the primary school leavers, for instance in 2002 the candidates were over 0.45 million expected to rise to 1.6 million in 2004 (British council, 2003). The 2002 ministerial policy statement notes that there has been a pleasant effect of now attaining an enrolment of 7.2 million pupils in primary schools. Consequently, the pressure on secondary schools in Uganda has been mounting over the years and is likely to increase. This is an outcome of the ever-increasing numbers of primary school leavers joining secondary education that it is worthwhile to invest in CISs so that information handling that requires somewhat sophisticated means, and which can be provided by the computer, is more efficient. Through establishment of a central database time may be saved because there can be multiple usage of the same data by all the school staff, and prevention of errors which may have occurred as a result of repeated registration of data by various staff (Visscher, 2001). This improved efficiency can be manifested in school effectiveness with a likelihood of having a better attainment of the school goals. It is likely that the number of young school managers in Uganda will rise beyond what it is today. In the yesteryears most school managers were above 40 years, the trend is that most are now below 35 years. This is because of the mismatch between the available very experienced teachers and the numbers of schools being put up today. For instance, Ministry of Education and Sports (1999:5, in Aguti, 2002) reports that in 1999, Uganda had 625 secondary schools but by the year 2001, the number had almost tripled to 1850 secondary schools (Ministry of Education and Sports, 2001 a: 3, in Aguti, 2002). It is thus crucial for these increasing relatively novice schools managers to make informed decisions that can be based on the school information system, which in addition also provides guidance on management activities. Visscher (2001) notes that the information system can also help to signal that certain aspects of schooling require attention. For instance, if certain standards have been defined in advance, such as the percentage of low marks within a class is too high, and transcribed into software, the computer can provide a warning to school managers if the standards are not being met. This may improve process control, lead to more timely corrective actions, and to a more effective school.

1.1 Organisation of Education in Uganda

The existing structure of the Ugandan education system has been in force since the early 1960s. In 1989, a commission was appointed by the government to review the entire education system and made proposals and recommendations famously known as the Kajubi report. The government accepted the recommendations in 1992 culminating into the Government White paper- Education for National Integration and Development. Government then produced a master plan for the Education sector. The plan constitutes an action-based approach to the implementation of the education policies formulated in the 1992 white paper. (Odaet, 1995)

The Ministry of Education and Sports (MoES) has got the managerial and administrative mandate to centrally run the education system. The MoES has a Minister of Education and Sports as its political head assisted by the 3 Ministers of State; in charge of Primary Education, Higher Education, and Sports. There is a Permanent Secretary (PS) who is the overall accounting officer for the ministry. The Commissioner for Education Planning and an Undersecretary in charge of Finance & Administration assist the PS. The Director of Education oversees the activities of six out of the eight departments of the ministry, each headed by a Commissioner. The eight departments of the MoES include; Finance and Administration, Educational Planning, Pre-primary and Primary Education, Secondary Education, Higher Education, Teacher Education, Special Needs and Careers Guidance, and Business Technical and Vocational Education Training Department. In addition, there are semi-autonomous institutions that execute certain responsibilities on behalf of and in liaison with the MoES. These include the National Council of Sports (NCS), Uganda National Examinations Board (UNEB), National Council for Higher Education (NCHE), National Curriculum Development Centre (NCDC), Universities, and Uganda National Council for UNESCO and the Education Service Commission (ESC).

1.2 Structure of the Ministry and its Departments

In line with the overall government of Uganda decentralisation policy, education sector functions decentralised are recruitment, deployment of primary school teachers, implementation of UPE and the school construction program. The implementation of these decentralisation programs is however hampered because it has to fit in the general sector guidelines issued by the centre. The School Management Committee, with the head teacher as its secretary, oversees school policy formulation and implementation. Its activities include supervising school budgets, reviewing education performance, overseeing student and staff discipline and making plans for school facilities expansion and repair. Head teachers draw up monthly reports to the District Chief Administrative Officers and forward a copy to the school management committee' chairperson (The Ugandan Experience of UPE, 1999).

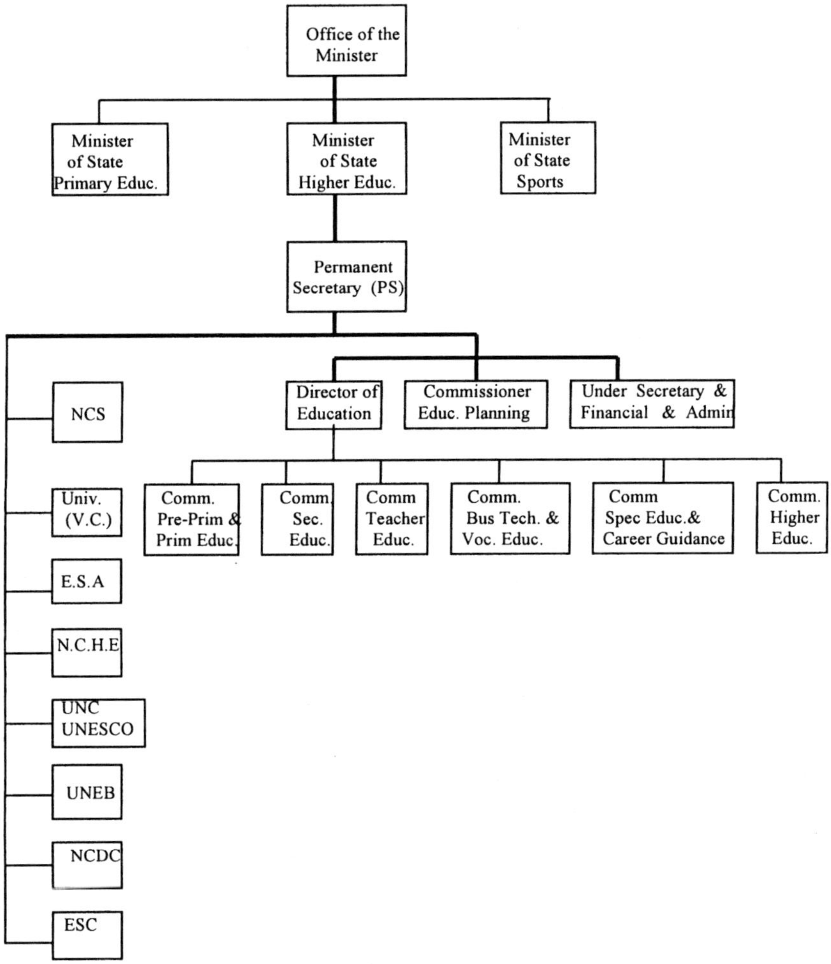

Figure 1: *Source: Ministerial Policy Statement 2002*

2 RESEARCH QUESTIONS AND RESEARCH FRAMEWORK

The study is guided by the following specific research questions, which have been formulated with regard to the variable clusters in the Visscher model (1996; 2001).

1. What computerised school information systems (CISs) are used in secondary schools in Uganda?
2. To what extent and how are these CIS used in secondary schools in Uganda?
3. What is user opinion of the CIS quality?
4. How were the CISs implemented?
5. What were the relevant features of the schools into which they were introduced relatively successfully?
6. What are the positive and/or negative effects of CIS usage?
7. Which factors prove to have a relationship with degree of CIS usage?
8. How can computerised school information systems and/or their use in secondary schools in Uganda be improved?

The study in this paper explores the usage of CISs in administration and management of secondary schools in Uganda using selected variables in the Visscher model (1996; 2001) on the factors determining the usage and impact of CISs in developing countries. While the Visscher model has been used in developed countries (Visscher 1999; 2003), its feasibility in the developing countries is tested in this study. Visscher notes that four factors determine the level of use of CISs and their effect in schools namely the CIS design strategy, CIS quality, implementation process features, and school organisation features. Most developing countries have not evolved a uniform CIS used in all the schools. On CIS quality, each system is used and appreciated in accordance with the perception of its users towards its features. Hence the use of a particular system is dependent on its applications, some of which the school staff may or may not use (Fung and Visscher, 2001). Fung (1995) and Visscher and Fung (2001) point out that the initiation phase in an innovation process is essentially related to commitment among the innovation users and their perception of the added value accruing from embracing the change. Like in many other attempts at change, the time variable is needed for sufficient understanding of the reasons for the change otherwise it is rejected. Riggs (1964, in Kereteletswe and Selwood, 2003) notes that in a prismatic society, it is not easy for old practices to give way to new or modern practices emphasising the time variable. Moreover, there is not a replacement of old practices by new ones but a displacement. Fung (1991) and Bird (1991) cited in Visscher (1995) argue that if the architect of the change process is supportive, that its successful implementation is guaranteed; and the same is just true if the school management does likewise. Moreover, with the wealth of expertise of CIS administrators, use of the system is expected to be impressive especially through their just-in-time assistance to the system users (Fung and Visscher, 2001). Visscher (1995) has presented user training as a factor that influences the implementation process of the CISs. Marx (1975, in Visscher, 1996b) points out that schools vary in their policy-making capacity, and that the areas in which schools develop their policies often differ in degree. It is this divergence in policy-making capacity that will strongly impact on the initiation of CISs in school policy making.

3 METHOD AND DATA ANALYSIS

The research is grounded on a sample survey. Uganda has fifty-six districts from which a selection of four neighbouring districts was made for conducting the sample survey. The researchers using a non-probability sampling technique identified 55 schools whose type and size, suggested that they could be using computers in school administration and management. It is evident that the majority of the biggest and well-developed schools in Uganda are located in the central districts of Kampala (the capital), Wakiso, Mukono and the neighbouring eastern district of Jinja; consequently qualifying as an area for drawing a sample for this study. Most importantly, innovations begin at the centre and spread to the periphery, hence the researchers thought that the field of ITEM being a recent innovation in developing countries to which Uganda belongs, it might not be spread over the whole country. Each participating school was sent one questionnaire, which was to be completed separately by one of the school management personnel namely the head teacher (principal), the deputy head or deputy principal, director of studies or any person knowledgeable about the CIS. The response rate was 100% after follow-up activities. Descriptive statistics were applied, namely frequencies and cross tabulations, corresponding to the selected variables studied in the Visscher model (1996; 2001). Moreover, a regression analysis was done on those variables considered to most predict CIS usage so as to confirm a linear relationship between the factors studied. The five selected variables cover aspects of the quality of CISs, features of the implementation process, and the characteristics of schools in which CISs have been implemented relatively successfully. Respondents' scores were transformed into normalised scores, allowing their mutual comparison, and thereafter variables assumed to meet the linear criteria on system usage were entered into stepwise regression analyses on the use of CISs by school management personnel.

4 RESULTS

The survey mainly focused on fifty-five big and well-developed secondary schools in Uganda. It is astonishing that 38% of the selected schools (22% government-aided and 16% private schools) declared themselves non-users of CISs perpetuating the notion that developing countries like Uganda are advancing at snail-pace in regard to ITEM. Despite this relatively low turnout, optimism was restored by a total of thirty-four schools (a user response rate of 100%) responding to the survey of whom 56% were privately owned and 44% government-aided, all returning well-filled questionnaires acceptable to the researchers. Schools with 500-1000 students on roll were 54% and schools having over 1000 students on roll were 46%. Follow up from the researchers notwithstanding, it was impossible to increase the response rate because all responded. Due to time and financial constraints, the researchers decided to focus on responses of the CISs users from the thirty-four schools because the selected and therefore research schools represented the whole range of schools in the population using the CISs based on their size and type. Moreover, without obtaining results from and paying attention to these (part of) selected schools in Uganda, such a study, in all probability, would be unfeasible. We now adapt the results to the research questions in section 2.1 above.

4.1 Computerised School Information Systems Used

The findings reveal that there is a variety of CISs that are used in secondary schools in Uganda, which are both locally and externally developed. It is interesting to note that over 70% of the systems used are locally developed either by commercial software vendors (74%), or the school staff (18%), or individuals with knowledge in computer programming (8%). The locally developed systems are called ledger works, sysplus, school management information system, student information management system, school management system, accounting s/w, dehezi and the multi-user computer system. Some of the local systems developers include Kampala computer centre, and individuals with knowledge about computer programming. Software programmes reportedly used as CISs in some schools include Microsoft products like Access, Excel, Word, and Microsoft Money and Office automation systems, or End User computing system from the U.S.A. Other externally developed CISs include Smart force training from India.

4.2 Degree of CIS Usage

Eight CIS-modules were identified which included student records, student assessment, student attendance, staff records, timetabling, programme schedule, financial monitoring and planning, and library management. Table 1 illustrates percentages of respondents reporting whether the modules are included or not included in the CISs used. The results portray that the most common modules on any CIS are financial monitoring and planning, student records and student assessment. The least available modules are library management and student attendance.

A further analysis of the extent of use shows a large percentage of use of the most common modules of CISs to support managerial decisions.

Table 1: Modules included in the Ugandan computerised school information systems

	yes	no
	%	%
Student records(personal data)	90%	10%
Student Assessment(test scores)	83%	17%
Student Attendance	46%	54%
Staff records	68%	32%
Timetabling	59%	41%
Programme schedule	67%	33%
Financial Monitoring and Planning	91%	9%
Library Management(records)	39%	61%

In Table 2, results on frequency of module usage to support managerial decisions portray that, 43% and 13% of the respondents use 'financial monitoring and planning' every week, and once a year respectively. 'Student assessment' is the most commonly used module every month with 31% respondents.

The 'programme schedule' is most used a few times a year by 40% and finally, the 'library management' module with 50% of respondents noting that they never used it at all for supporting managerial decisions. The financial monitoring and planning module is the most commonly used module, and student assessment is procedurally used every month to compute students' monthly test scores.

Table 3 shows the percentage of school management personnel using the CISs in hours per month. Of the 100% respondents in the sample, 60% indicated that they both directly and indirectly used CISs with variation in time of use. The questionnaire defined former as using the system oneself (school managers) and indirect use as use of information (mainly printouts)

Table 2: Managerial use of modules included in computerised information systems

	never	every week	every month	few times a year	once a year
Managerial use of students' records	12%	27%	19%	31%	11%
Managerial use of student assessment	12%	15%	30%	31%	12%
Managerial use of student attendance	38%	29%	12%	21%	
Managerial use of staff records	24%	14%	24%	33%	5%
Managerial use of timetabling	33%	10%	18%	29%	10%
Managerial use of programme schedule	27%		27%	41%	5%
Managerial use of financial monitoring and planning	7%	43%	20%	17%	13%
Managerial use of library management	50%	18%		11%	21%

received from other staff using the system.

The data in Table 3 below illustrates that the time investment for the direct use of the CISs is highest ranging between 1-10 hours per month implying less time in indirect use. On the other hand, the levels of indirect use are significantly higher between 11-30 hours per month. Even for the category 'greater than 30 hours' it is reasonably higher than direct use. This is an illogical result for a school manager but it is offset by the fact that the respondents were mainly heads of the computer studies departments in schools (an average of 59%) implying that they were knowledgeable about the available CIS. The other respondents namely the head teachers or principals, the deputy heads, and the director of studies constituted of 12%, 14%, and 15% respectively. This indicated that perhaps the head teachers or principals rarely directly used the systems available in their schools but frequently depended on the printouts provided by other users.

Table 3: Percentage of Direct and Indirect Users in Number of Hours per Month (n=33)

	Direct use	Indirect use
0 hour	3%	3%
<1 hour	6%	
1-4 hours	33%	12%
5-10 hours	27%	18%
11-20 hours	6%	21%
21-30 hours	12%	27%
>30 hours	12%	18%

4.3 Perceived CIS Quality

This research question concerns opinions of the school management personnel on quality of CISs. On the question of whether the system provides information they need 12% replied that it does a little, 50% to some degree, 27% much and only 11% said it very much provides this. About 70% of respondents expressed the opinion that their systems always worked. Of the remaining 30%, 64% had one to three system problems a month and 36% has between four and seven problems.

Users have the following opinion (Table 4) on several aspects of the quality of data retrieved from CISs. Over 75% of respondents consider the accuracy of the data to be (very) good and so do respondents between 50%

to slightly above 70% on other aspects such as up-to-date information, completeness of information, management support capacity, on-screen retrieval and print out speed. School managers ranging between 10-35% are neutral on all the attributes of CIS data quality, yet according to 5-25%; retrieved CISs data is (very) poor.

Table 4: Aspects of computerised information systems data quality

	(very) poor	neutral	(very) good
Accuracy of information	9%	15%	76%
Up-to-date information	12%	26%	62%
Completeness of information	21%	29%	50%
Management support capacity	13%	33%	54%
On-screen retrieval speed	24%	9%	67%
print out speed	6%	21%	73%

4.4 Process of Implementation

Research question four refers to the features of the implementation process through which the CISs have been introduced into the selected secondary schools in Uganda. Of all the respondents, 12% did not receive any training to use the CISs, 41% were trained for 1-4 hours, 30% of the users received between 5-20 hours of training to use the CISs while only 17% were trained for more than 30 hours.

Pertaining to problems with the CISs, 21% of the respondents were (very) unhappy about the ease with which they get help from within the school in case of difficulties, and 41% reported that it was (very) hard to get help from outside school. Generally, 60% of the CISs users often to very frequently solicit help from the system administrator. Similarly, 30-50% use self-support (work on the problem themselves) or seek assistance from colleagues within the school. On the contrary, approximately 60% of the school managers very rarely used support from the external colleague and/or the user manual/guide as sources of help. Concerning the extent to which the goals for the introduction of the CISs are clear, 88% noted they were very clear, In addition, 62% indicated that the means and activities by which these goals could be met are very clear, and 32% remaining neutral.

Table 5: Hours of training (%)

	Amount of training
0 hour	12%
1-4 hours	41%
5-10 hours	15%
11-20 hours	15%
>30 hours	17%

4.5 School Organisational Features

When the CISs were first introduced in schools, only 12% of the respondents did not expect the system to help them in their jobs. Over 80% of the schools used manual systems prior to the installation of the CIS and only about 15% of the schools had other CISs. An inquiry into the level of motivation to work with the system revealed that 62% were (very) motivated and 12% (very) unmotivated when the CIS was first introduced in their schools. Experience in using computers either at home or work is generally low.

4.6 Effects of CIS Usage

The use of the CISs has had several effects at school level. Table 6 presents some of the outcomes and it can be observed that higher percentages are registered on the positive side starting with 40%-60% of respondents indicating insight into how the school functions had improved. Over 80% of the respondents reported (much) better evaluation of school performance. Utilisation of school resources (over 60%), information for curriculum planning (53%), and between 20-50% on internal communication with colleagues was better. However, it is only internal communication with colleagues that registered a reasonable negative percentage of about 23%. Stress (66%) and workload (69%) have lowered through using the CISs

Note: the table does not contain the percentages for the 'same' response category. The difference between 100% and the sum of the percentages for the positive and the negative answers concerns the percentages of respondents who neither observed an improvement nor deterioration.

Table 6: School Level Effects of the Use of computerised information systems

	worse (negative)	better (positive)	much better (positive)
Insight into how the school functions	3%	43%	13%
Evaluation of school performance		53%	28%
Utilisation of school resources	3%	61%	13%
Information for curriculum planning	9%	53%	16%
Internal communication with colleagues	23%	23%	32%
Workload	6%	41%	25%
Stress	9%	47%	22%

4.7 Factors Related to Extent of CIS Usage

This research question focuses on the factors that have a relationship with the magnitude of CISs usage in Uganda. On closer scrutiny of how far the degree of CIS usage is determined by (some of) the influential factors in the Visscher model (1996a; 2001); those that the researchers identified as the most potential predictors of CIS usage were entered into regression analyses on direct and indirect use. Five variables were selected that included start motivation, computer experience, training, information quality and support from the systems administrator. The first four variables were based on earlier studies done which reported that they are predictors of CISs (Visscher et. al., 1999; 2003). Support from the systems administrator is considered because Uganda being a developing country and ITEM being a new field, direct users need immediate help. Upon computation, three variables were considered non-predictors of CIS usage in Uganda and consequently excluded from the model on both direct and indirect use. These variables are start motivation, information quality and computer experience. It is the implementation factors of amount of training and support from the systems administrator that present proof of explanation of variation in direct use by the school management personnel as illustrated in Table 7.

Table 7: Results of Regression Analysis on CISs usage

Variable	Coefficients	Direct use School managers
1. Amount of training	Beta*	0.38
	Bstand*	0.39
	Sign. *	0.02
2. Support from systems administrator	Beta*	0.75
	Bstand*	0.61
	Sign. *	0.00
	R square	0.35

*Beta = unstandardised Beta; Bstand = standardised Beta; Sign. = Level of significance

The results in Table 7 indicate that thirty-five percent of the differences in the extent of the school management personnel direct CIS usage are explained by the variances in the variables 'amount of training' and the 'support from the systems administrator'. Overall, the latter variable has proven to be the most powerful explanation of variation in CISs use as is almost twice as influential as the former (.39 versus .61).

5 CONCLUSION AND DISCUSSION

The findings in this exploratory study portray the fact that Computer Assisted School Administration (CASA) in secondary schools in Uganda is just approaching the initiation stage in CIS development (Visscher, 2001). This is well-illustrated by 38% of the selected schools that are non-users even in these districts with most of the well-developed schools in Uganda, which indicates that it would be even worse in the poorer districts. Moreover, the basic usage available is concentrated on clerical work.

Developing countries have lagged behind in school administrative computing (Visscher, 2001). However, 70% of the CISs in Uganda are locally developed and commercial software vendors comprise 74% of the developers. With this trend, one could suggest that the future of CISs in

Uganda is promising and that for the other developing countries, ad hoc CISs can be developed without multi-million investments.

The CIS quality is low; only one third note that CISs provide the information they need perhaps due to lack of a common design strategy. On the process of implementation of CISs, user training was limited, for example, about 12% of the users received no training and 41% were trained for 1-4 hours to use CISs. Respondents were (very) unhappy with the accessibility of internal and external help. Most of the respondents (60%) sought help from the systems administrator while some solved the problems themselves. Computer experience was quite low being a symptom of the less vigorous use of information technology in developing countries. The level of indirect use is higher than direct use (only 1-10 hours per month).

Respondents are (very) positive on effects of CISs. Evaluation of school performance and school management were reported (much) better. It remains to be verified if the findings hitherto highlighted can scientifically hold and whether other factors apart from mere CIS usage are important, if not equally important. Computers as tools that simplify work is indisputable but may not wholly be responsible for the school improvements noted above, otherwise all schools having CISs would be impeccably the best performers.

Support from the systems administrator and amount of training are factors that explain the observed variance in the direct usage of CISs in secondary schools in Uganda. It is therefore worthwhile that any investment in design and implementation of CISs considers increasing the amount of training for the intended CIS users, and hiring the services of systems administrators in schools where CISs are introduced.

Comparatively, studies on CIS usage in Hong Kong, Netherlands, and the United Kingdom (Visscher studies) have revealed that the degree of CIS usage is by large for clerical purposes. The direct and indirect use of the CISs in the Visscher studies varies with the system administrator and clerks scoring high on direct use while principals are more of indirect users. The results in the Ugandan study are not any different from these findings.

Moreover the Visscher studies returned training as a relevant variable, possibly because it can be used to motivate the target group to use the system and clarify the goals and methods of the innovation process (Fung et. al., 2002). Much as the study in Uganda notes that amount of training is an important factor determining direct use; it also echoes the support from the systems administrator as an extraordinary implementation factor. This latter variable has not been proven its significance in the Visscher studies but Haughey (2003) reports that Telem (1997) focussed his study on the new role of the school computer administrator. Haughey further notes that in comparably large high schools, a site technologist was often hired to deal specifically with the network and its applications, marking unusual data and checking if these data were followed up. This partly presents a defensible ground for the Ugandan finding.

In the Visscher studies, the systems administrator is second to the users solving the problems themselves. In the Uganda study, the systems administrator is the leading source of help partly explained by the naivety of the school managers in computer operation. Indirect use in the Ugandan study has not been explained by any factor, unlike in the Visscher studies.

It is recommended that the critical factors (amount of training and support from the systems administrator) are cautiously nurtured especially the remarkably determinant factor of training which is reported to have been a prevalent issue in evaluation of information technology systems in industry and commerce (Visscher et. al., 1999; 2003). The system administrator in the school, for instance, is very knowledgeable about the system and its components, and able to provide basic training to the school managers on how to use the system. Training should cut across technical competencies and practical capabilities to managerially use the retrieved data. However, it may demand additional expenses for the already hard-earned CISs, the most appropriate solution being to design and develop robust or less faulty systems with packages of electronic performance support systems from which the users incrementally seek knowledge.

Design and development of a comprehensive school information system comprising numerous modules and/or reports/lists that will be to a large extent, uniform to all schools. But this requires commitment of colossal sums of money, which developing countries may not readily have. Alternatively, governments of developing countries like Uganda could opt for importation and adaptation of sophisticated CISs from the developed countries to specific features of their school contexts. This may save money and time required in evolving a formidable CIS.

Finally, this exploratory study projects that if these recommendations are met, the probability that CISs usage will increase is very high. It is speculated that the findings of this study will stimulate further research on a wider population and in other developing countries for more authentic generalisations. Moreover the study has shown that the variables in the Visscher model are relatively appropriate for testing CISs usage and its impact on secondary schools in developing countries as well.

6 REFERENCES

Aguti, J.N. (2002). Facing up the challenge of UPE in Uganda through Distance Teacher Education programmes. Paper presented at Pan Commonwealth Forum on Open Learning: Open Learning: Transforming Education for development. Durban, South Africa.

Bisaso, R. (2003). Computerised School Information Systems Usage in the Administration and Management of Secondary Schools in Uganda: An Exploratory Study, University of Twente, Faculty of Behavioural Sciences, The Netherlands.

British Council, (2003). Enhancing the quality of management and governance of schools in Uganda. Available http://www.britishcouncil.org/Uganda/education

Fung, A.C.W. (1995). Managing change in "ITEM". In Barta, B.Z., Telem, M., & Gev, Y. (Eds.)(1995). Information technology in educational management (pp. 37-46). London: Chapman & Hall.

Fung, A.C.W. & Visscher, A.J. (2001). A holistic view of SISs as an innovation and the factors determining success. In Visscher, A.J., Wild, P. and Fung, A.C.W. (Eds.) (2001). Information Technology in Educational Management: Synthesis of Experience, Research and Future Perspectives on Computer-Assisted School Information Systems. Kluwer.

Fung, A.C.W., Visscher, A.J., Smith, D., & Wild, P. (2002). Comparative Evaluation of the Implementation of computerised school management systems. In Watson, D. & Anderson, J. (Eds.)(2002). Networking the Learner Computers in Education. Dordrecht: Kluwer.

Haughey, M. (2003). The Impact of ICT on the work of the principal. In Selwood, I.D, Fung, A.C.W., & O'Mahoney C.D. (Eds.) Management of Education in the Information Age. The Role of ICT. (Pp 63-81). London: Chapman & Hall

Ministry of Education and Sports (1999) The Ugandan Experience of Universal Primary Education. Kampala, Uganda.

Odaet, C.F. (1995). Uganda. In Neville T. Postlethwaite (Ed.) 1995) International Encyclopedia of National Systems of Education. Elsevier Science Ltd.

Visscher, A.J. (1995). Computer assisted school administration and management: where are we and where are we going? In Barta, B.Z., Telem, M. & Gev, Y. (Eds.) (1995). Information technology in educational management. London: Chapman & Hall.

Visscher, A.J (1996a). Information Technology in educational management as an emerging discipline. International Journal of Educational Research, 25(4), 291-296.

Visscher, A.J. (1996b). The implications of how school staff handle information for usage of school information systems. International Journal of Educational Research, 25 (4), 323-34.

Visscher, A.J. (2001). Computer-Assisted School Information Systems: the concepts, intended benefits, and stages of development. In Visscher, A.J., Wild, P. and Fung, A.C.W. (Eds.)(2001). Information Technology in Educational Management: Synthesis of Experience, Research and Future Perspectives on Computer-Assisted School Information Systems. Dordrecht: Kluwer.

Visscher, A.J. & Bloemen, P.P.M. (1999). Evaluation and use of computer-assisted management information systems in Dutch schools. Journal of Research on Computing in Education, 32(1), 172-188

Visscher, A.J. & Fung, A.C.W. (2001). Imperatives for successful implementation of school information systems. In Visscher, A.J., Wild, P. and Fung, A.C.W. (Eds.) (2001). Information Technology in Educational Management: Synthesis of Experience, Research and Future Perspectives on Computer-Assisted School Information Systems.: Kluwer.

Visscher, A.J., Fung, A., & Wild, P. (1999). The Evaluation of the large-scale implementation of a computer-assisted management information system in Hong Kong schools. Studies in Educational Evaluation, 25, 11-31.

Visscher, A.J., Wild, P., & Smith, D. (2003). The Results of Implementing SIMS in English Secondary schools. In Selwood, I.D, Fung, A.C.W., & O'Mahoney C.D (Eds.)(2003). Management of Education in the Information Age. The Role of ICT. (Pp 34-44). London: Chapman & Hall.

ITEM System Usage in the Ministry of Education in Botswana

Omponoye C. Kereteletse and Ian Selwood
Ministry of Education IT Unit, Gaborone, Botswana
The University of Birmingham, School of Education, Edgbaston, Birmingham, UK
I.D.Selwood@Bham.AC.UK

Abstract: In this paper some of the results of a study that evaluated system usage of the computerised information system implemented by the Ministry of Education (MoE) in Botswana are presented. The system was implemented to manage the teaching human resource. Evaluation of the use of this new system was based on the users' perception of their ability to use the ITEM system directly, or indirectly, and a detailed analysis of factors that influence system usage. The magnitude of external training, perceived quality of information provided, and computer experience of the MoE staff explained considerable amounts of variance in direct use of the system implemented by the MoE in Botswana. Whereas the amount of external training, and perceived quality of information provided and output options explained considerable amounts of variance in indirect use of the system implemented by the MoE in Botswana.

Key words: Educational management, system usage, system quality, implementation, organisation.

1 BACKGROUND

Botswana is a developing country with a highly centralised system for managing education. Due to the rapid expansion of the education system, the manual system of managing the teaching workforce was not working efficiently or effectively. In 1994, a new education policy had been adopted - 'The Revised National Policy on Education' (RNPE) (MoE, 1994). The RNPE reported a massive expansion of pupils in schools, but that academic standards were declining. Furthermore, RNPE noted that the effective management of the teaching resource was seen as paramount to expanding education and maintaining quality. However, in spite of the reorganisation of the Department of Teaching Service Management, problems persisted with regard to the service delivery of the department. The Botswana Ministry of Education (MoE) decided to implement a computerised system for managing the teaching resource, based on Infinium Software and this went live on 3rd May 1999, and the implementation process was analysed by Kereteletswe and Selwood (2003). This paper evaluates the system usage of the implemented computerised information system.

2 RESEARCH FRAMEWORK

According to Visscher, (1995) system use is related to system quality, implementation process features, and organisational process features. Hence, the impact of system quality, implementation process features, and organisational process features on direct and indirect usage of the implemented system were investigated. Three system quality characteristics: software quality, information quality, and quality of output options, were considered in the analysis. Five characteristics of the implementation process features were considered: external training, internal training, clarity of innovation goals, clarity of means, and technical team performance. Internal training and clarity of means were excluded from the analysis due to the incidence of numerous missing values. The variables that constituted the organisational features were the system (Infinium HR) goals, motivation before implementation, and computer experience.

3 METHOD AND DATA ANALYSIS

A total of 168 questionnaires were distributed to staff in the MoE Departments involved in the management of teachers. These were Teaching Service Management, Secondary Education, Primary Education, and Regional Education Offices. The questionnaire was completed by clerical staff, secretaries, personal assistants, middle managers, and top managers.

A response rate of 76% (127 out of 168) was achieved. Of the 127 questionnaires returned, eleven were excluded from the analysis as they had numerous blanks. Users rated their subjective state on various 6-point scales. The categorical data of the independent variables were coded and scores for the dependent variable 'direct and indirect use' on the interval scale (0 hours to greater than 6 hours per week) were converted to z-scores. This standardisation paved the way to the manipulation of the attitude levels across context, using each respondent's mean in the standard comparison. To analyse the data on the factors related to the extent of system use (system quality, implementation process and organisational process features) in the MoE, backward regression analysis was used.

4 RESULTS

4.1 How System Quality Features Relate to Direct Use

Table 1. ANOVA test on the null hypothesis concerning system quality and direct use

Model		Sum of Squares	df	Mean Square	F	Significance of F
1	Regression	18.404	3	6.135	4.056	.031
	Residual	167.892	111	1.513		
	Total	186.296	114			
2	Regression	16.848	2	8.424	5.568	.014
	Residual	169.447	112	1.513		
	Total	186.296	114			
3	Regression	14.834	1	14.834	9.776	.000
	Residual	171.462	113	1.517		
	Total	186.296	114			
		R^2	% R^2			
1	R squared (R^2)	.189	18.9%			
2	R squared (R^2)	.181	18.1%			
3	R squared (R^2)	.173	17.3%			

1. Predictors: (Constant), software quality, quality of output options, information quality
2. Predictors: (Constant), Output options, information quality
3. Predictors: (Constant), Information Quality

Dependent Variable: DIRECT

ANOVA was used to test the null hypothesis that there was no linear relationship between predictors (information quality, software quality and quality of output options) and direct use. In model 1, when all three predictors are entered, the significance level associated with the observed value of *F* is 0.031. In model 2, the significance level improved to 0.014, and a further improvement in the level of significance of F is 0.000, is noted in model 3. Thus, in all the three models, the null hypothesis can be rejected because the significance of F in the three models is less than 0.05, and we can conclude that there is a significant linear relationship between the set of predictors and direct use. However, an increase in the *F*-value is noted in models 2 and 3 when the variables software quality and quality of data output options are removed respectively. The *F*-value increases but there is little change in the sum of squares, and the df (degrees of freedom) was 3 in model 1, reduced to 2 in model 2 and then to 1 in model 3. However, Model 3 is adopted since the other two independent variables 'software quality' and 'output of data quality options' did not have any significant relationship with direct use of the Infinium HR system by MoE, as shown in Table 2.

Table 2. System quality features influence on direct use

Model	Main effects	Unstandardised Coefficients Beta	Std. Error	Standardised Coefficients Beta	t	Significance of F
1	(Constant)	3.792	.679		5.581	.000
	Information quality	.628	.251	.238	2.499	.014
	Quality of output options	.318	.283	.106	1.124	.164
	Software quality	.462	.456	.092	1.014	.313
2	(Constant)	3.358	.528		6.358	.000
	Information quality	.662	.249	.250	2.657	.019
	Quality of data output options	.326	.283	.109	1.154	.052
3	(Constant)	2.897	.345		8.387	.000
	Information quality	.746	.239	.282	3.127	.000

a. Dependent Variable: DIRECT

Table 2 shows the significance of *F* for the remaining independent variable, information quality in model 3 at 0.000 which is less than p=0.05. Therefore, there is a significant relationship between information quality and the direct use of the Infinium HR system in the MoE in Botswana.

More importantly, Table 2 also provides indications of the relationship between the variables: information quality and the direct use of the Infinium HR system in the management of teaching staff. This is explained using the unstandardised and standardised coefficients. At the MoE level, an increase of one point in the information quality variable implies an increase of 0.746 in the direct use variable. That is, if the 'direct use' variable increases by one point, it moves for example, from the '0 hours' of direct use valuc to '1-2 hours' value (or from '3-4 hours' to '5-6 hours' etc.) per week. In other words in terms of the standardised coefficients, an increase of one standard deviation in information quality produces an increase of 0.282 standard deviations in direct use above the mean. That is, 11.03% over the mean. In addition, 17.3% (R^2) of the variance in direct use is explained by information quality.

4.2 How System Quality Features Relate to Indirect Use

Table 3 shows the significance of F at p=0.000 (p=<0.05) for both models (1 and 2), suggesting that the null hypothesis (on indirect use) is rejected. Thus, there is a significant linear relationship between the system quality features and indirect use in the management of teaching human resource in the MoE.

Table 3. ANOVA test on the null hypothesis on indirect use

Model		Sum of Squares	df	Mean Squares	F	Sig.
1	Regression	23.951	3	7.984	6.837	.018
	Residual	129.614	111	1.168		
	Total	153.565	114			
2	Regression	22.318	2	11.159	9.523	.000
	Residual	131.247	112	1.172		
	Total	153.565	114			
1	R squared (R^2)	.329	32.9%			
2	R squared (R^2)	.292	29.2%			

1. Predictors: (Constant), Quality of output options, Software quality, Information quality
2. Predictors: (Constant), Quality of output options, Information quality
Dependent Variable: INDIRECT

In model 2 when the variable software quality is removed, the *F*-value increases from 6.837 to 9.523 and there is little change in the sum of squares, 23.951 to 22.318, suggesting the contribution of the variable, software quality, was insignificant (significance of F at 0.240) in the indirect use of the Infinium HR system (Table 4). The results of model 2 are therefore considered in the analysis.

Table 4. System quality features influence on indirect use

Model	Main effects	Unstandardised Coefficients Beta	Std. Error	Standardised Coefficients Beta	t	Significance of F
1	(Constant)	3.279	.597		5.492	.000
	Information Quality	.565	.221	.236	2.560	.040
	Software Quality	.474	.401	.104	1.182	.240
	Quality of output options	.697	.249	.256	2.804	.010
2	(Constant)	3.723	.465		8.008	.000
	Information Quality	.531	.219	.221	2.420	.001
	Quality of output options	.689	.249	.253	2.766	.027

The unstandardised coefficients for information quality of 0.531 in model 2 (Table 4) tells us that an increase by one unit of information quality increases the indirect use by an average of 0.531 points on the six-point scale ((1= 0 hours, 2= 1-2 hours, 3= 3-4 hours, 4= 5-10 hours, 5=11-15 hours, 6=

>15 hours) per week. In the same way, a one point increase in the 'quality of data output options' increases the indirect use of the Infinium HR system by an average of 0.689 points on the six point scale. Using standardised scores, an increase of one standard deviation in information quality or quality of output options produces an increase of 0.221 or 0.253 standard deviations respectively, in the dependent variable indirect use. Furthermore, 29.2% of the variance in indirect use is explained by information quality and quality of output options in model 2 (Table 3)

The findings with respect to the effects of system quality features show that quality of information from the Infinium HR system has a relationship with both the direct and indirect use of the Infinium HR system in the management of teaching personnel by the MoE. In addition, a variable closely related to information quality, 'quality of output options' had influenced indirect use of the system by the MoE end users. However, the variable, quality of software appears not to affect either the direct or indirect use by the MoE.

4.3 How Implementation Process Features relate to Direct Use

Table 5 shows the results of a three-step backwards regression analysis with the variable, clarity of innovation goals removed in model 2, and the variables clarity of innovation goals and performance of the Change Facilitator System (CFS) (the technical team) removed in model 3. Table 6 shows that there is no significant independent relationship between the removed variables and direct use of the Infinium HR system.

Table 5. ANOVA test on the impact of implementation process features on direct use

Model		Sum of Squares	df	Mean Square	F	Significance of F
1	Regression	36.608	3	9.51	7.049	.045
	Residual	149.687	111	1.349		
	Total	186.296	114			
2	Regression	36.430	2	12.862	9.613	.012
	Residual	149.865	112	1.338		
	Total	186.296	114			
3	Regression	34.250	1	21.558	16.016	.000
	Residual	152.046	113	1.346		
	Total	186.296	114			
3	R squared (R^2)		27.3	27.3%		

1. Predictors: (Constant), Performance of CFS, Amount of External training, Clarity of innovation goals
2. Predictors: (Constant), Performance of CFS, Amount of external training
3. Predictors: (Constant), Amount of external training.

Dependent Variable: DIRECT

The amount of external training seems to be the most powerful source of explaining the variance in direct use. The standardised coefficient of the variable external training is at 0.429 (Table 6), suggesting that an increase by one standard deviation in the amount of external training produces an increase of 0.429 standard deviations above the mean of direct use of the Infinium HR system. Therefore, an increase of one standard deviation in the amount of external training yields an increase of 18.79% of direct use above the mean (7.5 hours per week). Additionally, 27.3% (Table 5) of the variance in direct use of the Infinium HR system is explained by the independent variable 'amount of external training.'

Table 6. Impact of implementation process features on the direct use

Model	Main effects	Unstandardised Coefficients Beta	Std. Error	Standardised Coefficients Beta	t	Significance of F
1	(Constant)	2.577	.740		3.483	.001
	External training	1.136	.229	.441	4.959	.000
	Clarity of innovation goals	8.370E-02	.230	.033	.363	.717
	Performance of CFS	.419	.345	.104	1.215	.227
2	(Constant)	2.643	.714		3.701	.000
	External training	1.112	.218	.432	5.095	.000
	Performance of CFS	.435	.341	.108	1.277	.204
3	(Constant)	3.452	.330		10.456	.000
	External training	1.104	.219	.429	5.045	.000

4.4 How Implementation Process Features Relate to Indirect Use

Table 7 shows the results of a three-step backwards regression analysis with the variable, clarity of innovation goals removed in model 2, and the variables clarity of innovation goals and performance of the CFS removed in model 3.

Table 7. The impact of implementation process features on indirect use

Model		Sum of Squares	df	Mean Square	F	Significance of F
1	Regression	15.983	3	5.328	4.298	.382
	Residual	137.582	111	1.239		
	Total	153.565	114			
2	Regression	15.638	2	7.819	6.349	.042
	Residual	137.927	112	1.231		
	Total	153.565	114			
3	Regression	14.723	1	14.723	11.983	.000
	Residual	138.842	113	1.229		
	Total	153.565	114			

Model	Sum of Squares	df	Mean Square	F	Significance of F
R squared (R^2)	0.225	22.5%			

1. Predictors: (Constant), Performance of CFS, Amount of external training, Clarity of innovations goals
2. Predictors: (Constant), Amount of external training, Clarity of innovations goals
3. Predictors: (Constant), Amount of external training

Dependent Variable: INDIRECT

Furthermore, Table 8 shows that the performance of CFS and clarity of innovation goals have significance values of *F* at greater than 0.05, suggestive of the variables having no significant independent relationships with the indirect use of the Infinium HR system. The significance of *F* in model 3 is at 0.000, thus the null hypothesis is rejected. It is further observed that the sum of squares change is very small across the models (from 15.983 in model 1 to 14.723 in model 3) while the corresponding values of mean squares increased from 5.328 (significance of F= 0.382) to 14.723 (significance of F= 0.000).

Table 8. Impact of implementation process features on the indirect use

Model	Main effects	Unstandardised Coefficients Beta	Std. Error	Standardised Coefficients Beta	t	Significance of F
1	(Constant)	2.723	.709		3.839	.000
	External training	.667	.220	.285	3.036	.003
	Clarity of innovation goals	.203	.221	.087	.919	.360
	Performance of CFS	.174	.331	.048	.527	.599
2	(Constant)	3.030	.403		7.523	.000
	External training	.668	.219	.286	3.050	.003
	Performance of CFS	.188	.218	.081	.862	.390
3	(Constant)	2.814	.316		8.921	.000
	External training	.724	.209	.310	3.462	.000

The standardised coefficient for 'amount of external training' of 0.724 (Model 3, Table 8) implies that an increase by one point on external training variable increases the indirect use of the Infinium HR system by an average of 0.724 on the six-point scale. Alternatively, in terms of standardised scores, an increase of one standard deviation in amount of external training produces an increase of 0.310 standard deviations in indirect use of the Infinium HR system. This means indirect use of the system increases by 12.93% above the mean (per week).

The findings on the relationship of implementation process features suggest that amount of external training of the end users is a factor in explaining the variances in both the direct use and indirect use of the Infinium HR system in the management of teachers by the MoE.

4.5 How Organisational Process Features Relate to Direct Use

This section examines and analyses data collected on the impact of organisational process features on use (direct or indirect). The variables that constitute organisation features are the Infinium goals, motivation before implementation, and computer experience. These three independent variables were considered in the backwards regression analysis.

As noted on the footnote of Table 9, all organisational features variables were entered in model 1, perceived IS goals was removed in model 2, and then in model 3 perceived IS goals and motivation before implementation were both removed implying that these factors did not have a significant independent relationship on the direct use of the Infinium HR system. However, the significance of F is at 0.008 (Table 9), suggesting that the null hypothesis (direct) is rejected, as there is linear significant relationship between the predictors and dependent variable direct use.

Table 9. The impact of organisational process features on direct use

Model	Main effects	Unstandardised Coefficients Beta	Std. Error	Standardised Coefficients Beta	t	Significance of F
1	(Constant)	2.901	.865		3.353	.001
	Motivation before implementation	.363	.325	.104	1.119	.266
	Perceived IS goals	.188	.337	.051	.558	.578
	Computer Experience	.689	.241	.263	2.854	.005
2	(Constant)	3.274	.546		5.998	.000
	Motivation before implementation	.382	.322	.109	1.187	.238
	Computer Experience	.690	.241	.264	2.867	.035
3	(Constant)	2.776	.350		7.938	.000
	Computer Experience	.649	.239	.248	2.721	.012

Model		Sum of Squares	df	Mean Square	F	Significance of F
3	Regression	11.459	1	11.459	7.406	.012
	Residual	174.836	113	1.547		
	Total	186.296	114			
3	R squared (R^2)	0.338	33.8%			

1. Predictors: (Constant), Computer Experience, Perceived IS goals, Motivation before implementation
2. Predictors: (Constant) Computer Experience, Motivation before implementation
3. Predictors: (Constant), Computer Experience

Dependent Variable: DIRECT

The variable 'computer experience' explains 33.8% of the variance in direct use. This variable has a standardised coefficient of 0.248. Therefore, an increase by one standard deviation in the variable 'computer experience' results in an increase of direct use by 10.26% above the mean. The conclusion reached here is that an increase in computer experience of the end users would result in increased direct use of the Infinium HR system.

4.6 How Organisational Process Features Relate to Indirect Use

Table 10. The impact of organisational process features on indirect use

Model	Main effects	Unstandardised Coefficients Beta	Std. Error	Standardised Coefficients Beta	t	Significance of F
1	(Constant)	3.093	.793		3.900	.000
	Motivation before implementation	-.256	.298	-.081	-.861	.391
	Perceived IS goals	-.130	.309	.039	-.421	.675
	Computer Experience	.558	.221	.235	2.521	.113
Model		**Sum of Squares**	**df**	**Mean Square**	**F**	**Significance of F**
3	Regression	8.783	3	2.928	2.244	.161
	Residual	144.783	111	1.304		
	Total	153.565	114			
3	R squared (R^2)	0.057	16.7%			

1. Predictors: (Constant), Computer Experience, Perceived IS goals, Motivation before implementation

Dependent Variable: INDIRECT

The summary Table 10 on the main effects depicts significance of F of the predictors on indirect use at 0.161, which is not statistically significant at $p>0.05$. Therefore, the null hypothesis is accepted, that there is no linear relationship between organisational process features and the indirect use of the Infinium HR system in the management of teaching staff. In addition, the three independent variables, motivation before implementation, perceived IS goals and computer experience within the MoE have no significant impact on the indirect use of the database. Although 16.7% (R^2) of the variance in indirect use is explained by the three predictors it was not statistically significant.

5 CONCLUSION

Three factors thought to influence system quality - information quality, quality of software, and quality of output options were analysed with respect to their effects on direct and indirect use of the Infinium HR system. Both direct and indirect use was affected by information quality. In addition, a variable closely related to information quality namely quality of output options had influenced indirect use of the system by the MoE end users. However, the variable quality of software appears not to affect either the direct or indirect use by the MoE. With respect to the implementation procedure, the critical factor effecting indirect and direct usage was the amount of external training of the users. As regards organisational processes, the only conclusion that can be drawn is that an increase in computer experience of the end users would result in an increased direct use of the Infinium HR system, but no increase in indirect usage.

To conclude, this paper highlights some of the factors that influence direct and indirect use of the Infinium HR system as implemented for managing the teaching resource in the MoE in Botswana. However, it should be noted that the amount of use might have been influenced by other factors. Botswana is a developing country and as Riggs (1964) asserts, in prismatic societies there is a tendency of the new and the old to sit side by side. That is, although a new system has been introduced, the system remains unused by the user organisation. Unfortunately, space does not permit the investigation of this hypothesis here.

6 REFERENCES

MoE (1994). *The Revised National Policy on Education (RNPE).* Gaborone, Botswana Government Printer

Kereteletswe O.C. and Selwood I.D. (2003). The Implementation of Information Technology in Educational Management in Botswana in Selwood, I.D., Fung, A.C.W., & O'Mahony C. (Eds) *Management of Education in the Information Age - The Role of ICT.* Boston: Kluwer.

Riggs Fred, W. (1964) *Administration in Developing Countries: The Theory of Prismatic Society.* Boston: Houghton

Visscher, A.J. (1995). 'Computer assisted school administration and management: where are we and where should we go?' In *Information Technology in Educational Management.* Edited by Ben Zion Barta, Moshe Telem and Yaffa Gev. Chapman Hall for IFIP, London.

Data Quality in Educational Systems for Decision Makers

Geoff Sandy and Bill Davey
Victoria University and RMIT
Geoff.Sandy@vu.edu.au, Bill.Davey@rmit.edu.au

Abstract: Significant research has shown that effectiveness of an educational administrative system can be measured by acceptance testing. These research efforts have suggested that an additional measure should be of system quality. ITEM systems are used by Universities and funding bodies to make important decisions. Case study research reported here shows that there is a likelihood of poor decisions being made because of the continued existence of data quality problems. This means that a decision maker should be able to see what reliability is relevant to each piece of data. Data quality literature shows that data quality depends on some important and known factors and case studies show that only some of these factors are included in current ITEM systems.

Key words: University, data quality, administrative systems.

1 INTRODUCTION

Recently, a former Director of the CIA revealed that a real-life version of this fictional scenario was actually played out when a test tape was inadvertently installed and the screen at a similar center warned of a nuclear attack. As computers play a more and more important role in the real-world – a world in which the computer-generated outputs often present a picture of the real-world for critical activities – it is increasingly vital that that picture be correct! (Orr, 1996)

Although educational management seldom deals with nuclear warfare, decisions in education do depend on information and do have consequences. Each of the universities studied in this research has a revenue from the national and state governments of the order of $500 million and $200 million respectively (RMIT annual report 2002, VU annual report 2003). These funds are received as a result of statistics collected from and stored in the university information systems. One of the very few studies that examined the integrity of this data was conducted in 1992 by a team of researchers that examined statistics student by student. This study found: "This information was obtained for the five year study period but, when checked against faculty records, was found to be only about 50% reliable." (Burns, Davey, Hill, Leveson 1992). Obviously, in 1992 the University information systems were not reliable and very large amounts of money were being distributed on the basis of these poor figures. Each of the universities in this study has recently upgraded its information systems. This exploratory but timely study of the new systems reveals that whilst fundamental improvements have been made we are still not confident about their data integrity.

2 THEORETICAL FRAMEWORK

The general literature of data quality contains some coherent principles regarding the means of keeping data pure. According to the U.S. Defense Information System Agency (Cykana & Stern, 1996), the root causes of poor data quality can be attributed to four primary areas:

1. Process problems.
2. System problems.
3. Policy and procedure problems.
4. Data design problems.

There are a number of general Data Quality Rules that one can deduce from an FCS view of information systems:

DQ1. Data that is not used cannot be correct for very long;

DQ2. Data Quality in an information system is a function of its use not its collection;

DQ3. Data Quality will, ultimately, be no better than its most stringent use;

DQ4. Data Quality problems tend to become worse with the age of the system;

DQ5. The less likely some data attribute (element) is to change, the more traumatic it will be when it finally does change;

DQ6. Laws of data quality apply equally to data and meta-data (the data about the data). (Orr 1998)

Similarly Becker (1998) categorizes seven common data quality problems seen by end-users: (1) data corruption due to incorrect conversion, (2) historical and current data having different meanings, (3) the same data having more than one data definition, (4) missing data, (5) hidden data, (6) missing granularity, and (9) violation of integrity rules. Clearly both of these sources indicate the need to correctly structure data, and then to use the data regularly in support of daily operations. The need for structure starts with the intended uses of the data. To see what that means in an educational setting the case studies started with analysis of user complaints about the two old systems. From this analysis the data quality rules could be seen in terms of three main areas common to both the case studies.

First is the accessibility of the information required by the decision makers. Second, is the integrity of the information used by the decision makers and finally, is whether the information supports the business rules of the organizational unit. Each of these is discussed in section 4 with examples drawn from each of the case studies.

3 METHODOLOGY

To test this framework two universities were chosen for an in-depth study. Both had acknowledged problems with their administrative systems but had taken different paths to solving these problems. The researchers are both senior academics at the respective universities with significant administrative responsibilities. A range of administrative staff and academics provided input into the findings through interviews and other verbal input. A study was also made of documentation of the administrative systems. Specifically, data was collected about the accessibility and integrity of the information from the old systems. In addition data was sought as to how well the information supported the business rules of the organizational units of each university. This includes both the academic administration and the academic teaching units.

4 THE CASE STUDIES

Two universities in Victoria, Australia were chosen for the study due to the ability to obtain very detailed data and the recent revamp of their information systems. The universities have taken different directions in addressing the problems of data quality. VU has produced a data warehouse solution we will call the MIS. RMIT has used a People Soft product to support a business process reengineering model called the AMS.

4.1 Victoria University Data Warehouse (MIS)

In 2002 Victoria University (VU) introduced a Data Warehousing system and MIS (hereafter referred to as MIS). Funds were first voted for this project in 1999. The main data sets of the Warehouse are the Victorian Tertiary Admission Centre (VTAC) Popularity Polls, the VU Student Information System (VUSIS) and data VU provides to the Commonwealth Department of Education, Science and Training (DEST). Wherever possible official point of time data captures are used in preference to VUSIS data.

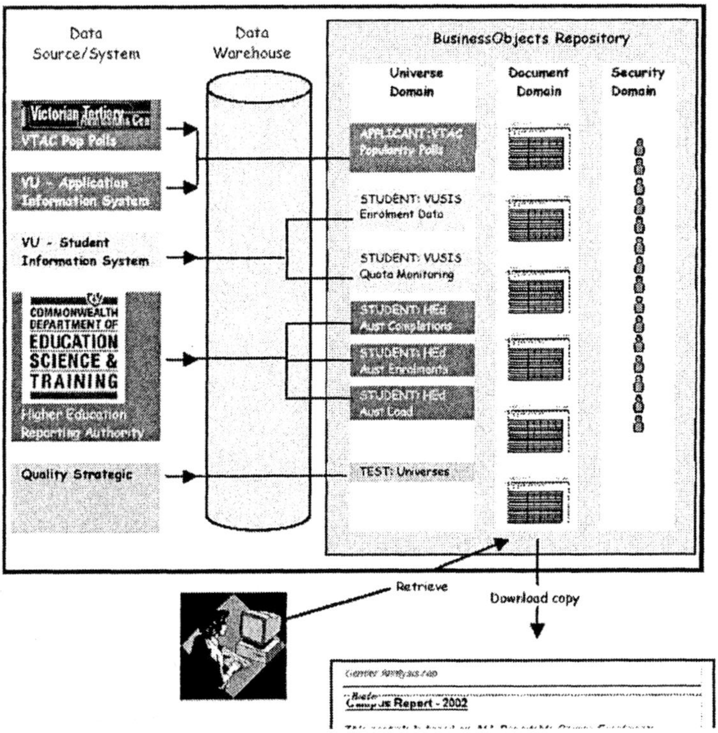

Figure 1: MIS at Victoria University

BusinessObjects is a software program that allows authorised users to retrieve and analyse corporate data. The BusinessObjects Repository is a database that controls all BusinesObject activities. There are three domains:

1. Universe Domain.
2. Document Domain.
3. Security Domain.

Users are concerned with corporate documents housed in the Document Domain. They can access and print standard reports and are able to create and access customised reports. The Course Analysis Reports for the Higher

Education Sector of VU is an example of a class of standard reports. They have been widely distributed and a response to their usefulness has been sought. The results have yet to be published.

The MIS provides relatively easily access and all relevant information is warehoused. The MIS provides information for each course for 3 years (2001-2003). Figure 1 shows that the MIS is a data warehouse, taking data from a number of sources and providing it to users in the form of Business Objects to the user.

4.2 RMIT University Academic Management System (AMS)

In 1998 RMIT Council adopted the Information Technology Alignment Project (ITAP) recommendations, including the acquisition of a functionally rich and inherently flexible integrated academic management system to manage the student learning experience and to facilitate the academic teaching process. In 1999, RMIT conducted a tender for a software replacement to the existing HP3000 legacy systems. The selected software was PeopleSoft Student Administration, with AST Consulting selected as the Implementation Partner.

Business Process Re-engineering (BPR) is a recognised management tool used by organisations to improve their performance across a range of indicators. The purpose of reviewing an organisation's business processes is to gain a comprehensive understanding of the way the organisation currently operates, to identify bottlenecks and difficulties in the current system and to redesign those systems to produce an improved outcome for the organisation and its stakeholders. The following abstract from the AMS process description website, http://www.ams.rmit.edu.au/business/bp_sr.htm, show the type and extent of processes that have been reengineered.

0	Current	Enrolment	Enrol Student -Single Subject-Enquiry
1	Current	Enrolment	Enrol Student -Single Subject-Web Based
2	Current	Enrolment	Enrol Student -Single Subject-Paper Based
3	Current	Enrolment	Enrol Student -Higher Ed Onshore Local (UGRD, PGRD, RSCH)
4	Current	Enrolment	Enrol Student -Higher Ed Offshore International (UGRD, PGRD, RSCH)
6	Current	Enrolment	Enrol Student -Preparatory (Incl VCE)
7	Current	Enrolment Variations	Context Enrolment - Registration/Variation/Exemption
8	Current	Enrolment	Enrol Student -Offshore (PREP, TAFE, UGRD, PGRD, RSCH)
9	Current	Enrolment	Enrol & Re-enrol Student OLA
10	Current	Re-enrolment	Re-enrolment preparation

There are approximately 500 of these high level processes in the list, each of which has a detailed process map, a small section of which has this level of detail.

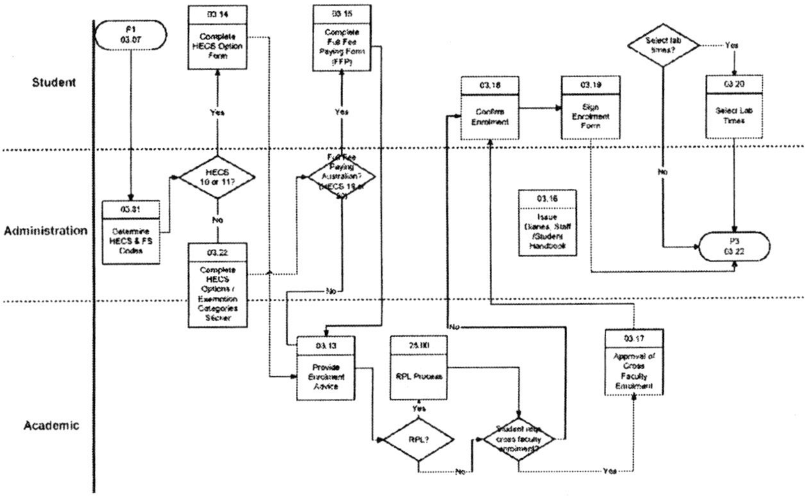

Figure 2: Typical process definition form the AMS

Accurate measurement is important for the University and specifically at the course level because the Australian Government like many others is intent on mandating many more quality control processes that must be reported upon by the University.

The AMS team made an important initial decision. That was to create robust process descriptions for every process prior to implementing that process in the new system. An unattributed adage "a computer allows us to turn a manual mess into an automated mess" is typical of the outcome of many systems that do not ensure robust systems before automation.

5 PROBLEMS WITH DATA QUALITY

The study focused on how the old systems performed in regards to three key aspects of data quality. Reference is also made about the new system. Appropriate information must be accessible to the decision makers. Information cannot be used by people who cannot find it. In both cases senior academics and administrators were found to not use systems because of their inaccessibility.

Similarly information will not be used if it suspected of lacking integrity. This can be due to the structural factors pointed out by Becker, or due to lack of use resulting in out-of-date and incomplete data. In both cases integrity concerns were prominent in the decision to introduce a new system.

Finally, information must support the fundamental business rules of the organisation. Both case studies showed that the old systems did not fully support the important business rules. The new systems were also prompted by a desire to have some business rules re-engineered and implemented in new systems.

5.1 Accessibility of Information

A Victoria university the legacy system, called VUSIS, was necessarily complex and therefore difficult to navigate. It presented difficulties to anyone but the most experienced users. Also some important information was not stored on VUSIS.

A Head of School (HOS) requires information on how many fee-paying students are enrolled in each undergraduate and postgraduate course. In addition a break-up based on onshore/ offshore is required. The information is to establish the degree of dependence on full-fee income for each course. A threat, like a SARS outbreak, may put a course or School at risk if there is a very high dependence on full fee income. Such information is also required because of a strategic decision to attract more students onshore (more profitable) than operate offshore. In the past such information was difficult to obtain because of difficulties associated with the VUSIS and that relevant information was stored in multiple places.

At RMIT the legacy system was an HP product, distributed through an interface called Reflections. Most people knew the system as Reflections. This system was available to one person in each department in the University. Because the system was mounted on very old hardware it became so slow as to be unusable during peak periods. Most departments reported that they used paper-based back-up systems for 'the real work' although the system was robust and reliable in the features that were offered. Accessibility of information was a problem with the Reflections system since an emulation program needed to be installed on each client machine and the server was very old technology. This meant that only a few people in each faculty were able to be connected. In practice this meant printing of lists for use by staff.

5.2 Information Integrity

Recently, the Senior Management of Victoria University decided to continue with the practice of annual increase of the ENTER score required of students to enrol in an undergraduate course. This is the score graduating secondary school students receive. An official document analysing the impact on each Faculty, Course and Campus was distributed. It sought to use 2003 ENTER scores to assess the impact of raising the ENTER from 65 to 70 in 2004. The Faculty of Business and Law's executive officer believed that the numbers in the document were inaccurate in regard to the Faculty. Using BusinessObjects the results revealed this to be the case Specifically, the numbers enrolling with an ENTER in 2003 was 51 not 103.

A manual check would confirm the accuracy of the MIS but this was not undertaken as it was considered too resource-intensive and laborious. However, the Faculty of Engineering, Science and Technology did undertake such a manual count. It revealed that the senior management data was very inaccurate and the MIS sound.

As with many institutions, RMIT determines program viability through a number of measures. These include survey data from graduates. In recent times a number of programs were marked for deletion due to unfavourable survey results. On enquiry it was found that the underlying survey results were from less than five graduates. This level of granularity is an issue with data quality. Any critical data values that are used for decision making should allow the manager to 'drill down' to determine how much reliability is supporting any given figure. This simple example was repeated in most of the decision making within the University. Eventually senior management decided that a new system was required to provide timely and accurate information.

5.3 Business Rule Support

One of the quality measures the success of a course is evaluated against is the student retention rate across the years of the course. DEST uses a measure referred to as the Apparent Retention Rate (ARR). It is an important business rule about what makes for a successful course.

The MIS project team at Victoria University has identified the need for the University to upgrade its information systems so it can accurately measure course completions. Currently, VU reports ARR data to DEST based on graduation information. However, it is recognised that the number of students who graduate may be less than the number of students who complete and that this may have an adverse affect on the retention rate. It is also recognised that the ARR is based purely on the student and not the student course combination. This means that a student who transfers to another higher education course will be counted as a continuing student.

At RMIT the issues of qualification to graduate, recognition of prior learning and prerequisite courses are all seen as academically essential. The old system supported none of the relevant business rules and full-time staff were allocated in every department to perform these tasks. The errors due to this massive amount of manual processing had become of concern to senior administrators and were seen as a justification of the new system. Prior to introduction of the AMS a considerable amount of effort was expended in determining and integrating business rules from around the University. Some business rules were found to be so complex that the University decided to simplify all rules. Documentation and standardization of business rules became an important step in producing an effective administrative system.

6 BENEFITS AND CONTINUING PROBLEMS OF THE NEW SYSTEMS

The MIS at VU represents an important development in minimising data quality problems. It confirms many of the data quality rules. This can be illustrated with reference to two examples previously discussed. The first concerns accessibility of information to make decisions on overseas full-fee students. The second concerns decision making needs on identifying high and low demand courses.

The MIS is an easily accessible system for important course reporting information than has been the past experience of users. The VUSIS system is necessarily complex and difficult to navigate. It presents difficulties to anyone but the most experienced users and does not contain all information.

Despite the benefits conferred by the MIS at VU there remain continuing data quality problems. Again this may be illustrated with reference to two examples that have arisen recently at VU. First, concerns the inability to define and accurately identify student attrition in a course. The second example is the failure to access in a timely and meaningful way, basic staffing information on a University, Faculty and School basis.

At RMIT, the AMS was transported from the United States where it had been used in the tertiary education sector. It is mounted on modern hardware and provides reporting features that have the potential to be very useful. The system is restricted in use, but reports are available to most officers of the university who might need the information. To this extent the data is used daily and any errors in the database do show up quickly.

The AMS sought to improve on this lack of availability by making information available through a web interface. The interface exists but security and training concerns have meant that only a few people in each department have password access to the system, particularly for input. This fundamental balance between security and universal access remains unsolved with the new system. The process of adapting a program from one system to another across international boundaries has lead to a very large problem. The University has found many problems with the interaction of adaptations. It has been decided to restore the original version of the programs and to change University processes to match those inherent in the original.

7 CONCLUSION

The literature suggests that the issues 'Accessibility of Information', 'Information Integrity' and 'Business Rule Support' underlie the important issues of data quality in university administrative systems. Two universities took different approaches to implementing a new administrative system. One designed a data warehouse to provide data objects to users, the other took a business process engineering approach, in each case to address real data quality concerns. In both cases an important design criterion was to make information more generally accessible and hence improve its quality. In both cases significant improvements were created in accessibility, and this was reflected in perceived data quality. The data quality model of using three area of concern was found to be a useful means for studying information systems in the tertiary education field.

8 REFERENCES

Becker, S. (1998), "A Practical Perspective on Data Quality Issues," *Journal of Database Management*, 9, 35-37.

Burns B, Davey B, Hill G, Leveson L. (1992). Articulation and Credit Transfer, Northern Industry Education and Training Link Melbourne.

Cykana, P., Paul, A., and Stern, M. (1996), "DOD Guidelines on Data Quality Management," *Proceedings of the 1996 Conference on Information Quality*, Cambridge, MA, 154-171

Orr, Ken (1998) "Data Quality and Systems Theory - A Paper by Ken Orr, Ken Orr Institute"; in Communications of the ACM, May 1998.

RMIT (2002), Report of the RMIT Council for the period 1 January to 31 December 2002 http://mams.rmit.edu.au/wmhpedjibaj9.pdf.

Tatnall, A. and Davey, B. (1995). "Executive Information Systems in School Management: a Research Perspective". *World Conference on Computers in Education VI. WCCE'95. Liberating the Learner*. Tinsley, J. D. and van Weert, T. J. London, IFIP / Chapman & Hall: 579-588.

Victoria University (2002). Annual Report, http://www.vu.edu.au/home/Media_and_Marketing/Online_Publications/2003_Annual_Report/indexdl.asp.

Visscher, A. J. and Bloemen, P. P. M. (1999). "Evaluation of the Use of Computer-Assisted Management Information Systems in Dutch Schools." *Journal of Research on Computing in Education* **32**(1): 172.

Planning as the Base for Efficient Management of ICT

The case of ULPGC

Jacques Bulchand, Jorge Rodríguez
Universidad de Las Palmas de Gran Canaria
jbulchand@dede.ulpgc.es

Abstract: Challenges produced as a result of the vertiginous advance in computer and communication science are extremely difficult to meet, especially for public universities. In this paper, we propose a methodology for the development of strategic information system (IS) and information and communication technology (ICT) plans in higher education and we present the application of this planning procedure to the Las Palmas de Gran Canaria University. A formal planning process is needed in higher education to meet the needs of all agents participating in the universities. Thus, the proposed methodology is composed of nine steps and involves the whole of the university community, not just IS/ICT technicians. These nine phases, derived from strategic planning procedures, are preplanning, external environment assessment, internal evaluation, strategic interest themes identification, mission and vision statements declaration, strategic axes identification, goals and strategies definition, project and specific actions definition and implementation and evaluation. In this paper we also present in detail the process carried out in ULPGC using the proposed methodology and the results in "The Plan for Info-Tech Systems and Communications ULPGC 2003-2006", which is at present in its implementation or execution phase.

Key words: Information systems, information and communication technology, strategic planning.

1 INTRODUCTION: THE NECESSITY FOR IS/ICT PLANNING

Lately, we are seeing higher education institutions going though a series of very important changes. On one hand they are subject to growing economical restrictions. On the other, there is a vast necessity of information systems (IS) and information and communication technologies (ICT) in all the environments of university life (Bates, 2000).

Under this perspective, information systems and information and communication technologies (IS/ICT) development requires careful planning. This planning should involve the whole university community. Indeed, they should be given the chance to opine about which are the problems that must be attended in the short term and what should be the financial resources distribution.

Besides allowing participation, IS/ICT planning lets us achieve six goals (Andreu, Ricart and Valor, 1996; Cassidy, 1998; Ward and Griffiths, 1996). First, an alignment between the IS/ICT strategy and the corporate. Second, guaranteeing the necessary resources so that the ICT area is able to face rapidly changing environments. Third, finding an efficient and feasible structure for the IS/ICT area. Fourth, improving the communication between management and the IS/ICT technicians. Fifth, dealing with a critical and expensive organizational resource. And sixth, obtaining an organizational knowledge by doing the planning process.

1.1 Barriers to IS/ICT Planning

Although it may seem that the above stated goals are very important, it is verifiable that very few organizations carry out formal IS/ICT planning procedures. What is the reason for this behavior? Basically, the resistance to this kind of planning found in managers and in IS/ICT technicians.

IS/ICT technicians resist because organizations have tried to apply in this area every possible management technique, such as outsourcing, downsizing or total quality management. Unfortunately, results obtained have not really been significant. Due to this, technicians tend to be skeptical and consider each new initiative and strategy as a trend which is in vogue but which will shortly disappear (Boar, 2001).

Managers, on their hand are not favorable either to IS/ICT planning. They do not really see the impact that IS/ICT have and there is a credibility gap in ICT use. Plus, they do not view information as a business resource to be managed for long-term benefit, as economical and human resources are (Ward and Griffiths, 1996).

1.2 Problems When There is Not an IS/ICT Plan

Once the main goals of the planning process and the main existing barriers to them have been defined, some authors describe the problems organizations that do not have strategic IS/ICT plans will face (Ward and Griffiths, 1996). First, there will be a loss of business opportunities and the organization will incur a competitive disadvantage in respect to competitors. Second, there will be a lack of integration between systems and inefficient management of data. This is duplication of efforts, lack of precision, delays and information not useful for business management. Third, development priorities will not arise from business needs. Instead, projects to be developed will arrive from available technologies and from the search of an application for them (Cassidy, 1998). These three kinds of problems should help convince managers about the need of carrying out IS/ICT planning processes.

2 PLANNING METHODOLOGY

We now propose a methodology to develop information systems and information and communication technology plans in higher education institutions. We base our work in the existing methodology for the development of strategic plans applying it to the information systems and technology area (Bates, 2000; Bryson, 1998; Bryson, 1995). Thus, we propose a methodology composed of nine phases that we now present.

Each of these phases requires a series of techniques and tools. These will be referred to in each of the phases although they will thoroughly described in next section.

2.1 Preparation for Planning

This phase can be considered previous to the planning process. Its main goals are three. To define why we are going to carry out the planning, to determine the exact process that is going to be used and to define the involved work teams.

2.2 External Environment Assessment

The second phase is external environmental assessment. Its main goal is to detect existing trends and to check their influence on the university being studied. In this phase, we obtain two of the SWOT matrix components: opportunities and threats. The techniques and tools to be used in this phase are other university IS/ICT plan examination, observation and in-depth interviews.

2.3 Internal Evaluation

The third phase is dedicated to internal evaluation. Its goal is to analyze current and under-developed IS, user perceptions, infrastructures, current human resources and economical resources dedicated in the last few years. As a result of this phase we will obtain strengths and weakness of the SWOT matrix. The techniques and tools to be used in this phase are several. Gibson and Nolan's model, value chain model, Rockart's critical success factors model, discussion groups, in-depth interviews, questionnaires, other university IS/ICT plan examination, detailed examination of all the existing documents regarding the IS/ICT area and direct observation.

2.4 Strategic Interest Themes Identification

The fourth phase is meant to identify strategic interest themes, which can be considered as the union of challenges and trends. Challenges appear formally expressed in the institution's strategic plan, if it exists, or in its SWOT matrix. Trends, on the other hand can be identified through the Delphi method and through in-depth interviews. Techniques to be used in this phase are four. Examination of the institution's strategic plan and its SWOT matrix as well as other university IS/ICT plans and articles by experts in the area, in-depth interviews, questionnaire and Delphi method.

2.5 Mission and Vision Declaration

The fifth phase is dedicated mission and vision statements declaration. Mission is a precise definition that justifies the existence of the organization's IS/ICT area and where functions provided by it to the rest of the organization is found. Vision is where the organization wants to arrive in the long-term. Techniques to be used in this phase are four. First, in-depth interviews. Second, examination of other university IS/ICT plans. Third, observation of tasks usually accomplished by IS/ICT staff. Last, the questionnaire that will be sent to the whole community.

2.6 Strategic Axes Identification

The sixth phase consists of strategic axes identification. These axes are a few pillars over which the future can be organized. When possible, they should be derived from the institution's strategic plan. Else, in-depth interviews must be used.

2.7 Goals and Strategies

In the seventh phase, goals and strategies are proposed for each of the axes defined. Usually there will be between three and five goals for each axis. Goals concerning IS, ICT and information management must be present. Techniques to be used are in-depth interviews, questionnaires, Delphi method and other university IS/ICT plan examination.

2.8 Projects and Specific Actions Definition

In the eighth phase, a series of projects and specific actions are defined for each of the strategies previously outlined. Each of them is assigned a budget, a responsible and one or more indicators that allow us to control them. These specific actions are derived from the questionnaires, interviews and observation of internal documents and from examination of other university IS/ICT plans. All of them will be validated in the Delphi method.

2.9 Implementation and Evaluation

The ninth and last phase is called implementation and evaluation. Its goal is to guarantee that proposed actions are put into practice and to evaluate obstacles found. In the evaluation phase we use the indicators that have been generated for each action. We suggest using the Balanced Scorecard, which allows us to get and integrated vision of all the indicators.

3 FIELD WORK

All through the developed proposal, we have pointed to several methods and techniques to be used in each of the phases. However, it is not necessary to develop them individually for each phase. Instead, carrying them out just once though the planning process is enough to achieve, simultaneously, all the intended goals. We now present each of the techniques and tools to be used, outlining an approximate proposal of when they should be developed.

3.1 University Strategic Plan

We have already mentioned that the best situation is when the university has a strategic plan and that it is aligned with the IS/ICT plan. In this case, the strategic plan and the IS/ICT plan will be developed in parallel. Thus the strategic plan will take into account the IS/ICT area, so challenges needed for strategic interest themes and strategic axes will be developed in the institution's plan.

If the strategic plan did not take into account specifically the IS/ICT area when developed, we will probably have to add a strategic axis specifically focused on systems and technologies. Last, if we do not have an institution's strategic plan at all, the strategic interest themes and the axes for the IS/ICT plan will have to be drawn from the external and internal analysis of the institution using other research techniques.

3.2 Internal Documents

Internal documents are an important source of information for internal evaluation and for mission and vision definition. Documents to be analyzed are the statutes and normatives and the IS/ICT area job post relation.

3.3 Direct Observation

Direct observation of the work carried out by the IS/ICT staff is useful to complete the results obtained from the examination of internal documents. With it, we also find out which are the tasks really done by the IS/ICT staff above what is officially stated.

3.4 Other University IS/ICT Plans

Examination of other university IS/ICT plans is one of the most useful information sources in the planning process. This is because the environment in all universities is fairly similar. If we do not have an institution's strategic plan, we will use this examination for the axes definition, too.

3.5 Discussion Groups

The main goal of discussion groups is to detect the problems associated with IS/ICT use in the university under study. Due to this it is a technique to be used during the internal evaluation phase. We understand discussion groups should not try to find solutions to problems, since in initial phases the main goal is to find out the current situation and not to solve existing problems. We also advise that ICT technicians do not participate in these groups.

We propose carrying out a minimum of five discussion groups with university community members. Two would be dedicated to administrative staff, two to teachers and researchers and one to students.

3.6 In-Depth Interviews

In-depth interviews should be carried out to rectoral team members, department directors and faculty deans. Not all these members must be interviewed, since the number could be considerable. Instead we propose selecting a smaller number through a directed random selection process. The goals of the in-depth interviews are to validate problems detected, to detect perceptions and sensations that relevant university members have about the university's IS/ICT, to analyze what these members expect from the university IS/ICT and to find some solutions to the main problems already detected. These interviews should be carried out once we have ended and analyzed discussion groups.

3.7 Questionnaire

A questionnaire is sent to all members of the university community, and its main goals are to confirm problems that arose during the discussion groups, to allow all university members to take place in the elaboration of the plan, to find out the opinion that the community has about some trends that are happening and to help in defining goals and action plans.

3.8 Delphi Method

Last, we propose developing a Delphi method in the ending part of the planning process, when a first outlining of goals, strategies and action plans has already been made. In this case, we think the participants should be experts in university IS/ICT, relevant rectoral team members and some external members, such as experts from local government, nation-wide system experts or university IS/ICT suppliers.

3.9 Analysis Tools

We consider using three analysis tools in the IS/ICT planning process in universities: the value chain model, the critical success factors and Gibson and Nolan's model.

4 ULPGC IS/ICT PLAN

We now describe the process taken to develop the Universidad de Las Palmas de Gran Canaria's (ULPGC) IS/ICT plan.

4.1 Development of the ULPGC IS/ICT Plan

We now describe the steps taken to validate this methodology through its application to ULPGC.

The proposed plan was developed in the eight months between November 2001 and June 2002. During this time a direct observation of the IS/ICT area of the university was carried out, and during the first four months internal documents were examined.

Five systems and technology plans of higher education institutions from the United States were examined. These five examined plans were obtained from the Internet and were those of Berkeley, MIT, University of Arizona, Penn State University and East Tennessee State University.

IS/ICT and institutional strategic plans were developed with a certain overlapping, so some degree of alignment was achieved. During November 2001, five discussion groups with non-expert users were carried out. The first two of them were with researchers and teachers. The next two were with administrative staff and the last one involved students.

From these discussion groups, a structured list of more than 120 items was created. These items were classified into 10 subjects, each item reflecting a problem detected by users or a wish about how IS/ICT should work.

Using these problems and the desires found in the discussion groups, a semi-structured questionnaire composed of 31 questions was elaborated. This questionnaire was used in a series of in-depth interviews that were carried out in December 2001 and January 2002. These in-depth interviews were carried out to 8 rectoral team members, 6 deans and 6 department directors, for a total of 20 interviews.

Last, in April 2002 two simultaneous processes started. On one hand, a questionnaire was sent out to all the members of the University. On the other hand, a Delphi method was developed.

This questionnaire was only filled using electronic media; basically the institution's web page. A total of 544 answers arrived: 234 from teachers and researchers, 143 from administrative staff and 167 from students.

For the Delphi method, an expert panel composed by 22 experts in IS/ICT from university and non-university environments was used. The first round took place in April and May 2002 and the second one in June 2002. In each of these rounds, experts where asked about three different items. First, trends in general environment and their possible influence in our university. Second, about the main goals to be carried out. Third, the actions needed to achieve the goals and qualitative and quantitative indicators for each of them. In the first round, economical and temporal estimations where asked for and in the second round a confirmation of these was required.

Also two of the three proposed tools were used, the value chain model and Gibson and Nolan's model. The critical success factors model was not used.

4.2 ULPGC IS/ICT Plan

To end this paper, we now present the main contents of the Information and Communication System and Technology Plan of the ULPGC. Following the proposed methodology, the Plan has been structured into four axes. In each of them goals have been defined. In each goal action plans are defined. For each plan an execution time has also been estimated (short, medium and long term). Last, for each action plan we have a series of concrete actions, with a budget and a timetable for those to be executed in 2003.

4.2.1 SWOT matrix

From the analysis developed by IS/ICT heads, from the discussion groups and from other university IS/ICT plans, we got the main environment trends that affect the university's IS/ICT. The analysis was considered externally (2 threats and 8 opportunities were found) and internally (8 strengths and 20 weaknesses were found).

4.2.2 Mission and vision

We define the ULPGC mission as "Give University Community a stable, productive and efficient ICT environment that makes teaching and researching easier, provides services to university community and to society, and helps knowledge management processes".

Vision is defined as "We intend to place our University in the top-ten in the IS/ICT area in our country, at the same level as reference universities in our context. ULPGC should be innovative in its daily tasks and must promote information and knowledge society in its environment."

4.2.3 Axes

We found four axes in total. Three were derived from the institution's strategic plan, those related to teaching, researching and management and services to the community. The fourth axis is specifically for IS/ICT and has been called "Technology and Available Resources".

4.2.4 Goals and actions

A total of 12 goals were defined between the four axis previously mentioned. Each of these 12 goals has a series of actions. In total, we have proposed up to 60 actions and 36 indicators to evaluate them. The Plan is available for download (in English and Spanish) at http://www.ulpgc.es.

5 CONCLUSIONS

Using a systematic approach to the development of system and technology plans in universities can be a great aid to achieve a successful distribution of limited financial resources in an expansive area such as that related to new technologies. But a better resource distribution is also achieved. Other important results are also obtained. First, the whole university community participates in the process. Second, due to their participation, they get to know the plan.

Also, a few effects have to be taken care of. On one hand is the hangover effect. This is thinking to some stage that the objective of the planning process is to develop the plan, when the goal is to implement the plan. On the other, when implementing the plan, we discover our limitations, that is, we are able to think fast, but we execute very slowly.

6 REFERENCES

Andreu, R., Ricart, J.E., Valor, J. (1996). Estrategia y sistemas de información. Barcelona, Spain. McGraw-Hill, Interamericana de España, S.A.

Bates, A.W. (2000). Managing technological change. Strategies for college and university leaders. San Francisco (CA), EE.UU. Jossey-Bass Publishers.

Boar, B. (2001). The Art of Strategic Planning for Information Technology. New York (NY), USA. John Wiley & Sons, Ltd.

Bryson, J.M. (1988). "A strategic planning process for public and non-profit organizations". Long Range Planning, 21(1), pp. 73-81.

Bryson, J.M. (1995). Strategic planning for public and nonprofit organizations (2ª edición revisada). San Francisco (CA), USA. Jossey-Bass.

Cassidy, A. (1998). A practical guide to information systems strategic planning. Boca Raton (FL), USA. St. Lucie Press.

Ward, J., Griffiths, P. (1996). Strategic planning for information systems. Chichester, UK. John Wiley & Sons.

Educational Management Systems and the Tutorial Class

Bill Davey and Arthur Tatnall
RMIT University and Victoria University, Australia
Bill.Davey@rmit.edu.au, Arthur.Tatnall@vu.edu.au

Abstract: Recent research by the authors has shown that University administrative systems are not designed with a view for use in the direct educational process. To attempt to discover the mechanisms for this failure in IT systems an in-depth case study was conducted. The study involved an extremely well documented University administrative system, intended to support the tutorial classroom, called the Administrative Management System (AMS). Based on a well known PeopleSoft product the implementation and development of the system allowed a study of the dynamics within the educational institution. It was found that the vision of IT support for the classroom has not been achieved and that the process of developing a large system for the University involved steps that would, almost inevitably, lead to an emphasis on data gathering rather than relevant reporting.

Key words: Administrative management systems, university administration, university classrooms, teaching support.

1 INTRODUCTION

In studying the development of information systems it is quite common to find that a system has not fulfilled its potential because, although technically well designed, it failed to meet the needs of its users (Meredith and Mantel 1995). Even the best designed system that does not do what all its users want is of little overall value, and an important part of systems development is finding out the needs of all the users: "You must thoroughly understand the business needs before you can create a useful system" (Post

1999). In an earlier ITEM paper (Davey and Tatnall 2003) we pointed out how the information systems literature stresses the necessity of involving users in the process of designing information systems (Fuller and William 1994; Lindgaard 1994; Lawrence, Shah and Golder 1997). If this is not done then these systems will not be as useful as they could be. Lawrence et al. (1997) point to a need to consult with all users while Lindgaard (1994) notes that a large body of research has shown that potential users do not make best use of information systems unless they feel that these systems have been designed with their involvement and in their interest. Tatnall (2001) points out that there is a body of research indicating that when centrally designed systems are seem as unresponsive to the needs of a group of users then these users will ignore this system and devise means of their own to achieve what they want. There is plenty of evidence that this happens frequently in many university departments (Davey and Tatnall 2003).

Recent research (Davey and Tatnall 2003) has shown that many university administrative systems are not designed with a view to being used in the direct educational process: to be of use in the tutorial classroom. Newton et al. (2003) point out that partly because of the way the data in university administrative systems is stored and accessed, absolutely no use can be made of these systems to improve teaching and learning. They note that a tension thus exists between the different purposes of management systems in both school and higher education, and that systems that are designed primarily with a view to the provision of management information are unlikely to be of use for classroom purposes. One Australian university set out with the intention of creating a system to provide support for academics, and this paper reports on a detailed study of its development and an investigation into the reasons for the large gap between the intentions of the system and the final outcome.

2 THE GAP BETWEEN VISION AND REALITY

A definition of academic management was set out by a high level university committee, producing a vision of what academic management might mean. Among the nine attributes of the system to be developed were:

Section 4 Defining characteristics of academic management

3. Successfully managing an educational services contract

- Students receive personalised advice from course teams based on information and alerts from the AMS.
- Students monitor their own academic performance with up-to-date, accurate information on progress.
- Students are provided with formative feedback at key learning milestones (including assessments).
- Students receive early advice of academic progress.
- Course teams monitor students' progress and workload based on rules they set and are alerted to need for early intervention.
- AMS supports these processes, including triggering and recording formative feedback.
- AMS stores details of the learning agreement, any negotiated amendments, and facilitate automatic re-enrolment.
- Progress of employees is reported to enterprises as agreed.
- The AMS maintains links between individual learners and the employers' educational services contract.

5. Supporting career-long relationship management

- Expectations of a lifelong relationship with RMIT are introduced to all students before completion of their course.
- Faculties, departments/ schools and course teams integrate and coordinate planning for alumni activities and networking.
- The AMS maintains records of all alumni and client enterprises.
- Staff work with students to provide career guidelines at graduation and career planning services on an ongoing basis.
- Staff continue to provide alumni with information about university learning opportunities at RMIT to support their career on an ongoing basis to encourage further engagements with RMIT.

7. Maximisation of well-being of RMIT's students, clients and staff

- AMS provides students and clients with comprehensive information on services, facilities and program or subject specific occupational health, well-being and safety issues and costs.
- Students are supported to identify special needs.
- RMIT responds to the plan and implement assistance as needed.
- AMS assists course teams identify and support diverse student needs.

Table 1: RMIT's vision of academic management

Interviews were conducted with senior and junior academics, administrative officers and several members of the development team.

When shown the features above, all respondents reported that none of these features were actually extant in the Administrative Management System (AMS), nor was anyone aware of plans to include features that might support these ideals. Clearly there had been an implementation which ignored a large part of the originally envisaged functionality, and this was the functionality that an academic might be interested in when looking to improve the work done in academic classrooms.

In fact, the specifications of business processes included just these:

- Recruitment – automated information access supplemented by expert advice on programs, and university services including housing, finance, etc., and handling of individual queries.
- Selection and management of selection (based on established selection criteria and processes – with the ability for individual academic selection decisions remaining).
- Problem-solving and management of individual students. Enrolled students are allocated to a Student Case Manager who is their first point of contact for queries and problems.
- Customer Relationship Management – to facilitate and maintain RMIT's relationships with enterprise clients, including the supervision of the educational services contract.
- Timetabling.
- Program Team Management – including projects, quality assurance and monitoring cohort progress.
- Electronic courseware development and cataloguing.
- Provision of expert advice on AMS functionality, and ongoing training to Faculties Department and central service areas. 'Super Users'/Business Analysts of the AMS (Functional Analysts who have formed part of the implementation team and returned to their faculties/service areas with expert knowledge of the system).
- Research support.

Note that none of these points have to do with classroom activities.

This is more starkly brought into focus when looking at the timelines for the project:

AMS Process	Available:
Updating of student details	Late Oct '01
Attendance Confirmation - updating and enquiry	Late Oct
Grade Rosters	Late Oct
Download of grade rosters in new format	Late Oct
Entry of results via Client Server, or upload of results (in either previous HP format file or in the AMS download format file)	Late Oct
Advisement reports etc.	Late Oct
Negative Service Indicator maintenance & enquiries	Late Oct
Student Account Enquiries - by staff (Client Server)	Late Oct
Student Account Enquiries - by student via web	Dec
Reports and on-line enquiries	Late Oct
Pilot of GradeBook for nominated courses	Early '02
Direct admissions for nominated programs	Late Oct
VTAC admissions and offers	Late Oct
On-line International Applications (possible interim arrangement initially)	Late Oct
International Applications	Late Oct
Re-enrolment by student via web on campus	Dec
Re-enrolment by staff member via client server	Late Oct
New enrolment by student via web on campus	Feb '02
New enrolment by staff member via client server	Late Oct

Table 2: Timeline for project implementation

Note that *all* of the processes envisaged are of straight data capture. It seems that the grand dream of an IT system supporting the whole education process had resulted in a routine student records storage system.

3 FINDING REASONS FOR THE GAP

The formal project team chart (above) shows how thinking on the AMS development became a reality. The diagram includes only officials recruited from the vendor or the administrative levels of the University. In theory any academic advice could be garnered from the faculty reference group.

The Minutes of the Academic Management System Reference Group of 2/2000 show that of 41 members of the reference group, one Dean was represented by a department head but no other academic with teaching, or teacher supervision roles, was a member. By rollover time the reference group had grown to 62 members, none of whom were active teachers. At this meeting, it was announced that:

> *"The Functional Analysts are a key component of this Phase and will be consulting with various relevant experts across the University. A high level of automation is envisaged in order to streamline the procedures. Functional Analysts will be looking at the rules which the University already has in place, will be analysing whether these rules are consistent, informal or on an individual basis and will be working towards consistent procedures across the University system. The consistency of University procedures will lead to successful automation."*

Again, the functional analysts were drawn exclusively from administrative support staff of the University. Research has shown (Martilla and McLean 1977) that it may be more effective for *users* to determine those factors they think important to the effective use of information systems. In a case study by Shah (2001) such a study of user input led to the identification of issues such as communication between the Information Systems Department and users, the speed of response of particular sections of the system and the existence of specific reports. A question arises as to the prevalence of features of a system that have importance to users, but have not been emphasised by the developers of the system. It seems that, in this case, the definition of user became one that excluded any officer directly related to teaching within the University.

4 RETURN ON INVESTMENT

We then looked for reasons for the sudden lurch from a vision of academic administrative support into the much more mundane world of student records capture, the first clue was found from documents explaining some advantages of the new system. The Return on Investment (ROI) indicated that a saving of 86 person years of effort per annum could be achieved within 5 years. This figure was based on a significant reduction in the number of paper transactions (currently 1.2 million documents per annum) associated with student administration.

The reduction in the amount of paperwork was to be achieved by:

- Business Process Re-engineering leading to the rationalisation and streamlining of academic procedures.
- Reduction in the number of appeals based on procedural errors.
- Increased self service for students including financial transactions, enrolment and class selection.

- Reduced staffing required for enrolment and re-enrolment.
- Monitoring and enforcement of final result submission deadlines (approximately 20,000 results were incomplete at 1st April 2000).
- Reduced errors in enrolment resulting in fewer enrolment variations.

The major impacts on academic and teaching staff were considered to be:

- Direct input of assessment results thus obviating double handling and the need to check results input by admin staff.
- Immediate access to class lists without the need for intermediaries.
- Monitoring of timely completion of assessment.
- Automatic academic advisement with reduced call on academic staff to provide time to advise students on enrolment issues.
- Automated enrolment requiring much less academic staff time.
- Increased administrative assistance by redeployment of effort and re-skilling of administrative staff.

It can be seen that each of these justifications for the system was oriented around cost savings from automation. There was no discussion of intangible benefits, and benefits to classroom teaching at all.

5 THE ROLE OF ADMINISTRATIVE SYSTEMS IN TEACHING SUPPORT

As we noted in a previous discussion of aspects of this topic (Davey and Tatnall 2003), Fulmer and Frank (1997) point out that while these systems have been effective in business-related tasks such as inventory control, personnel management, cost analysis and audit, they have been "… far less effective at depicting the conditions of teaching and learning. … They have not provided quality data for analysing and intervening in processes of teaching and learning." It should be noted that Fulmer and Frank were referring to administrative information systems in schools in these comments, but our research shows them to be equally true of many university systems.

In an earlier ITEM paper (Tatnall and Davey 1995) we also argued that educational management systems should make more use of the 'higher levels' of information system and provide decision support and executive information facilities rather than just transaction processing. These higher levels of support could provide a much better level of support for teaching. Newton et al. (2003) also suggest use of higher level functions such as decision support. Speaking mainly of school-based systems, they suggest that knowledge based systems may offer possibilities for tracking of student progress and diagnosis of learning problems. We would argue that such functions would also be of value in university systems.

6 A CUTTING-EDGE EXAMPLE

An extract from the process description for the monitoring of student progress indicates the thinking at the time of the requirements definition:

> *"Each student who fails to meet academic requirements is sent a certified letter. All correspondence is certified to ensure that students obtain documentation from the University. A return receipt is returned to the relevant Faculty to ensure that documentation was received."*

Clearly the developers here are seeing student progress monitoring as a system that requires monitoring of only the paperwork. There could have been mention of diagnosis from the data or supplying quality improvement data, but there was not. Since none of this was imagined, the process definitions excluded any real academic support.

Another clue as to what was envisaged by the system development team can be seen from the training schedules. This list of training courses shows that the system was seen as a means of recording data, rather than supplying information.

AMS001	AMS Basic, People & Student Data
AMS003	Managing Organisations
AMS004	Communication, Comments & Checklists
AMS005	Committees & Events
AMS007	Managing Applications (Direct Local)
AMS008	International Applications
AMS009	Managing Evaluation and Matriculation - run as pilot only in 2001
AMS010	Managing Student Records & Enrolment
AMS012	Class Scheduling - run as pilot only in 2001 - open for other staff mid-2002
AMS015	Student Financial Basics
AMS018	Billing, Payment & Refunds
AMS019	Administering Payment Plans

Table 3: Course numbers and names

7 CONCLUSION

This case study shows that administrative systems in university education are not immune to the vagaries of information systems designed for any other industry sector, and suffer the same problems if all stakeholders are not involved in their design. They are often not designed to take into account the possibilities of using their output to improve what goes on in the tutorial classroom. A 'grand plan' was envisaged by the University where a quick changeover to a robust data gathering and reporting system would quickly lead to improvements through web-based automation of interactions with clients (mostly students) so that the system would yield high-level academic returns. The reality that has been found by almost all sectors that take on a BPR (Business Process Re-engineering) exercise is that the data capture and reporting systems are non-trivial but still determine the possibility of leading on to higher-level use of the information. A further finding from the case study is that the inclusion of stakeholders at all times in the project seems necessary to maintain focus on the vision and avoid intricate, but often unhelpful, detail from becoming the only outcome. It is also noted that education organisations seem to be composed of two streams of management: teachers and administrators. These two streams seem, in the case study example at least, to have little idea of the priorities of the other.

8 REFERENCES

Davey, B. and Tatnall, A. (2003). Involving the Academic: A Test for Effective University ITEM Systems. *Management of Education in the Information Age: The Role of ICT.* Selwood, I., Fung A. C. W. and O'Mahony C. D. Assinippi Park, Massachusetts, Kluwer Academic Publishers / IFIP: 83-92.

Fuller, F. and William, M. (1994). *Computers and Information Processing.* Massachusetts, Boyd & Fraser.

Fulmer, C. L. and Frank, F. P. (1997). Developing Information Systems for Schools of the Future. *Information Technology in Educational Management for the Schools of the Future.* Fung, A. C. W., Visscher A. J., Barta B. Z. and Teather D. C. B. London, Chapman & Hall / IFIP: 122-130.

Lawrence, D. R., Shah, H. U. and Golder, P. A. (1997). Business Users and the Information Systems Development Process. *The Place of Information Technology in Management and Business Education.* Barta, B. Z., Tatnall A. and Juliff P. London, IFIP / Chapman & Hall: 118-127.

Lindgaard, G. (1994). *Usability Testing and System Evaluation.* London, Chapman & Hall.

Martilla, L. A. and McLean, E. R. (1977). "Importance Performance Analysis." *Journal of Marketing*(January).

Meredith, J. R. and Mantel, S. J. J. (1995). *Project Management: a Managerial Approach.* New York, John Wiley & Sons Inc.

Newton, L. and Visscher, A. J. (2003). Management Systems in the Classroom. *Management of Education in the Information Age: The Role of ICT.* Selwood, I., Fung A. C. W. and O'Mahony C. D. Assinippi Park, Massachusetts, Kluwer Academic Publishers / IFIP: 189-194.

Post, G. V. (1999). *Database Management Systems.* London, McGraw Hill.

Shah, S. K. (2001). "Improving Information Systems Performance Through Client Value Assessment: A Case Study." *Review of Business* **22**(1/2): 37-42.

Tatnall, A. (2001). Design Strategies. *Information Technology in Educational Management: Synthesis of Experience, Research and Future Perspectives on Computer-Assisted School*

Information Systems. Visscher, A. J., Wild P. and Fung A. C. W. Dordrecht, The Netherlands, Kluwer Academic Publishers: 97-113.

Tatnall, A. and Davey, B. (1995). Executive Information Systems in School Management: a Research Perspective. *World Conference on Computers in Education VI. WCCE'95. Liberating the Learner*. Tinsley, J. D. and van Weert T. J. London, IFIP / Chapman & Hall: 579-588.

Quality Management in Virtual Education

Management Indicators for Continuous Improvement

Lucía Melián, Víctor Padrón and Tomás F. Espino
UNIVERSITY OF LAS PALMAS DE GRAN CANARIA
lmelian@dede.ulpgc.es

Abstract: The important mission of the university institution in society as a body creating and transmitting knowledge justifies higher education being one of the main players in the application of new information and communications technologies (ICTs) in an attempt to exploit the significant advantages that their development can bring to the activity. However, the virtual university faces the challenge of analyzing how the new educational format alters the knowledge learnt in quality management in traditional higher education. New parameters, models and indicators will have to be defined, and new competitive bases will have to be promoted.

Key words: Total quality management, virtual higher education, student satisfaction.

1 INTRODUCTION

ICTs represent a unique opportunity for the management and creation of knowledge. In effect, the Internet is a super-highway giving access to all types of information, encouraging interactive communications at a world level, reinforcing and boosting understanding, comprehension and knowledge and so contributing to raising world quality at all levels.

From that basic premise, learning has also been subject to this phenomenon. It is obvious that the university, as an institution creating and spreading knowledge, grasps this opportunity to strengthen its role. To that end, it is experiencing and incorporating ICTs, especially the Internet, in its teaching and research work, taking advantage of the flexibility, dynamism and interactivity of the medium to promote communication between educational agents, both inside and outside the institution (Sánchez Allende, García Manso and Díaz Moreno, 2003).

However, *virtual learning in higher education defines a more competitive market* since the wider offer contributes to the virtual student being a demanding customer classified as a consumer requiring a university product and service of excellent quality. As a result, this leads to the need to study quality management within virtual universities. The academic literature shows this question (Pond, 2001; Roffe, 2002).

2 TOTAL QUALITY MANAGEMENT IN THE VIRTUAL UNIVERSITY: A PROGRAM FOR RESEARCH

Total quality management can be defined as a management philosophy that bases its raison d'être on customer satisfaction as a winning formula to achieve a competitive advantage in the market, involving all the organization and external agents such as suppliers and distributors, among others. The practicality of this model is that it is a multi-company management philosophy; in other words, applicable to any sector, and so, on asking whether TQM has a role to play in virtual university education, the answer is, of course it has.

Firstly, the virtual university is still an institution with a management directed at accomplishing its organizational mission – the creation and transmission of knowledge – which is performed in a digital context with its own characteristics. Secondly, the main client, the student, is more demanding than ever as a result of fierce competition in the market. Consequently, the student takes on a determining role as the key auditor of the academic institution's actions and is demanding not only in terms of quantity but also of quality because of the change in the nature of the service.

With reference to the need and formula for, and the implications of identifying the customer's requirements and demands, a review of the academic and professional literature revealed a series of basic premises. First of all, quality from the customers' perspective is defined as the difference between their expectations and their perceptions of the actions of the company under study. Secondly, quality is a multi-attribute concept; a construct of the second order resulting from the practice of the company in a set of areas of action, dimensions and attributes (Parasuraman, Zeithaml and Berry, 1985, 1988). In this respect, although some authors support the universality of one set of dimensions and attributes for every type of service (Parasuraman, Zeithaml y Berry, 1988), others support scales adapted to the specific context of the study, justified, in part, by the very idiosyncrasy of the field of study (Carman, 1990; Babakus and Boller, 1992). In this respect, the differential nature of virtual education indicates the identification of the typical attributes and dimensions (Table 1).

Table 1. Characteristics of the virtual learning environment

QUALITY	CONCEPT
DYNAMIC	Up-to-date knowledge is transmitted in real time. The content and material are subjected to recycling and innovation as changes take place. It is impossible to be in the digital context and not take advantage of the sources of information provided by the Internet to capture and process information relevant to the content of the educational program.
INTERACTIVE	Students are in touch with teachers, other students, with the on-line resources of the Internet and with the institution's services. This is possible from the moment that the Net allows the user 24-hour access to the website, promoting interactive communication, which increases the added value of the educational offer.
PERSONALIZED	The student perceives a more personalized relationship insofar as there are methods and systems that permit direct, individual dealings with the teaching staff, other students and the institution itself. Moreover, as a result of the interactivity, the institution is on a direct line with each student, gathering information that enables it to identify possible interesting alternatives, adopting and adapting individualized formats.
COLLABORATIVE	The Internet favors collaboration, the exchange of ideas and discussion by providing the means and the systems, (chats, video-conferences, forums, debates...) to channel them. With collaborative work, the student will acquire skills such as the ability to criticize and work in a team, among others. In this way, constructive knowledge is generated, stemming from sharing it.
SELF-LEARNING	The student is more active in asking questions and obtaining help in virtual learning. He/she assumes more responsibility for his/her learning by having to seek information, show an initiative to work in a team and identify his/her own resources. The student can decide when and how to progress with his/her educational project, once again revealing the status quo of the Internet user: self-service and self-control.

At this point, and based, on the one hand, on the acceptance of customer satisfaction as the reference point for the internal management of the virtual university, and on the other, on the recognition of the properties of on-line education, this work addresses two basic objectives: (1) the theoretical proposal of a scale to measure quality in the university from the student perspective and, (2) the identification of the competitive bases of the internal management of the on-line educational institution that contributes to customer satisfaction.

To that end, it was decided to use a complementary methodology. Firstly, there was a review of the theoretical and practical works on success factors in virtual education in the academic literature and an examination of virtual education websites in order to construct the scale of quality. Secondly, based on the gap model of Parasuraman, Zeithaml and Berry (1985), and after a study of the literature related to the resources and capabilities necessary to operationalize a virtual university, the criteria of internal management were linked to the evaluative criteria of the student.

The works reviewed included the contributions of Lieblein (2000), Sánchez Allende, García Manso and Díaz Moreno (2003), Tascón Trujillo (2003), as well as the empirical research of McGorry (2002) and Song et *al.* (2004).

3 PARAMETERS OF ACTION IN VIRTUAL HIGHER EDUCTION: AREAS OF ACTION AND COMPETITIVE BASES

Given the idiosyncrasy of higher education in the digital context, there is an analysis to identify the criteria to evaluate organizational excellence from the student perspective, and the factors of its internal management that contribute to student satisfaction.

3.1 Attributes and Dimensions of Quality in Virtual Higher Education

A review of the relevant academic and professional literature and an examination of websites devoted to on-line university education led to the extraction of a model that presents quality as a higher order construct comprising a set of dimensions – institutional quality, functional quality and relational quality – and sub-dimensions with their respective explanatory attributes.

As well as serving as a reference for organizational action, it offers the added value of explaining what each section –dimension and sub-dimension- contributes to and subsequently attracts the client.

3.1.1 Institutional quality as the fundamental core

Institutional quality affects the actions of the on-line educational institution regarding its making its activity known, projecting an image to the market and seeking a competitive position.

It represents the basic management nucleus from which every organizational action materializes since it refers to the disposition to offer determined academic products and services as well as those that are non-academic but relevant to an educational activity; it materializes in the image and the offer (Table 2).

Table 2. Institutional quality

SUB-DIMENSIONS AND OBJECTIVES	ATTRIBUTES
IMAGE	The student can access the administration and secretariat services to handle procedures and formalities.
Inform the institution's main client, i.e. the student. Create a market image. Transmit security and responsibility to the student. Advertise the academic products and services. Convince the student of the institutional capacity to undertake an e-learning project	The student has alternative, effective means of access to the institution's representatives. The institution gives relevant information about the organization, such as its history, credentials and activity performed, resources, study programs, academic and financial results of previous years, services, and faculty staff. The institution takes responsibility for protecting student data on the Internet and authors' copyrights. The institution programs visits to the campus, making university life more tangible. The institution has a digital platform that allows it to perform its administrative, academic and social work in an optimum manner.
OFFER	The educational offer is of social interest, meeting the needs of the job market.
Supply a flexible offer adapted to the students' limitations regarding time and location. Deal with the economic, social and cultural areas demanded by professionals and that arouse interest in learning. Exploit the resources that other institutions can provide. Create and transmit knowledge.	There is a wide range of study plans and vocational activities. The student is offered up-to-date, interesting offers such as: job offers, research groups, masters and specialized courses. The student is offered access to, and participation and collaboration with, other universities. The student is offered access to, and participation and collaboration with companies and institutions.

3.1.2 Functional quality as a means to channel the activity

Functional quality evaluates the execution of the on-line educational activity; the form and method that brings institutional quality into effect is operationalized. Therefore, in this dimension, we assess the institution's fulfillment of its raison d'être. Three sub-dimensions are used for this: design, material and teaching (Table 3).

Table 3. Functional quality

SUB-DIMENSIONS AND OBJECTIVES	ATTRIBUTES
DESIGN	The website design is attractive, entertaining, thus encouraging navigation.
Guide the student. Avoid confusion and transmit security.	Navigation is simple and intuitive. The operating technique is correct. The page download is relatively quick.

SUB-DIMENSIONS AND OBJECTIVES	ATTRIBUTES
Take the student where he/she needs to go. Save students' time.	
MATERIAL	The learning material is relevant and up-to-date, showing the important activities and facts.
Offer material that arouses student interest. Offer material that reflects international economic and social life. Avoid unnecessary inconvenience to the student when he is allowed access to the material at a suitable time and in an adequate form.	The design of the material is suitable for a virtual learning context, for example, using a hypertext format with links to documents of interest. The teaching material is completed with access to documents, reports and experiences of other institutions and companies. A virtual library of great bibliographical depth is available, permitting access to the documentation necessary for optimum performance of the learning task. Before the beginning of the course, the student has material that can still have points of interest updated. The teaching material is legible. It has easy understanding.
TEACHING	The teacher shows a clear mastery of the material, both in terms of the content and in responding to the student's queries and questions.
The student feels secure and comfortable. The student feels that personalized teaching assistance is available. The student feels motivated. The student integrates the content with technology in a natural way. Promote constructive, discussible, conciliatory thinking.	The teacher conveys secure and trust. The teacher accepts criticisms. The teacher stimulates collaborative learning. The teacher stimulates teamwork. The teacher encourages constructive argument. The teacher encourages debate by, for example, introducing topics related to the subject in chats, forums or video-conferences. The teacher motivates the student's interest and boosts learning. The teacher adapts the syllabus to reality by incorporating current topics into the program.

3.1.3 Relational quality as a vehicle to promote loyalty

Relational quality is the third level of organizational action to be evaluated. Although it could be included as part of functional quality because it operationalizes university life, its identification has been considered individually for one basic reason: it comprises the essence of the new information and communications technologies, which is personalization and interactivity.

In other words, the personalization and the interactivity are the subdimensions of the relational quality. The personalization adapts the academic offer to individual demands and the interactivity helps to do it.

The result of this philosophy is an attempt to create a virtual climate that favors the retention of the student as a customer that always finds a learning opportunity in the institution's offer, which is developed through personalization and interactivity (Table 4).

Table 4. Relational quality

SUB-DIMENSIONS AND OBJECTIVES	ATTRIBUTES
PERSONALIZATION Virtual teaching becomes a personal means of learning. Technology is the vehicle for an individualized approach to learning, not for automation. The student feels that the organization is making significant efforts to adapt to his/her personal demands and needs. The student feels that he/she is being appraised and guided in this new learning context.	The teacher guides and advises in both support material and study habits in order to achieve effective learning. The student has access to a technical assistance service that advises him/her in the use of ICTs. The teacher employs an individualized treatment of the student, monitoring and following up his/her progress. The teacher keeps the student informed of his/her academic progress (works, marks obtained, personal comments...) The student has access to his/her academic records as well as to information regarding his/her administrative paperwork. Flexible teaching methods are used so that the student can participate in line with his/her timetable restrictions. The student is permitted to configure the program, appraisal system and activities to suit his/her restrictions and needs. The student is informed, at the suitable time and in a correct form, of relevant topics of interest throughout the academic year.
INTERACTIVITY Maximize the principal characteristic of the new technologies: the possibility of interacting without problems of space and time. Create an atmosphere of a virtual campus, of collective social life. Encourage free expression, debate and communication. Facilitate access for everybody to everything.	Interactive communication between students (discussions, chats, video-conferences,..) is promoted, creating opinion groups and means of dialog. An informal space is created for communication among participants in the system, with the creation of a notice board, chats,..). Interactive communication between teachers and students is promoted (discussion forums, video-conferences,..).

3.2 COMPETITIVE BASES OF THE VIRTUAL UNIVERSITY FROM THE GAP MODEL

The Gap model, developed by Parasuraman, Zeithaml and Berry (1985) for physical environments and later modified by Zeithaml, Parasuraman and Malhotra (2000, 2002) for virtual environments, defines the quality perceived by the user as the result of the size and direction of four organizational discrepancies or gaps associated with information, design, operations and communication: (a) Gap 1, the information gap, is the difference between the users' expectations and the managers' perceptions of the users' expectations (b) Gap 2, the design gap, is the difference between the managers' perceptions of the users' expectations and the specifications of quality established in the design, (c) Gap 3, the operations gap, is the difference between the design specifications and the service actually provided; and, (d) Gap 4, the communication gap, is the difference between the service provided and that which is communicated to the users.

In this way, the quality perceived by the user, also called Gap 5, is the result of the difference between the service provided and the expectations and is the accumulated effect of the four previous gaps. This means that the gap model would combine the following parts in a common framework: (1) evaluation of e-quality and its consequences (the user part) and (2) the organizational deficiencies that could reduce e-quality (the organization part).

Once the customer perspective is analyzed and taking this model as a reference, its use in the case of the virtual university lies in extracting the key aspects in the internal management in order to achieve optimum action in the evaluative criteria that the student takes a reference.

These key aspects give a detailed description of the competitive bases that a virtual university must control (Table 5).

Table 5. Competitive bases of virtual university management

CAUSES OF THE GAPS	STRATEGIES TO NARROW THE GAPS: COMPETITIVE BASES
GAP 1 Insufficient market research. Inadequate use of the research. Lack of interaction between managers and users. Inadequate upward vertical communication.	Study the level of student satisfaction (e-mail surveys, analysis of complaints and suggestions,...). Study the level of expectations and demands of novel students. To promote interaction between management and students there must be forms of access (e-mail, telephone, fax,...), as well as virtual encounters via video-conferences. The institution's top management must increase meetings and communication with teaching and administrative staff to obtain proposals and suggestions.
GAP 2 Deficiencies in the commitment of the management. Perception of non-viability. Absence of objectives or errors in the establishment of requirements or standards.	The university management must be trained in quality management. The university management must believe in Total Quality Management. The university management must know their resources. The university management must value their resources. The university management must pursue and procure resources from others organizations. The university representatives must define their areas of

CAUSES OF THE GAPS	STRATEGIES TO NARROW THE GAPS: COMPETITIVE BASES
	action (such as: teaching, administrative services, virtual services like the library, notes/handouts on the net, links with other organizations). The university representatives must establish objectives or standards in each area of action that are coherent with strategy.
GAP 3 Functional ambiguity and conflicts. The staff members do not really know the scope of their functions. The technology required to perform the operations is not in place. Inadequate systems of supervision, control and reward. Lack of a sense of teamwork.	Clear delimitation of the programs of subjects, with discrimination of content. The organization's members must know the scope of their functions (of content and technologies). The remuneration of the teaching staff must be linked to productivity (for example, according to the number of video-conferences offered, or the number of on-line tutorials). The virtual university must have a complex, interactive digital platform. Teamwork facilitates the optimum result by means of, for example, the saving of resources and the synergies of technological learning.
GAP 4 Deficiencies in lateral communication between departments and sections. Differences in procedures and policies of the different areas. Tendency to promise too much.	All the university staff must know and agree on the marketing plan. A series of minimum criteria for teaching must be established (for example, interactivity and personalization in dealing with the student). Continuous improvement must be reinforced in order to reach higher levels of action; only then can high promises be made.

4 CONCLUSION

There are two lessons to be learnt by reading this work. Student satisfaction with the virtual university requires optimum action from the institution in three areas: institutional quality (image and offer), functional quality (design, material and teaching) and relational quality (personalization and interactivity). To meet those demands, the university must strengthen a set of competitive bases, including the following: collaboration, training, participation of management, participation of teaching and administration, continuous improvement, information, alliances with strategic partners such as other universities or companies for projects or exchanges. However, the combination of TQM and virtual higher education constitutes an important area of study. In this respect, it is necessary to perform future analyses of aspects such as the application of the EFQM, certification and accreditation subject to the norms, and how strategic alliances contribute to excellence.

5 REFERENCES

Babakus, E. and Boller, G. W. (1992). An empirical assessment of the SERVQUAL scale. Journal of Business Research, 24, 253-268.

Carman, J. (1990). Consumer perceptions of the service quality: an assessment of the SERVQUAL dimensions. Journal of Retailing, 66 (1), 33-55.

Lieblein, E. (2000). Critical factors for successful delivery of online programs. The Internet and Higher Education, 3 (3), 161-174.

McGorry, S. Y. (2003). Measuring quality in online programs. The Internet and Higher Education, 6 (2), 159-177.

Parasuraman, A., Zeithaml, V. A. & Berry, L. L. (1988). SERVQUAL: a multiple-item scale for measuring consumer perceptions of service quality. Journal of Retailing, 64 (1), 12-40.

Parasuraman, A., Zeithaml, V. A. & Berry, L. L. (1985). A conceptual model of service quality and its implications for future research. Journal of Marketing, 49, 41-50.

Pond, W. K. (2001). Twenty-first century education and training. Implications for quality assurance. The Internet and Higher Education, 4 (3-4), 185-192.

Roffe, I. (2002). E-learning: engagement, enhancement and execution. Quality Assurance in Education, 10 (1), 40-50.

Sánchez Allende, J., García Manso, A. & Díaz Moreno, P. (2003). Educación virtual: el nuevo apoyo a los estudios universitarios. In L. Joyanes Aguilar & M. González Rodríguez, (Eds.), II Congreso Internacional de Sociedad de la Información y del Conocimiento, libro de actas (pp.284-289). Spain: McGrawHill.

Song, L., Singleton, E. S., Hill, J. R. & Koh, M. H. (2004). Improving online learning: student perceptions of useful and challenging characteristics. The Internet and Higher Education, 7 (1), 59-70.

Tascón Trujillo, C. (2003). Aulas virtuales en la Universidad. Nuevos roles y competencias docentes en la teleformación. In L. Joyanes Aguilar & M. González Rodríguez, (Eds.), II Congreso Internacional de Sociedad de la Información y del Conocimiento, libro de actas (pp.263-270). Spain: McGrawHill.

Zeithaml, V. A., Parasuraman, A. & Malhotra, A. (2002). Service quality delivery through web sites: a critical review of extant knowledge. *Journal of the Academy of Marketing Science*, 30 (4), 362-375.

Zeithaml, V.A., Parasuraman, A. & Malhotra, A. (2000). *E-service quality: definition, dimensions and conceptual model.* Working paper. Cambridge, MA: Marketing Science Institute.

Emerging Knowledge Networks as a Background For Educational Management

Learning from Information Industries

Mikko J. Ruohonen
Department of Computer Sciences, FI-33014 University of Tampere, Finland
mr@cs.uto.fi

Abstract: Knowledge-based organisations are facing constant changes in their operations and management models. Industry structures are converging which means new business processes and organizational structures. Hence, interorganisational competitive advantage demands cross-organisational learning and management. Knowledge workers need to create new competencies and management processes need to be contextualized. Knowledge work characteristics are applied in the context of the information and communications technology (ICT) industry. Finally an explorative framework for knowledge work leadership is developed and tentative empirical guidelines are reviewed.

Key words: Knowledge work, ICT industry, inter-organisational competitive advantage, organisational contexts, management approaches.

1 TRANSFORMATION OF THE ICT INDUSTRY

The use of information and communications technology (ICT) has emerged as an important target of management. In addition to improving cost-effectiveness, it also offers great potential for innovations (Ruohonen & Salmela 1999). E-business is starting a change process in which organisations must think about operations models, organisational processes, and ways to meet and serve customers needs (Kalakota & Robinson 2001).

Functional hierarchies have turned to be more organised networked structures. The functional growth of a company is often based on buying competing companies, mergers, or branch rationalisation to make strategic alliances. Mass production has turned into a customer-oriented operation and even mass-customised (Pine & Gilmore 1997, Contractor & Lorange 2002). Different collaboration and outsourcing strategies will become more important (Kern & Willcocks 2002). Collaboration is not just based on transferring transactions between companies, it is also sharing knowledge, uniting and integrating processes and developing joint measures for operations. We call it an era of knowledge management networks (Ruohonen & Salmela 1999, Warkentin et al. 2001).

The information production and services industry, later information industries, is one of the drivers and enablers of the aforementioned change. Different products and services of the companies which handle information technology, telecommunications, digital contents industry and related fields provide opportunities for new innovations. It means that a strong commitment and ability to network reliably with their partner organisations should exist. The management of co-operation between organisations becomes a key factor in this challenge. Formal agreements between organisations are just a start - the building of knowledge networks demand new qualities both from organisations and their managers. The next four qualities (Dyer & Singh 1998) are important as the source of the competitive advantage between the organisations:

- Relation-spesific assets i.e. investing in the specific relationship of partners.
- Knowledge-sharing routines between partners.
- Complementary resources supplementing core competencies of each partner.
- Effective governance of the relationship.

The knowledge creating companies should manage of all these qualities. This is also the case when organizing your educational management services, for example, when the organisation either co-operates within an ICT development project or has a constant outsourcing service relationship with a customer company. This is reflected, among others ways, in the administration and maintenance of electronic exchanges, in the management of communication network services or in the fostering the use of intranets.

2 MANAGEMENT OF INTERORGANISATIONAL COMPETITIVE ADVANTAGE

2.1 Relation-Specific Assets

The co-operative relationship between organisations is not merely by control of formal agreements, as the organisations must also bind themselves into the long-term cooperation. Starting of outsourcing services begins the co-operation relationship with many options to change this relationship. Pricing, cost control and exit provisions just provide a skeleton for a tighter co-operative relationship. It must be possible to evaluate the outsourcing operations and at the same time be possible to make selective outsourcing possible. The outsourcing which produces added value leads to changing of the models and the co-operation relationship, and the cutting short of costs remains "business-as-usual" (Lacity & Hirscheim 1993, McFarlan & Nolan 1995). The service provider must be able to learn the organisational model and processes of customer organisations. At the same time customer organisations have to be ready to become acquainted with the products and service alternatives beyond the approach of traditional transaction costs. The professionals' working in the service organisation must be in line with customer responses. The service organisation should take care of the customer's schedules and timetables. Both parties must accept that when building co-operation, one must commit oneself to invest in that relationship continuously, both economically and mentally. Very few co-operative projects start moving without incidents and succeed by a first attempt. The success of the co-operation is strengthened especially by mutual trust which is claimed to be a necessary condition to the genuine co-operation project.

2.2 Knowledge-Sharing Routines Between Partners

Currently many organisations organise their information systems services behind common web-based portals. This takes place, for example, in the public administrative and educational services, supply of the tourism industry, procurement of the car industry, paper, metal and electronics industries. Unfortunately these exchanges or portals tend to be only cyber-crossings. Hence, the customer arrives at this crossing from which he chooses the following direction and never returns. The exchange of knowledge should be two-directional in knowledge networks. Stakeholders must learn from each other for improved service of customers and better competitiveness. If the holder of the portal considers the meeting place only as the strengthening of his own position on the market, the portal becomes rather a bulletin board which is full of ads. However, if the portal is designed to be a problem-solving space it requires community knowledge sharing practice of the portal partners. The transfer of customer knowledge, for example, to competitors, is extremely difficult because knowledge interrelates to context. Many organisations, such as Avnet/Marshall, have operated within the field and developed their services continuously for a long time towards proactiveness, right pricing of services and anticipation of customer needs (El Sawy et al. 1999, Turban et al. 2002). So the added value is not based on control of the transaction cost, it is searched beyond control of the traditional value chain (Stabell & Fjeldstad 1998).

2.3 Complementary Resources or Capabilities

The resource-based theory from the firm (Barney 1991) calls for those resources which are valuable, rare, hard to copy and effectively organised from the point of view of the competition. The core competence has often been created in time, self-steered and even by chance. It is particularly difficult for management to see the importance of competencies created at the floor level. The learning created in action and while facing customers provides a foundation for success. However, these competencies can become obsolete if competitive or technological changes affect our business environment. The competitive advantage of knowledge networks is created through a clustering process in which two or more organisations with complementary competencies begin to compete against other competitors' clusters with similar interests. This creates a match-making and grouping process. First the exchange of knowledge will be clustered around different technology options but at the following stage one already must think what kind of customer groups we are taking care of. The complementary competencies can open new markets and technology areas. Traditionally we avoid situations in which espionage or stealing of corporate core competencies is obvious. On the other hand, there are viewpoints according to which external competencies should be produced in the hyper-competitive businesses (D'Aveni 1995, Matusik & Hill 1998).) Japanese car manufacturers are able to distribute knowledge inside a trusted network while in the US business environment formal agreements and sanctions dominate business (Dyer and Singh 1998).

2.4 Effective Governance of the Relationship

Competitive advantage is not achieved if costs of cooperation exceed the level of other similar ones by competitors. So a project, such as the service portal, must be governed effectively, for both the technical infrastructure and the contents (i.e. services). Co-operation rules of practice must be created while different stakeholder groups control their own interests. It is good to have a mediating organisation - an official broker which functions formally or based on partner relationships. The ways of action have pointed to persons in charge of organisations and the processes must be clear and explicit to every partner. The broker must be able to operate fast without constantly arranging meetings when cooperation proceeds and the customer interface changes. Situations in which this customer setting has to be evaluated and checked will be created continuously.

3 A FRAMEWORK FOR KNOWLEDGE WORK LEADERSHIP

3.1 Contextual Approaches Needed

The ICT industry has been stamped by a strong turnover. The knowledge workers have looked for more inviting jobs for themselves and for new possibilities opening in the field. The motivation base is, or at least has been, mainly economical. Companies have had to persuade the experts of the new economy by better salaries and share options. A number of ICT companies have experienced the first phase of the knowledge company lifespan. In this phase nearly any way of working went through and customers were willing to pay for that. This was very evident in late 1990s in the so-called dotcom-companies. Search for "the new economy experts" ended up with acceptance of poor quality management and productivity guidelines. Project management and business know-how was not really appreciated while it was more interesting to strive for Initial Public Offerings and sky-rocketing rise of shareholder value. Most of the companies were very small in size, with no business management experience and personnel of very young age and narrow qualifications. Hence, there was no clear management practice. The companies were more like bunches of good friends or families. However, now ICT companies also try to create other attraction factors than economic advantage. The economic advantages are a kind of hygienic factors as such but in addition to them the sensibility of the work and ways of action, the character of the work community, the culture of the organisation and management style and the general attractiveness of the business branch are evaluated. Knowledge management is also the evaluation of your company management approaches, not just technology. The new start-up companies enjoy the advantage of quick implementation of new practices. Those organisations with a longer time in business have probably created different organisational rules which are slow to change. More experience and knowledge is needed concerning management practices in different information industry contexts (Ruohonen et al. 2003).

3.2 The Explorative Framework

The following generic framework is an exploration of the empirical findings from case companies (Ruohonen et al. 2003). The framework is proposed to be continuously evaluated against empirical findings and elaborated to a more advanced description. The dimensions for categorizing different contextual knowledge work management approaches are defined by external variety (competitive business forces) and internal variety (personnel differences). Competition has put pressure on all information organisations, but especially on those which made a fresh and glorious start (dotcom-companies). Most of the companies have failed now and faced the rules of competition. Competition makes companies aware of good quality and project deadlines. Personnel differences refer to those emerging challenges which are rising from differences in age, culture, job career, professional backgrounds, even gender and race in some societal contexts.

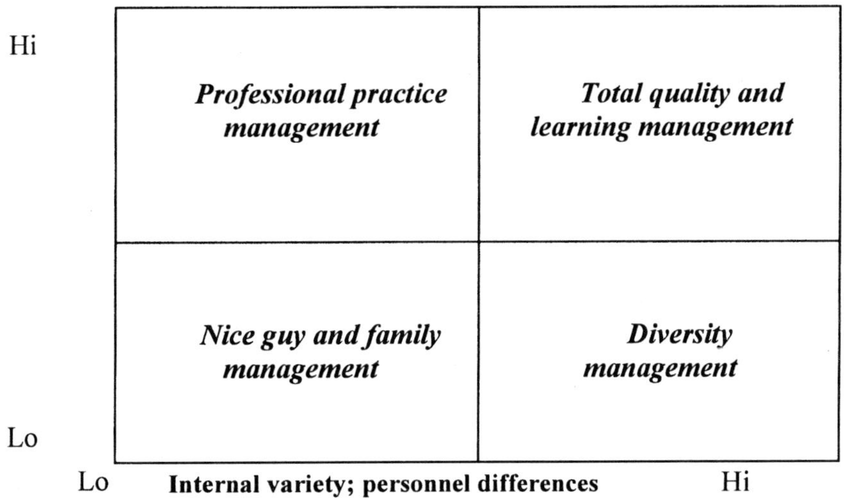

Figure 1. A framework for knowledge work leadership approaches

3.2.1 Nice guy and family management

This corner of the framework represents the typical start-up company. In those companies customer intimacy might be great and knowledge sharing is easy while the company is small in size. All people can participate in joint problem solving and project sessions. However, in these companies recognition of complementary resources is seldom done explicitly. Normally there is a shortage of resources which force buying companies to use these services. Governance of projects, such as e-commerce projects, is normally poor. Quality is low and timetables are flexible. These companies first provide value due to market inequivalencies, but when markets develop and customers learn to demand more, quality management becomes problematic. Management of people is based on "nice guy feelings", normally managerial structures are avoided and there are no systematic administrative processes. Office hours are very flexible and people like to use their freetime with their colleagues or even stay overnight in the office. Management follows the guidelines of how to work with your friends or even family members.

3.2.2 Diversity management

This describes the situation which has been typical for some of the growing dotcom companies. They have increased their size by buying smaller companies and in the same time got publicly listed. The rapid growth has created problems of communication and management structures and also clash of cultures. Many small family management companies have been destroyed by these acquisition maneuvers. Interorganisational competitive advantage emerges from the four competitive factors previously described. Relation-specific assets grow but they are fragmented according to certain specialist and competence groups i.e. customers are not really customers of the new merger-based company. Projects are more diverse in nature and demand variety of personnel competencies. Knowledge sharing might grow problematic due to rapid growth and different learning styles of personnel. It is increasingly more difficult to gather complementary resources for a larger customer project. Governance can still be poor, and that affects the quality provided. The challenge is diversity management, both projects and human resources become more diverse and managers need to know more about different psychological, social and cultural phenomena which are reflected in their daily work.

3.2.3 Professional practice management

This corner is the possibility for a rather homogenous personnel in harder competition. If companies can create more systematic approaches, improve their strategies, structures and processes in line with customer demands they might survive. However, this means that some of the workers are not happy while they can not do what they want. Project managers need to be aware of project deadlines, strong enough to resist last minute changes and very authoritative when people are producing over-quality. The advantage of these companies is longer customer relationships which have educated both parties to do their best. Professional rules, patterns and even support systems can help knowledge sharing inside the company and with customers. Complementary competencies are identified and constant review of service quality is executed. Governance is more systematic but enables freedom when necessary. In these companies world-class innovations are possible. Professional practice management develops the company further.

3.2.4 Total quality and learning management

This is the most challenging while it requires both the management of business competition but also different diverse personnel management approaches. These companies are normally the big players in the field which provides many branches of services to customer companies. They normally also have very diverse personnel working abroad. These businesses need to take care of both "old" systems and emerging new economy systems. They analyse, support and consult strategy making. Many of these take care of outsourcing and application service provision. They hire people for customer companies. Relation-specific assets are usually managed by account managers who are responsible for certain customer projects. Projects and customers are categorized. They have initiated both formal (IT-based) and informal (face-to-face) knowledge sharing practices with information systems support. Complementary resources are strived through team building, task forces and evolving organisational arrangements. Governance uses total quality management and critical chain reviews. Quality is defined either by excellence criteria or with meeting customer demands. In the same time these companies face a clear threat of becoming too bureaucratic, therefore active learning management processes are needed too. Especially processes which support reflection are needed. Both quality and learning management makes the manager an acrobat on one hand trying to keep costs and schedules, while on the other hand enabling creativity, freedom of ideas and professional learning.

4 FINAL REMARKS

A theoretical framework was reviewed for emerging knowledge work and leadership cultures in the ICT industry. Competition and increasing pressure to make network economy demands new competencies. Interorganisational competitive advantage requires cross-organisational learning and working processes. Knowledge work has to face productivity challenges. Managers need to identify the context they are working in order to align with personnel competences. An explorative framework was provided and described against theoretical groundings and empirical findings of an on-going research project. The framework will be elaborated with further research on emerging knowledge work and management practices.

5 REFERENCES

Barney, J.B. (1991) Firm resources and sustained competitive advantage. Journal of Management 17(1), 99-120.

Contractor, F.J. & Lorange, P. (2002) The growth of alliances in the knowledge-based economy. International Business Review 11, 485-502.

D'Aveni, R. A. (1995): Hypercompetition: Managing the dynamics of strategic maneuvering. New York: Free Press

Dyer, J.H. & Singh, H. (1998): The relational view: Cooperative strategy and sources of interorganisational competitive advantage. Academy of Management Review 23(4) 660-679.

El Sawy, O.A., Malhotra, A., Gosan, S. & Young K.M. (1999): IT-Intensive Value Innovation in the Electronic Economy: IT-Intensive Value Innovation in the Electronic Economy: First Prize, 1997 SIM International Paper Awards Competition.

Kalakota, R. & Robinson, M. (2001): E-Business 2.0. Addison Wesley Longman, Reading, Massachusetts.

Kern, T. & Willcocks, L. (2002) Exploring relationships in information technology outsourcing. European Journal of Information Systems 11, 3-19.

Lacity, M.C. & Hirscheim, R. (1993) Information systems outsourcing myths, metaphors and realities. Wiley, Chichester.

Matusik, S.F., Hill, C.W.L. (1998): The Utilization of Contingent Work, Knowledge Creation, and Competitive Advantage. Academy of Management Review 23(4), 680-697.

McFarlan, F.W. & Nolan, R.L. (1995) How to Manage an IT Outsourcing Alliance. Sloan Management Review 36(2), 9-23.

Gilmore, J.H. & Pine, J. II (1997): Four Faces of Mass Customization, Harvard Business Review Jan-Feb 1997, 91-101.

Ruohonen, M. & Salmela, H. (1999): Yrityksen tietohallinto. Edita, Helsinki.

Ruohonen, M., Kultanen, T., Lahtonen, M., Rytkönen, T. and Kasvio, A. (2003) Identity and Diversity Management for New Human Resource Approaches in the ICT industry. In F. Avallone, H. Sinangil & A. Caetano (eds) Identity and Diversity in Organisations. Milan: Guerini Studio.

Stabell, C.B. & Fjeldstad, Ö, D. (1998) Configuring value for competitive advantage. on chains, shops, and networks. Strategic Management Journal 19, 413-437.

Turban, E., King, D., Lee, J., Warkentin, M. & Chung, H. (2002) Electronic Commerce – a Managerial Perspective. Prentice Hall.

Warkentin, M., Sugumaran, V. & Bapna,R. (2001) E-knowledge networks for interorganizational collaborative e-business. Logistics Information Management 14(1/2), 149-162.

A Collaborative Environment for New Learning Ecology and E-Pedagogy

Toshio Okamoto and Mizue Kayama
Graduate School of Information Systems, The University of Electro-communications, Japan
School of Network and Information, Senshu University, Japan
okamoto@ai.is.uec.ac.jp

Abstract: Nowadays, we realize change in learning ecology by making progress in Internet technologies and advanced media. A learning ecology moves from individual learning to collaborative learning via the Internet. So we are urged to create a new e-pedagogy. This paper proposes and discusses functionality for collaborative learning, then discuss what e-pedagogy is, based on new learning ecology. In this discussion, we emphasize the re-use function of data logging occurring during a collaborative learning process. Moreover, we consider the educational meanings and methodology to explore essentials of collaborative learning. We introduce a platform for a collaborative learning environment called RAPSODY-EX (REX) that we have developed. The features and functions of this platform are described, and then we discuss the extendibility of the platform for a collaborative environment from the issue of e-pedagogy we propose.

Key words: e-pedagogy, learning ecology, collaborative learning, knowledge transfer,

1 INTRODUCTION

The Internet is becoming a catchphrase in the world of school education, which makes distance education possible to anybody at anytime and from anywhere. As such, a new learning style 'e-Learning' emerged under the new umbrella concept of 'Learning Ecology and Pedagogy', where the Internet raises the level of communications and collaborations among people via technology. Nowadays, the word/system of 'e-Learning' is rapidly spreading due to popularization of the Internet. As for advantages of the

Internet, people can communicate with each other anytime and anywhere. Moreover people can share, rebuild, stock and reuse various kind of information. Here, it seems that the concept of e-Learning gets citizenship in society instead of CAI (Computer Assisted Instruction). Along with this stream/trend, we recognize the necessity of construction of a new learning society such as learning individuals, learning organization and learning community. Above mentioned, we can say that the Internet is a kind of *Treasure Island* of educational resources from a worldwide stance, though it includes much harmful information.

2 PURPOSE OF THIS STUDY

The aim of this study is to propose the concept of new learning ecology and e-Pedagogy in the center of collaborative learning via the Internet. A learning environment where includes various IT devices and some kinds of computer network (Internet, LAN, WAN, and so on) has produced a new learning ecology such as exploring/discovery learning, collaborative learning and so on. According to these changing situations, a new and persuasive pedagogy has to be created. In this paper the idea of e-pedagogy is proposed. Based on this concept, we introduce the RAPSODY-EX (REX), which is a platform for a collaborative learning environment (Okamoto, Cristea, & Kayama 2000). A distributed collaborative learning (CL) environment is expected to facilitate learning activities for knowledge building and meta-cognition through mutual understanding among learners. In this environment, management/integration of the learning resources/information becomes an important task for the purpose of promoting learners' decision-making activities and teachers' mentoring activities. The especially stressed functions are as follows: for evaluating learning process, restoring collaborative activities, plug-in API, referring/reusing information and so on.

3 NEW LEARNING ECOLOGY AND E-PEDAGOGY

Varieties of knowledge will be taking a form of multimedia in a highly technological, network society. And this knowledge can be obtained through so-called VOD (Video On Demand). Moreover, wide varieties of educational applications and teaching systems will be provided. The problem, however, is that we need the ability to grasp the essence of that knowledge. Also this knowledge should not be enclosed only in a human understanding of the world. An ability to create a new knowledge out of that understanding is now sought. The knowledge in a closed textbook will be transferred to this real world. It is important to form live knowledge. To make science and technology attractive to youth needs a synthesizing pipe, that is, a systematic resource to totally canalize the scientific minded to that new knowledge.

In the Post-Modern age, our new learning viewpoint is as follows.

a) Group modeling and collaboration for social activities.
b) Exploration-minded experimental learning.
c) Learning (urged) by asking, explaining and teaching to make a new insight.
d) Interactive diagnosis and open learning model.

From those aspects, we must construct the curriculum with a view for e-pedagogy based on the following educational considerations:

- Topic oriented structure: contents are synthesized according to topics. Many topics are organized systematically and make comprehensive contents as IT-education.
- Scenario oriented structure: making scenario-like contents and offering well balanced unit subjects.
- Minimum essentials: extracting minimum essential unit subjects as "informatics for all" and making a comprehensive subject together with other common subjects.
- Comprehensive subjects based on existential subjects: an integrated subject, making a comprehensive selection by taking units as thought necessary from other subjects such as math, science and so on.

These are views to make a comprehensive subject. Therefore, it is hard to say what is best. Information technology, however, is a familiar matter so that it should be something attractive to children/ students' mind. It should not be what sounds fictitious.

4 WHAT IS COLLABORATIVE LEARNING

4.1 Some Definitions and facilities

In terms of what Roschelle & Teasley defined as "collaboration" to be "…. a coordinated, synchronous activity that is the result of a continued attempt to construct and maintain a shared conception of a problem" (Roschelle & Teasley 1995). Dillenbourg takes up the following 4 points as the features of CL, which are a situation, interactions, process (learning mechanism) and effects of CL (Dillenbourg 1999). Cowie & Rudduck note that "collaboration in leaning is the opportunity to learn through the expression and exploration of diverse ideas and experiences in cooperative company...." (Cowie & Ruddick 1998). It is not about competing with fellow members of the group and winning, but using the diverse resources available in the group to deepen understanding, sharpen judgment and extend knowledge.

In consideration of those views, Okamoto pointed out that CL should emphasize 1) process/situated context, 2) individual learning achievement such as knowledge acquisition, skill formation and concept formation, learning set, 3) versatile cognition for both of holistic and serialistic thinking schema, 4) understandings of objective relationships among self/you/he or she, and 5) effects of observation learning (reflection/self-monitoring) (Okamoto et al. 2000). CL doesn't depend on place and time. Especially in an Internet environment, the type of asynchronous ecology of CL is more useful rather than the synchronous one such as a videoconference. Moreover, in the process of CL, individual learning may be sometimes embedded, based on a certain curriculum in schools, and vise versa. Table 1 shows the dimensions on features of CL.

Table 1. The dimensions on features of CL

Activity-cognitive level	Activity-social level
• Discussing	• Observing/Suggesting
• Planing/Designing	• Role-taking/Cooperating
• Data/Idea sharing	• Coordinaing/Controling
• Evaluating/Finding solution	• Social interacting
• Building knowledge	• Facilitating/Supervising

In general, we can divide the activities in collaborative learning into two classes of cognitive level and social level. Based on these activities, the resources required in a CL environment are as follows:

- Technologically mediated dialogue channel
- Shared workplace for a group
- Personal workplace
- Learning materials/ learning tools
- Analyzing tools of data/information
- Learning materials/ learning tools
- Repository/memory for data/information revealed in CL
- Reference channel for the collaborative repository
- Modeling tools for monitoring the process

4.2. Methods for Supporting Collaborative Activities

There are two approaches on CSCL. One is to emphasize the interactions among learners. Another is to stress the efficiency of knowledge acquisition and the certainty of knowledge acquisition. The former approach aims at clarifying the effect of an interaction and promoting the effect of an interaction as well. There are many researchers focusing on realizing the transparent and seamless purpose of efficient communication. For example, they use agent technology, natural language analysis, statistical text mining and others. The latter approach focuses on providing a medium for the interactions among learners so as to promote and/or increase the efficiency of knowledge acquisition. There are various functions and mechanisms developed for these purposes. In order to support collaborative activities, the following functions are necessary:

- Offering the workspace of an individual and the workspace of a group.
- Supporting mutual transfer data, information and knowledge in the workspaces.
- Including various information media (libraries, applications, tools and so on) to the platform.
- Shared screen image / shared operation.

5 A PLATFORM FOR THE CL: RAPSODY-EX

RAPSODY-EX (REX) is a platform of a CL learning environment. Our focus is on the management function for a collaborative workplace in CL. The features of REX are as follows:

- Management of Learning Session: this feature enables a student to participate in collaborative activities on REX.
- The communication library (API) for the shared application/tool: this feature allows plug-in applications/tools for CL (shared applications) to REX.
- The hierarchical control mechanism of learning log data: this feature allows distribution/ record/reference of learning logs based on the learning condition/context.

The main function of this platform is the management of collaborative workplaces and learning sessions (Kayama & Okamoto 2002, UEC 2004). Once a CL mediator/instructor defines the collaborative activity on REX, a learning session can be generated in REX for the learners. For each learner, a learning session is instantiated on each REX client. A learner expresses his/her opinions/views through shared applications on a learning session. A collaborative workplace, containing two or more learning sessions, keeps and manages the context of CL. The REX server specifically performs the management of a collaborative workplace and a learning session, consisting of some management modules for different information on REX. Moreover, it also contains a maintenance module with a set of CL cases and a management module of a learning session

A learning session represents a space for group member activities. Each learning session is generated as a response to the learner's needs / instructional goals on REX. After this, it is registered to the REX server. A learning session contains one or more shared applications representing a unit of CL activities on REX. A learning session is described by an attribute and a state. The conceptual scheme of a learning session is shown in Figure 1. An attribute is a set of information used for characterizing a learning session. This includes some static information, such as the start time of CL, the participating member of a learning session, the name of a shared application, and a URI (Uniformed Resource Indicator) to the substance of a shared application.

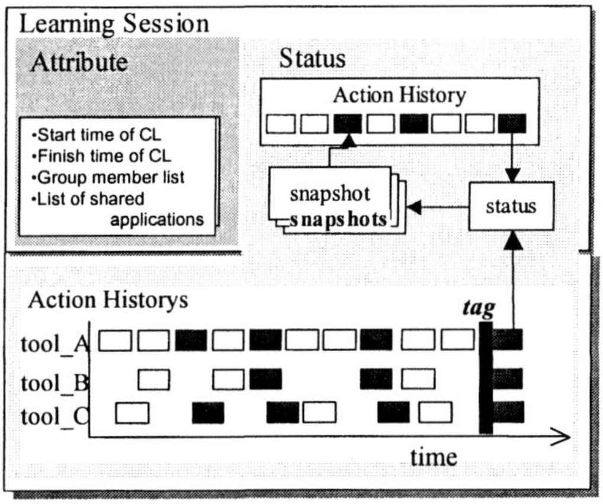

Figure 2. The conceptual scheme of a learning session

The assurance of keeping learning context and the reuse of learning logs are realized by this hierarchical management of learning logs. Additionally, some components of the collaborative environment (eg. shared applications/ tools, and learning management tools for CL) are implemented more easily and effectively.

6 MODELING OF COLLABORATIVE ACTIVITIES IN REX

6.1 Learning Activities of CL

Generally, CL by the Internet enables synchronous and asynchronous learning modes. In an asynchronous learning pattern, the communication/ interaction medium consists of an e-mail system, a BBS and others. However in a synchronous learning mode, communication/ interaction among learners is achieved via simultaneous learning tools.

In this research, CL is defined from a different aspect. The simultaneity is emphasized in our case. A synchronized type is defined as an extended case of a synchronized type. Thus, the design principle of REX has to maintain a collaborative workplace. A learning session is an operative object of a collaborative workplace in REX. In this object, the learning activities are expressed as the series of actions for achieving the learning goal. The learning activities for a student are represented as follows:

- *<Join>* ::= acts participating in CL
- *<Suspend>* ::= acts which do_not/ are_impossible_to contribute to generation of an outcome of CL although learner has participated in CL.
- *<Leave>* ::= acts which stop the participation for the CL.
- *<Refer>*::= acts which refer to the outcome and/or the process of CL.

6.2 Learning States of CL

The state of CL is represented by combining four activities: Practicing, Broken, Accomplished and Aborted. The feature of each state is summarized in Table 2.

Table 2. The features of the learning states of CL

State of CL		**Practicing**	**Broken**	**Accomplished**	**Aborted**
Learning Goal		NO	NO	YES	Cannot
Participant		YES	NO	NO	NO
A	*Join*	OK	-	-	-
C	*Suspend*	OK	OK	-	-
T	*Leave*	OK	-	OK	OK
.	*Refer*	OK	OK	OK	OK

A *Practicing* state in the process is to achieve a learning goal, which is defined as a set of *Join* mode, *Suspend* mode and *Leave* mode. A *Broken* state in the process is to achieve a learning goal. In this state all of the group members are in *Suspend* mode. At an *Accomplished* state, a learning goal is achieved. In this state, all of the group members are in *Leave* mode. At an *Aborted* state, a learning goal cannot be achieved and any learning activity will not happen. In this state, all of the group members are in *Leave* mode. Moreover, a *Refer* state is executed at all learning states.

6.3 The Functions for Collaborative Modeling by REX

Some functions are necessary for smooth and efficient interaction/ communication and effective acquisition of some kinds of meta-cognition skills. The first function should be the identification of learning states and learning activities at a collaborative workplace, which offers useful and valuable information for CL support. Thus, the platform can apply some appropriate support for a group/learner.

We assume that it is important to secure the information shared among learners in CL. Shared information here includes result/production/ solution during learning, which are set as attributes of a learning session at REX. Table 3 shows examples of status of a learning session. In this situation, the simultaneity of learning activity is guaranteed. Action is used for the operation/screen_image shared among learners during CL. Action history is used for maintenance of a series of learning activities. Then the information is stored as status of a learning session. Status is held in the result/ production/solution of CL. Therefore information can be offered as a current learning context to a newcomer in CL. Status is also recorded as a snapshot. REX shows a user result/production/solution at the current state. Moreover, REX shows a series of results/productions/solutions by using snapshots. By using this type of information, a learner is able to check the past learning situation for his/her reflection and confirmation. Tag shows integrated learning result of a learning session consisting of some shared applications.

Table 3. The usage of the attributes of a learning session.

Granularity of Log data	PURPOSE	
	Synchronous CL	Asynchronous CL
Action	Operation/Screen sharing (each shared application)	-
Action History	Maintaining of Action (each CL)	Confirmation of a series of Action (each shared application)
Status	Maintaining of results/solutions Giving a context to a newcomer (each shared application)	-
Snapshot	Maintaining of results/solutions	Confirmation of results/solutions (each shared application)
Snapshots	Confirmation/Reflecting of results Maintaining of contexts (each shared application)	Confirmation of a series of results/solutions (each shared application)
Tag	Maintaining of results/solutions Giving a results to a newcomer	Confirmation of results/solutions (each learning session)

	(each learning session)	

On the other hand, we consider the situation where the simultaneity of learning activities is not guaranteed. In this situation action history, snapshot (s), and tag are also used for supporting CL. Action history is used for a check of a series of action during CL. These actions were previously performed by another group of learners.

Snapshot(s) is used for checking the result/production/solution in learning processes, the learning progress and the change of learning context. A tag is used for examining the results/productions/solutions in learning processes of a learning session.

7 CONCLUSIONS

In this paper, we propose e-pedagogy based on new learning ecology and a platform for a collaborative learning environment. First the idea of learning ecology and e-pedagogy are discussed. Then, some fundamental functions of CL are considered. Furthermore REX is shown as an example of the CL platform and the extendibility of this platform is discussed.

In this paper, a CL is considered with the simultaneity of learning activities for achieving a learning goal. Based on the proposed e-pedagogy, the learning activities in CL are examined and the model for CL was discussed.

We have started our important research in consideration of our experiences (Okamoto, Cristea & Kayama 2001), and are gradually building the specified items towards a future standardization (ISO/IEC 2004). The considerations and issues we discussed in this paper are just the first steps towards standardization. Our future research directions are to provide a technical mechanism to reuse the learning logs (status, action history, snapshots and tag) for supporting CL and to realize the concept of e-pedagogy in this learning ecology.

8 REFERENCES

Cowie, H. and Ruddick, J. (1998) "Co-operative Group Work; an overview", BP Educational Service, Sheffield University.

Dillenbourg, P. (1999). Collaborative learning - Cognitive and Computational Approaches" Pergamon.

ISO/IEC JTC1 SC36 WG2 (Collaborative Technologies): http://collab-tech.jtc1sc36.org/

Kayama M. & Okamoto T. (2002) "Collaborative learning support in the internet learning space: a platform for a learning environment and knowledge management in the educational context", International Journal of Industry and Higher Education, Vol.16, No.4, pp.249-pp.259.

Okamoto T., Cristea A.I. & Kayama M. (2001) Future integrated learning environments with Multimedia, Journal of Computer Assisted Learning (Ed. Robert Lewis), Blackwell Science, Vol.17, No.1, pp.3-12.

Okamoto, T., Cristea, A.I. and Kayama, M. (2000) "Towards Intelligent Media-Oriented Distance Learning and Education Environments", Proceedings of ICCE2000.

Roschelle, J. and Teasley, S.D. (1995) "The construction of shared knowledge in collaborative problem solving", In C.E. O'Malley (Ed.) Computer-Supported Collaborative learning, pp.69-97, Springer-Verlag.

UEC (2004) http://www.ai.is.uec.ac.jp/ipa/ipa3/

Information Society in Extremadura

Towards a Future of Solidarity and More Freedom

Jose A. Diaz
Digital Literacy Plan, Junta of Extremadura

Abstract: This paper describes a strategic project for an information society in the Spanish Region of Extremadura. One important aspect of this project was the development of GNU/LinEx and associated Free Software. The paper describes the advantages of this Free Software.

Keywords: Public intranet, regions, educational technology network, Free Software.

1 INTRODUCTION

A strategic project in Extremadura to access the Information Society is based upon the principles of networking and technological literacy, and its main aim is better life quality for Extremadura inhabitants, from an equality and freedom viewpoint.

For this reason a series of actions have been taken in the Region. On the one hand a powerful communication infrastructure has been developed: the Regional Intranet. This intranet is able to connect more than 1400 points distributed throughout the 383 localities belonging to our Autonomous Community. On the other hand programs reaching educational and socio-economic targets have been started.

The keystone of this strategy was clearly found in education. Information and communication technologies will contribute in a decisive way to improve the quality of education. So, the design of the Educational Technological Network (RTE) started off by providing one computer per two students in Secondary Schools. The Technological Literacy Plan (PAT) was also designed to take into account the needs of groups to whom this new technological world was less familiar. With this aim its 33 New Centres of Knowledge are distributed throughout the territory of Extremadura, especially in rural areas. Finally, in order to include the other social layers, Vivernet's task is that of supporting business in the digital era, the New Initiatives Promotion Centre being responsible for analysing and guiding the Information Society Strategies of Extremadura, depending on the present changing circumstances.

In this set of circumstances the GNU/LinEx Project (Free Software) is framed on this context as an answer to the need to avoid external dependencies, like proprietary software, which are not subject to any kind of public control.

2 CONTEXT: THE SOCIO-ECONOMIC FEATURES OF EXTREMADURA

Extremadura possesses a land area of 41,634 km^2 and a population of 1,073,574, meaning a population density of 25.78 inhabitants per km^2. The regional territory makes up 8.3 % of Spain but its population is 2.6 % of the total. Population is distributed throughout 383 localities, but only Badajoz (136,316 inhabitants) has more than 100,000 inhabitants. 57 % of people in Extremadura live in villages of less than 10,000 people. According to population, Cáceres is the second town with 82,034 inhabitants and the regional capital, Mérida is third with 51,056 inhabitants.

The economy of Extremadura has been undergoing an evolution in recent years. It was the best Spanish Autonomous Community in regard to European convergence in the areas of educational, social and business projects during the period 1985-1999. These projects are bringing about development, positioning the region at the same level of equality and freedom, based on the premise of introducing the region in the new technologies revolution. They are fostering the possibility of coping with the knowledge revolution now and in the future.

3 THE INFORMATION SOCIETY GLOBAL STRATEGY OF EXTREMADURA

In 1998 during the general politics debate the President of Extremadura, Juan Carlos Rodríguez Ibarra, announced that the Extremadura Government's efforts would be directed towards positioning the region among the leaders of the technological revolution known as the information society. Such a revolution would involve the whole population and it would be based upon the principles of networking and technological literacy, in order to improve citizens' welfare.

We had lost our chance to be included in the industrial revolutions and this was the moment to take advantage of an extraordinary chance to join this revolution. The knowledge society was not based on commodities like coal or oil, but information and computer networks. This situation positioned any individual person at the same level everywhere, and with the same successful opportunities, regardless of the place where the they lived.

The proposal was ambitious, and a series of actions was taken to provide the region with telecommunications infrastructures as well as with the necessary programs to reach the educational and socio-economic aims.

3.1 Technological Framework: Intranet of Extremadura

Development of the 'Intranet of Extremadura' started in 1999 with the main aim of providing high bandwidth access (2 Mb) in regional localities through the public educational centres, public health centres and public administrative centres managed by the Government of Extremadura. At the end of 2001, the intranet was fully set through 1800 network points and all Extremadura localities, almost 400, have access to high bandwidth and high speed Internet connections.

Technically speaking, the intranet is an optical fibre ring which connects each public administrative centre to a single access point which is located in the Data Processing Centre, Mérida. Radio link technology is used where there is a lack of optical fibre. In this way, there is a network of transmitting-receiving antennas throughout the region connecting the single access point to the different localities. In a similar way WIFI technology is used to connect separated buildings of each educational centre in certain localities where the intranet is accessed in a central building, but there are other dependent buildings around the same centre.

In the future there is a possibility of using the remaining bandwidth of the intranet to offer Internet connections to localities which lack high speed technologies like ADSL.

3.2 Strategic Framework

While the design of the regional intranet was being prepared, a set of programs were started off, addressed different areas of the Society of Extremadura. These programs cope with the technological literacy of the population, the promotion of business opportunities based on new technologies, the spreading of information society and new technologies, and improvement of the education system.

3.2.1 Technological Literacy Plan

The Technological Literacy Plan (PAT) was first started by the Regional Government at the end of 1999. Its main aim was to provide each citizen with universal access to information technologies. The technological literacy process is based upon a structure of centres, called New Centres of Knowledge (NCC). Throughout the region there are 33 new centres of knowledge, especially in the most far-from-city rural areas and the outlying urban areas.

These centres offer to their users, mainly adults, training in new technologies according to their needs. Generally speaking they cope with basic use of computing tools. Remarkably, we could say that a high number of old people have learnt to use computers, to surf the web, and to manage their email accounts in these centres.

There is a computer technician, but also a public relations officer in each NCC. There are also seven computers with Internet connections and the usual peripherals – scanner, printer, digital camera, etc. Since GNU/LinEx was introduced the centres have used Free Software without having any problems. Since GNU/LinEx began 50,000 people have participated in events designed by the NCCs. The users have welcomed the operating system in a positive way.

3.2.2 Vivernet

Vivernet, "The New Era Business Laboratory", was born in the second half of 2000. Its main aim consists of promoting new technology entrepreneurs. In its headquarters, physically settled in Badajoz and Cáceres, the new business stays for an average of 15 months. The entrepreneurs receive legal and financial training, and also technological training.

Vivernet spreads the use of GNU/LinEx, and develops Free Software for the regional SMEs (Small and Medium Enterprises) in training courses and events related to this kind of business software.

3.2.3 New Initiatives Promotion Centre

Perhaps the New Initiatives Promotion Centre is a less known project because it works directly for the Public Service. It is responsible for analysing and defining Information Society strategies. It also promotes the use and development of information technology in different social areas. During the last 2 years the Centre has developed the eExtremadura program, which is an action financed by European funds. This program consists of joining together different regional agents – trade unions, enterprises, town councils, university – in order to develop new technology projects. In the second convocatory after the introduction of GNU/LinEx, more than 50 projects from a total of 400 mentioned use of GNU/LinEx or Free Software.

Today, the New Initiatives Promotion Centre is managing technical development of the GNU/LinEx project. This project has as partners the Education, Science and Technology Regional Ministry, the New Centres of Knowledge, Vivernet, and Fundecyt.

3.2.4 Educational Technological Network

The Educational Technological Network is the most characteristic project of the Education, Science and Technology Regional Ministry. Its main aim consists of introducing the educational system into the knowledge society. Action was taken to train teachers in the use of ICT, and to promote creation of content to be shared on the net (www.extremadurasi.org).

The most ambitious action consists of changing the concept of 'computing classroom' into one of 'computer into the classroom'. This means a ratio of one computer per two students in Secondary Education Centres, a fact that has an influence even in the architectural design of the new buildings. The classrooms are larger and the building structure supports the needs for electric and networking wiring. In the classroom, there is a new larger design of desk for computers and for the students' usual needs. In the old centres the design of the desk is slightly smaller.

Getting to this point, there was a need to solve the problem of software to be installed on the computers. Proprietary software was not a solution and an economical alternative for 80,000 machines was needed. That alternative was Free Software.

4 GNU/LINEX PROJECT

At the end of 2001 the intranet was fully operational, the projects of the Information Society Secretary were consolidated, and 14 new educational centres were almost finished, according to the 1-computer-per-2-student ratio. About 400 machines were to be introduced in the new centres.

We had not stopped growing when a big problem appeared. On the one hand as technological projects, there was an important software dependency, in most of cases owned by a *single company*. We had to spend a great sum to pay for the licences for each of the machines.

On the other hand, a more important aspect, the educational system had introduced and installed 80,000 machines which needed operating systems, but also productivity software to work with.

The large amount we had to spend 'bit everybody's eye' and obviously the license costs were almost unreachable, particularly if we take periodical license updating of products into account. So, an alternative solution was needed. Instead of proprietary software the only possibility was Free Software.

We had being using Free Software already in server environments with excellent results. But we had not tested a Free Software solution for end users lacking computing knowledge. Our main need was a desktop solution based of Free Software and oriented to users with office automation requirements.

In this sense, about November 2001 we got in touch with the company Ándago. They had experience in implementation of Free Software in desktop machines in the Ministry of Public Service. Once the authorities of the Regional Ministry gave their approval, they started to develop the first version of GNU/LinEx.

4.1 Be Legal, Copy LinEx

This was the slogan for the GNU/LinEx launch on March 17th 2002. It makes reference to the advantages of using Free Software, and the possibility of redistributing the software and code with full freedom. LinEx first version was based on the Debian Potato distribution and included GNOME as a graphical environment. To be honest, the version had lots of limitations, but it was a starting point.

A couple of months later the first advantages of Free Software were proved. Two Secondary teachers had developed a new version of LinEx based on the first one developed by Ándago, with improvements in all aspects. These teachers were included in the GNU/LinEx technical staff, which depends on the Education, Science and Technology Regional Ministry. In September 2002 the GNU/LinEx 3.0 Woody version was presented in SIMO. It was based on Debian Woody and included GNOME 1.4 as a graphical interface.

4.2 What is GNU/LinEx?

Technically speaking, GNU/LinEx is a Free Software distribution based on Debian GNU/Linux. It includes a set of programs and a graphical interface, GNOME, oriented to non-technical end-users. Debian is a distribution created and developed around the world by a large group of voluntary programmers, researchers, and especially teachers. Debian was chosen because, on the one hand, there are not trademarks associated with this distribution and, on the other hand, because this initiative provides high quality standards to its software.

Nevertheless, the standard Debian distribution was not suitable for all our needs so the GNU/LinEx development team's work consisted of adapting Debian to the needs of the Government of Extremadura. The first task to be undertaken was selecting software to be included in the single CD-ROM that GNU/LinEx was distributed on. Out of almost 9000 software packages compounding Debian, 800 have been selected. These are the packages included in the GNU/LinEx Distribution. The next task was the development of a graphic installer to make the installing process as easy as possible to avoid inexperienced user's intervention. Finally, new icons have been added to the desktop. These icons make reference to the cultural background of Extremadura: for example, Espronceda is a word processor, Zurbarán is a graphic design tool, Guadalupe is an email program.

Once we did this we gained an easy-to-install product with a variety of productivity software able to cope with almost every need of an office or an educational system user.

Today, the main technical features of GNU/LinEx, version 3.0r1+g2.2, are as follows:

- Linux Kernel 2.4.20
- Graphical Interface GNOME 2.2
- A set of GNU free applications:

    (Semi) automatic graphic installer
    Word processors
    Spreadsheet
    Presentations
    Accessories
    Web browser
    Email program
    Instant messenger
    Domestic financial management
    Image editor
    VNC
    and much more...

4.3 GNU/LinEx on the Net: www.linex.org

Running in parallel to GNU/LinEx presentation was the www.linex.org portal. Information on the project is collected here and in this web site you can download GNU/LinEx from different servers, and obtain technical support for users' frequently asked questions. You can also access the GNU/LinEx documentation, manuals and tutorials.

A Technical Support Service will be accessible through the web portal very soon. Users will be able to ask questions which would be answered through the web site, as well as via their emails.

5 GNU/LINEX IS A COLLECTIVE PROJECT

When the Regional Government started off the project of working with Free Software in the Public System, GNU/LinEx became vey well known on the net. From this time the Government decided to adopt Free Software in a decisive way. Certainly regarding the educational environment, Extremadura is a world pioneer in installing a free operating system in classrooms. The GNU/LinEx project has appeared on the front page of national and international newspapers such as the Washington Post or the International Herald Tribune. It is of interest to several Governments and to national and international organizations that have declared their intention of cooperating with the development of this initiative.

The first collaboration for the development of Free Software was a Protocol signed by the Regional Governments of Extremadura and Andalusia in March 2003. According to the Protocol, Andalusia would use Extremadura's advances to develop their own distribution, called GNU/Guadalinex, to be launched in September 2003. To produce the protocol, Andalusia and Extremadura have joined a shared technical team to coordinate and share advances in both Autonomous Communities.

Beyond the Spanish frontiers, there are lots of cooperative agreements with the Government of Brasil, as well as contacts with Argentina, Colombia and Peru.

The GNU/LinEx project is not only supported by Governments, but also by user and business associations: GULEX or SINUH, Extremadura GNU/LinEx user associations, or Hispalinux, the Spanish user association.

The business role in this project is a most relevant one. From the very beginning, we observed the use of Free Software in a local enterprise environment as one of the main advantages, especially for the already limited technological sector. In this respect one of the results is development of tools oriented to SME financial management, accounting, payslips, etc.

Other companies, such as OKI, contacted the GNU/LinEx project. They have contributed by the development of their printer software installers for GNU/LinEx. ACER has included GNU/LinEx as pre-installed software in their laptops. Lambdaux Software contributes interchanging technologies between GNU/LinEx and Lux, the pre-installed distribution in AIRIS laptop models. Summing up, big companies pay attention to the important base of users of Free Software as a business opportunity.

6 FREE SOFTWARE FOR THE PUBLIC SERVICE

In Extremadura, our experience in using and distributing GNU/LinEx brings us to several conclusions about the introduction of Free Software in the Public Service, and there are more pros than cons:

(a) Public funds management. The Public Services has a duty to manage the citizens' money to obtain the maximum benefit for everybody. Investing in Free Software, the Public Service System gives society back the profits in font code appearance. This is a way to invest in local R&D because the Public Service is using the services of software companies in the region. As the font code is open the application costs are more economical.

(b) GPL vs. Proprietary License. When buying proprietary software licenses, the Public Service System depends on the business policies of a single supplier. These could change at any moment. But GPL licenses make independence from suppliers possible, so that the Public Service could negotiate and make a choice of the best service.

(c) Third party software licenses are not compulsory. If the Public Service System uses proprietary software to communicate with citizens, citizens are obliged to use proprietary software to communicate with the Public Service. But if Free Software is used the citizens have an option to chose.

(d) The Public Service has also a responsibility as a big consumer. If it takes action it could support technological sectors based on Free Software.

(e) Summing up, Free Software promotes positive attitudes like knowledge sharing and network cooperation. It is a new, profitable business model based on services related to software. This gives regions like Extremadura the opportunity to be at the same level as other regions in the world.

In light of these conclusions, the question to be answered is: Why do we have to rent proprietary software if we have a choice for Free Software?

Basic Architecture for ICT Integration in the Canary Educational System

Pedro Baquero, Alfredo Santana, Ignacio Zubiria and Manuel Prieto
Consejería de Educación, Cultura y Deportes. Gobierno de Canarias

Abstract: This article describes a global solution that covers the ICT infrastructure necessities of the educational community. The focus has started from the principle that the school has autonomy in the development of its educational project. And, at the same time, there are networks of people and schools that belong to a corporation system. The global solution consists of a basic technological architecture composed of three evolutionary projects (the Individualized Networks of the Schools, the Integrated Broadband Network and the Management System). The strategic bases for the design have been that the basic necessities of the educational community and the deployment of ICT infrastructure should be synchronized with the objectives for transforming the educational system. This study has been framed inside MEDUSA project. This project is an initiative of the Government of the Canary Islands (Spain) to extend the ICT use in the educational system.

Key words: ICT infrastructure, schools, educational system, corporate networks.

1 INTRODUCTION

In the last years a quick incorporation of ICT (Information and Communication Technologies) to the educational system has taken place. In this article the design of a global basic architecture for integrating ICT in the non university educational system is described. The strategic bases for the design have been that the basic necessities of the educational community and the deployment of ICT infrastructure should be synchronized with the objectives for transforming the educational system. Thereby, in the global design, different parts of ICT infrastructure have been integrated together with processes that eliminate obstacles for ICT integration in education. As reported in Pelgrum (2001) obstacles are not only infrastructural. In his study 38 obstacles were reported. The top 10 obstacles consisted of a mixture of material and non material conditions. The material conditions were insufficient numbers of computer equipment and of Internet accesses. As non-material conditions were a lack of skill of teachers and lack of supervisory and technical staff. While the material conditions are fulfilled with the deployment of ICT infrastructure, the non-material conditions require the 'deployment' of human resources, services and management processes. Therefore, infrastructure, services, human resources and management processes have been included in the technological architecture. The result has been a basic technological architecture composed of three evolutionary projects: the Individualized Networks of the Schools, the Integrated Broadband Network and the Management System. From a common strategy, each one of these projects has its own evolutionary strategy. This basic technological architecture has been designed considering that at the same time we are planning, designing, building, using and operating. This study has been framed inside the MEDUSA project. This project is an initiative of the Government of the Canary Islands to extend ICT use in the educational system.

Section 2 summarizes where the MEDUSA project is framed and what its objectives are. Section 3 describes bases for the strategic design of the basic technological architecture. Section 4, 5 and 6 describe respectively the Individualized Networks of Schools, the Integrated Broadband Network and the Management System. Finally in section 5 is the conclusion of this work.

2 THE MEDUSA PROJECT

Canary Islands is a region of Spain formed by seven islands. It is located in the Atlantic Ocean, 1,250 km from Europe and 210 km from the African coast. It has a population of 1,694,477 inhabitants, 40% of them concentrated in the metropolitan zones of the two main islands. The territory is strongly fragmented due to its insularity and geography (ISTAC, 2003). The non-university educational system (Cabrera & Afonso, 2002; ISTAC, 2003; CECD, 2003) is formed by 850 administrative workers, 301,622 pupils, 19,660 teachers and 1,264 schools. At the beginning of year 2001 the penetration was 23.6 students per computer with a significant number of obsolete computers. On the other hand, available computer material in schools was used to cover derived necessities of ICT conception as a curricular subject, ICT not being approached as a didactic instrument in different areas and curricular subjects. Schools did not have a data infrastructure that facilitated installation of ICT equipment. In year 2000 the number of schools with Internet access was about 24%, and only 2.2% had a WEB site. On the other hand, while there were some teachers with positive ICT attitudes, there were other teachers who had resistances of different intensity toward ICT use.

The Canary Islands educational system is framed inside the Spanish educational system (Cabrera & Afonso, 2002; CIDE, 2002) characterized by a decentralized model of administration that distributes the responsibilities mainly among National Government, Regional Governments and the educational centres. National Government has exclusively reserved the exercise of responsibilities that safeguard the homogeneity and substantial unity of the educational system. Regional Government deals with, among other duties, the administrative ownership in their territory, administration of personal, orientation and attention to the pupil, helps and grants, etc. Regulations have been establishing the principle of autonomy of schools. They have capacity for decision-making in curricular aspects. Educational centres or schools should elaborate three different documents where their pedagogic and curricular organization is reflected: the educational project, the curricular project and the didactic programming. It is therefore at the school where the initiative is focused on including ICT for support for the educational project. Regional Governments will be able to motivate and to support this type of initiative.

At the present time the Government of the Canary Islands, through the Department of Education, Culture and Sports, is developing the MEDUSA project (CECD, 2003), which is a specific ICT project for non-university education. It is basically conceived as an integral programme where all the educational elements are identified. This project is bounded to the educational administration and the public schools of Canary Islands. As shown in table 1, it is a project with very wide objectives. This project is framed inside CANARIAS DIGITAL programme (GC, 2003) in accordance with the strategic policy for facilitating the incorporation of the Canary Islands to the Information Society. The MEDUSA project is being developed in two Phases: Phase I (2001-2004) and Phase II (2004-2006). At the end of Phase II all schools will have Internet connection and a WEB site and there will be a ratio of less than 12 pupils per computer. It is mainly funded by the European Commission, through FEDER (Fonds Européen de Développement Régional) and FSE (Fonds Social Européen) programmes. At the present time THE MEDUSA project is at the beginning of Phase II and it is at a level which allows its evaluation.

3 OBJECTIVES OF THE PROJECT

The ultimate and general aim of 'Proyecto MEDUSA' is to integrate ICT in educational non-university environments in the Canaries in an effective way. This integration should lead us to qualified teachers and students in a short/middle-term period of time, so that they are used to logical and critical use of tools and technological resources, and that will permit new ways of teaching and learning, and that will also help to establish new ways of communication and contribution with other educational agents.

MEDUSA OBJETIVES
To create a mark of coordinated performance and of collaboration among the different departments in matters related with the ICT
To adapt the school environments for the integration of the ICT like didactic resource, as curricular content, as communication vehicle and like instrument of academic and administrative administration
To endow with solid infrastructures to the centers of that facilitate the access from the educational agents to the Society of the Information
To promote the use of the ICT in the schools using creative, interactive and flexible learning environments in the different teaching levels in the areas and curricular matters
To educate to teachers for using rationally and logically ICT, qualifying them to elaborate and to adapt educational applications
To approach of resolvedly form and practically the development and organization of contents using new tools and communication supports
To promote the use of the ICT in the areas of academic and administrative administration of the centers
To promote innovation projects and educational investigation using the ICT to define pedagogic models of integration of these technologies and also organization models in the centers
To facilitate the access to educational telematic networks, databases, electronic mail, etc. developing in students and teachers the capacity to access, to recover, to organize, to try and to transmit the information for educational use
To explore and to consolidate the ICT for the pupil with special educational needs

Table 1. MEDUSA Objectives

The immediate pursued benefits are, among others, to generalize access to information and contents in the Internet, to create flexible and more interesting ways of teacher training, to improve the administrative and academic management of schools, to facilitate the publication and exchange of experiences, and the creation of virtual communities for the different educational agents, apart from creating communication infrastructures to bear the Project. In the middle-term the effects should correspond with the capacity of citizens to continually learn, and to adapt themselves to the new work situations and relationships born from the evolution of the technology.

3.1 Strategic Focal Points of the Project

A project of this dimension requires a set of actions that become the basic pillars for a correct execution of it, and these actions are carried out in a coordinated and complementary way. That is why Departments and/or General Management take part and collaborate in any of the areas of action of the Project (communications, infrastructure, equipment, teacher training, schools management, and so on). This contribution is coordinated by the management and executive team of the Project.

The first action initiated in the project is the creation of infrastructures and equipment in the Management Department of the Project, in the Central Services of the Department of Education, in the 'Teachers Centres' and in schools. This is the most difficult process, and it permits us to arrange and enable all those logical and physical elements that will provide the technological basis for the Project to revolve.

The second basic pillar consists of training teachers, students and other agents involved in the execution of the Project. Users training is conceived as functional, practical and adapted to the contexts, to the materials and environment in which the Project develops.

Training contents and offers are flexible. They are collected in an annual Training Plan, provided with a modular structure to facilitate teachers in making up their training itinerary. This Plan is continually updated and improved. The course contents are organized in several 'training lines' which are slightly differentiated. Thus a first line is defined as 'instrumental training'. Its objective is to qualify teachers and other educational agents so that they are able to use equipment and generic applications up to an acceptable level of safety. A second line, also instrumental, intends to provide certain users with more intense training upon equipment and specific basic applications related to services and better use of Network resources.

A second training guidance is that of 'Use and exploitation of Administrative and Academic Management Applications', to take advantage of the functionalities of these applications, so that users are able to modernize and improve schools management and school libraries.

The third line of formation is oriented to 'ICT integration in the syllabus'. It intends to promote an open attitude, among teachers, toward the

S.I. and let them know general or specific applications so that they can use them in their teaching activities. A second more advanced training level will enable teachers to feel at ease in certain environments and produce their own applications.

'Technologies as a curricular subject' is another orientation in teacher training. It has to do with the need to undertake contents related to Technology in Secondary Education, data processing and other specific subjects included in specialized teaching.

Keeping in mind the basis on which the Project develops, training through the Internet is prompted. This kind of training is tremendously important and useful in a geographically dispersed area such as the Canaries. The use of training through the Internet will be shared with presential training, and a mixture of both. In general, any training activity will be backed up with tools ready to be used in the Internet, and that will provide users with different services.

The provision of contents is another strategic focal point of the Project. The shortage of educational and specific contents related to ITC, or borne by them, has not favoured the approach to ICT in schools, as well as integration and use of ICT as instrumental support in the different subjects. The policy of content provision is undertaken in different ways. On one hand, a percentage of ICT content will be released via publishers; another set of content will be self-developed, adapting them to context or participating in similar national or European projects. On the other hand, available content located in the Internet, which is conveniently catalogued and classified, can be also used.

In this sense, the promotion and support of innovation and educational research projects will be another source of provision, with the added value that these materials are already contextualized in specific classroom situations, so that the level of motivation is very high, because they will be suggested by teachers that work with them.

'Proyecto MEDUSA' is carried out and fulfilled when launching educational activities in the classrooms, involving students in those activities. Students are the main recipients of the Project; and it is in the environments created in schools, in the classrooms and in the network, where the Project acquires its true dimension. The progressive transfer of the use of the technological elements to the classrooms is considered fundamental. The ultimate aim is the natural media integration in the classrooms for teaching purposes.

In order to encourage and support the deployment of the Project on a personal level, there is a team of advisers (teachers specialized in the use of technologies in the classroom and educational levels) who advice with the support and collaboration of the 'teachers centres'.

4 TECHNOLOGICAL BASES FOR THE STRATEGIC DESIGN

Our vision has started from the school autonomy in the development of its educational project. Efforts should concentrate on the teaching-learning process using ICT. And, at the same time, there are people and school networks that belong to a corporate system. The ideal technological solution should give answers to two environments: the school and the corporate environment. The methodology has started locating the characteristics that should complete the necessities of these environments. At the same time the solution should go beyond endowing schools with an ICT global infrastructure and that should be framed inside all the objectives of the MEDUSA project eliminating obstacles for ICT integration (Pelgrum, 2001). Thus, to execute this technological solution, a series of characteristics has also been identified and they should complete the development of the project. The educational system has a series of particularities that make it a unique environment with its own characteristics and differences with respect to other organizations:

- There exist a larger number of schools with, in general, not very reliable communications lines.
- There exists great diversity of software. They are mainly educational applications instead of the productivity software (e.g., office applications) used in most of other organizations.
- The ICT applications are continually being installed and uninstalled. If there does not exist an adequate management, the computer environments become unstable.
- The educational community has important levels of autonomy. Their initiative and favourable attitudes can lead to an intensive ICT use.

Therefore solutions based on decentralized environments have been considered. Solutions based on centralized systems like ASP (Application Service Providers) have been discarded mainly because they need robust communications and standard applications (Harney, 2002).

At the beginning of the year 2001 we saw that there were low levels of ICT infrastructure in the Canary Islands educational system. There has been a considerable effort to endow all schools with equipment and infrastructure. As seen above, schools are framed inside a system that provides them autonomy with respect to the development of their educational project, the ICT educational project would be included inside. On the other hand, it is at the school where the direct contact with the pupil takes place and, therefore, where the teacher can apply and use ICT inside his particular strategy of working and teaching.

Schools and the administrative departments are all members of the educational system. The corporate network should facilitate the creation of knowledge networks. This network should favour the exchange of data and experiences and the improvement of corporate administrative processes. Also, it should expand access to the Internet for all schools. This network should be opened to incorporation of new services.

The technological solution should be fully integrated with the objectives of the MEDUSA project. The rhythm of development will depend, apart from the available budget, on the technology and also on other factors such as the market, the investment capacity of the operators and the services demanded by the citizen and public administration.

An objective for the future is to create a basic technological architecture for the educational system of the Canary Islands. It should be the infrastructure that gives a global solution of connectivity and support to all ICT applications and services. This basic technological architecture should have the following parts:

- A technological solution inside the school that is sufficiently uniform and at the same time completes the educational autonomy of the school, the mobility inside the school, the flexibility and robustness characteristics. Given the great number of schools, it will be carried out by gradual deployment. Each of these schools will be integrated in the educational system through a corporate network.
- The corporate technological solution should assure the integration of services and universality to the whole educational community. It will give a response to the necessities of broadband. Also, it will allow the mobility of users outside their schools.
- A technological and organizational solution that should be friendly with all type of users, especially the basic user, should be designed to support intelligence approaches in administration and operation and should support characteristics of the development of a project.

Following this model as reference, the final technological architecture will contemplate each one of the identified parts. This architecture will evolve toward a global solution that will be materialized with the development of three clearly differentiated projects:

- The Individualized Networks of the Schools.
- The Integrated Broadband Network.
- The Management System.

With these three projects all the characteristics would be aimed towards necessities of the school environments and the corporate environment. The previous technical projects become evolutionary projects when they converge on a global solution that is continuously evolving.

These three evolutionary projects should be consistent with the technological trends and thereby fulfill the long term characteristic. As clear trends we have the evolution of services toward IP technology (Goncalves & Niles, 1998), increase of broadband in access and incorporation of wireless accesses (Zamir, 2000). In the election of the technological solution these three trends has been considered.

5 INDIVIDUALIZED NETWORKS OF SCHOOLS

The deployment of ICT equipment and infrastructure for all schools has been defined. Each school should be endowed with ICT infrastructure to carry out its ICT educational project. There exist diverse types of schools in the Canary educational system, although the most important are primary and secondary schools. In a general way each school has an administrative staff, seminars or teachers' rooms, an assembly hall, a library, classrooms and computer classroom. A standard technological solution has been designed to adapt each school to its ICT educational project. This standard solution consists in:

- A local-area server. Its administration, including backup copies, is carried out remotely and centralized from ICT Centre (as described in section 6.2). The local-area server has the necessary services for educational autonomy of the school. Teachers and administrative personnel have their own accounts and their own directory where they can house all their information.
- A MEDUSA classroom with access to the educational network composed by about fifteen computers. The MEDUSA classroom has a standard configuration. The objective of this classroom is the support for teaching to all subjects. In general, these subjects do not have ICT curricular contents. It is intended that the MEDUSA classroom should be a very stable and robust environment, in this way a very strict permission policy exists for the installation of applications. On the other hand, each school used to have a computer classroom for specific computer teaching. In some cases these computer classrooms have also been endowed with equipment. Each school establishes its administration policy for computer classrooms, so computer teachers can be as free as possible. These classrooms are integrated inside the ICT infrastructure of the school and are isolated through a router to avoid conflicts with the rest of the network.
- Access to the corporate network is given for administrative services, library and seminars. In general, the corporate applications work in a

WEB architecture. Each seminar is endowed with a minimum of a computer with access to the corporate resources of the the Government of the Canary Islands. Also, the library is endowed with a computer and with the access to the corporate application of bibliographical resources.

- Access to the educational network is given to all the 'classroom corners'. In general, the 'classroom corner' is located next to the teacher's table and blackboard. Each classroom is endowed with one or two double network points placed in the 'classroom corner'.
- Endowment with computers and peripherals. Schools are endowed with computer equipment for general use. This equipment is usually made up of a limited number of computers, peripherals (printers, scanner, etc), a notebook computer and a projector.
- The MEDUSA classroom and computer classrooms are wired to give service to all computers. Each classroom is endowed with two or four network points placed in the 'classroom corners'. Each room (library, seminars, assembly hall, administration and address) is endowed with a minimum of two network points. The whole school is endowed with structured cabling together with electrical infrastructure. Structured cabling category 5/clase E has been used. The local-area network is Fast Ethernet (100 Mbps) implanted with switches. It is tried to endow with at least a double point of network to all the dependences. This way guarantees that the school has a high flexible infrastructure that allows mobility among the different classrooms and rooms can evolve toward bigger speeds than 100 Mbps (Saunders, 1996) and is easily manageable through changing remotely configurations of switches.

Therefore, a uniform solution has been created in all the schools. The experience has allowed checking that this solution is adjusted to all ICT educational projects of the schools. The aspects that vary from one school to another are the number of computers and peripherals. The characteristics of the computers also varies due to market improvements that take place during the lifetime of deployment. A complete inventory control is acquired remotely through using intelligent agents in each computer. It facilitates the administration of the equipment. Permission policies have been created to have robust environments. Thus, the teachers can not directly administer and install applications in computers, in servers and in MEDUSA classrooms. Anyway, each school can install its own educational applications for which a management model has been created that permits more autonomy to the school. Different user profiles have been defined: the basic, the advanced and the administrator user. All the pupils and most of the teachers are basic users. Only the advanced and administration users can install applications in MEDUSA classrooms in function of the aggressiveness level of the installation with the operating systems.

Local solutions in computers are based on Microsoft Window XP. The operating system of servers is Microsoft Window Server 2000. At the present time, individualize accounts are only created for administrative and educational personnel of schools. Also, a reduced number of standard work groups can be created: one for teachers, one for administration and one for pupils. In few schools there exist collectives of teachers that request bigger levels of autonomy in the creation of services and groups. In general, these collectives coincide with teachers that have bigger capacities for ICT administration. Thereby, in Phase II the design has been improved with services that allow creating services more personalized at the schools. Solutions based on the new characteristics of Microsoft Window 2003 and Window Server 2003 with Active Directory 2.0 will be implemented. They will allow creating more flexibly different groups. Also, a better versatile creation of accounts will allow individualized accounts for pupils and a larger number of working groups.

The possibility of transparently changing the position of users and equipment is required. Two mobility profiles exist: the 'mobile' and the 'nomadic'. Although both allow mobility of users with transfer of communications of an access point to other, their mobility profile is different. The users of mobile networks we called 'mobiles': that is, they communicate while they are in movement. The users called 'nomadic', they move, stop and then communicate. The 'mobile' concept still has not been developed completely through such wireless technologies as WI-FI (IEEE 802.11 standards) (Dubendorf, 2003). These solutions have only been used to save distance. It is foreseen in Phase II to implant WI-FI areas in classrooms. The mobility characteristic that has been developed is the 'nomadic' using fixed accesses. This is linked with the experience that some teachers have acquired using notebooks and projectors. These teachers demand a bigger number of them for its use in 'classroom corners'. This demand of more equipment takes place several months after the school has been endowed with them. In Phase II a concrete action enlarging the supply of notebooks and projectors in schools is foreseen.

6 INTEGRATED BROADBAND NETWORK

The Integrated Broadband Network (IBN) connects all schools of the MEDUSA project. These schools are constituted mainly by head offices and schools. The IBN allows connectivity among them, with the corporate services of the Government of the Canary Islands and with the Internet. Educational personnel and office workers have access to the services of the

Government of the Canary Islands. All the users are connected to the exterior through a unique access to the Internet. The essential servers of the architecture are located in head offices from where all information arrives for the whole educational community (figure 1). The basic aspects that have been developed in the IBN are IP network, broadband access network to schools, mobility and security.

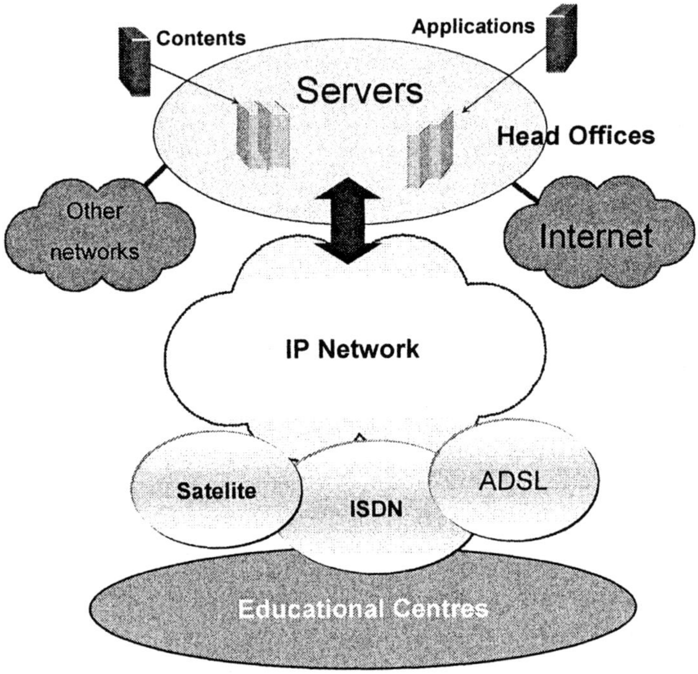

Figure 1. Integrated Broadband Network Architecture

6.1 IP Network

The IBN architecture is based on the use of IP protocol in the backbone and broadband technologies in accesses of schools. This solution fulfils the integrate characteristic. All the data services of the schools are integrated and come out through the same access using the IP protocol. At the present time voice services have not been included in this network. Future strategies will integrate voice using IP protocol. This way makes sure of the evolution of this network toward the IP scenario, where VoIP will be able to be incorporated in the future (Zamir, 2000).

6.2 Broadband Access Network

Schools have been endowed with broadband accesses. Currently, of the total of schools, 1,264, about 32% of them have access to the Internet through the IBN. 87% have ADSL accesses and the rest have ISDN accesses. At the moment, 13% of the 1,264 schools do not have either ADSL or ISDN coverage, they are in most of the cases schools located in rural areas. In the Canary Islands other available broadband technologies exist (e.g., cable modem and LMDS), although at the moment the operators that offer these technologies only have coverage in metropolitan areas. Thereby, in Phase II access by satellite has been considered as a better alternative for rural areas. The use in each access is continually monitored and it allows us to adapt the broadband necessities of each school.

ADSL access network architecture is based on points of interconnection (PoI) with the telecommunications operator. From each PoI ADSL, connections are established to each school. The capacity of each PoI is subscribed to a telecommunications operator. This solution allows having ADSL access that guarantees upstream and downstream speeds superiors to those that the telecommunications operators offer directly to their customers (Maxwell, 1999). Each PoI gives service to a zone of the Canary Islands, although ADSL coverage is not total in each area. In the future, superior demands of 2 Mbps could be carried out with other technologies like VDSL (Very high speed Digital Subscriber Line) access or increasing the number of ADSL access (e.g., 2xADSL) in each school. It is intended at the end of year 2006 that all the schools will have broadband accesses through the IBN.

6.3 Mobility

Users can be connected from any internal point to the network or from any external one (e.g., their home) conserving all functionalities as if they were in their habitual working place. Also relevant are concepts of 'mobile' and 'nomadic' user. The mobility concept that has been developed in the IBN is 'nomadic'. At present the IBN does not target the 'mobile' user. Not all users have the same necessities. Pupils, teachers and administration personal require two access points: one external to the network, in general their home, and the other internal, their school. This way, solutions can be implemented so that teachers and pupils can work or learn from their home. In these cases access can be made from outside. In some cases solutions have been developed based on VPN (Virtual Private Network) (Fowler, 1999) for pupils with special needs.

Another group of users also require mobility among schools. In this last case mobility is guaranteed through active directory policies where each user profile is replied in all the local-area servers of each school. The replica that is carried out is incremental and scheduled nocturnally with the purpose of not saturating access. At present the active directory is implemented with Microsoft Windows Server 2000 with Active Directory 1.0. These current active directory policies permit teachers move from one school to another, so they can be connected to the other school network. First they are registered with their user names, then they will be able to carry out all the functions that they have enabled inside the IBN. These policies also permit creation of collaborative working groups among teachers of different schools. In Phase II it is intended to enlarge this function for creation of collaborative working groups to pupils. It is not intended in Phase II to develop the widest mobility concept: the data 'mobile' user. At the moment only the mobile telephony service is embraced through corporate telephony services.

6.4 Security

Two logical networks have been created inside the IBN: a network that it is called the educational network and another called the corporate network. The objective is to avoid pupil access to the Government of the Canary Islands corporate network. This way unwanted access by pupils to the corporate services is avoided. In Phase II the educational network will come out to the Internet through a content filter. Each school will define, inside its autonomy, the contents that are not accessible for its pupils. The corporate network gives access to the corporate services of The Government of the Canary Islands. Permission policy has been implemented through the active directory profiles that allow protection of users and equipment. Internet access is always carried out through a firewall located in central services of the Government of the Canary Islands. Security is reinforced with the ICT Centre which maintains centralized control.

7 MANAGEMENT SYSTEM

The Management System guarantees a unique vision of THE MEDUSA project and the fact that the implementation of ICT infrastructure fulfils its objectives. Inside the Management System, it is important to include methodologies of ICT management (Boar, 1993; Davis & Yen, 1999). It also guarantees the availability and the quality of service (QoS) of all ICT services. One of its main missions is to reinforce the educational autonomy and friendly characteristics of the schools and security characteristics of the corporate environment. The Management System carries out a centralized control of the schools that are geographically very disperse. It is also important to give schools autonomy within a philosophy of high protection for the equipment, so that risks of voluntary or accidental manipulations will be diminished. Service philosophy is based on facilitating access of any user regardless of their computer literacy. The Management System is supported by the MEDUSA Office and ICT Centre.

7.1 MEDUSA Office

MEDUSA Office manages and has a unique vision of the entire THE MEDUSA project. It achieves different functions which emphasize the following (figure 2): executive, transformational, decentralizing and educational functions.

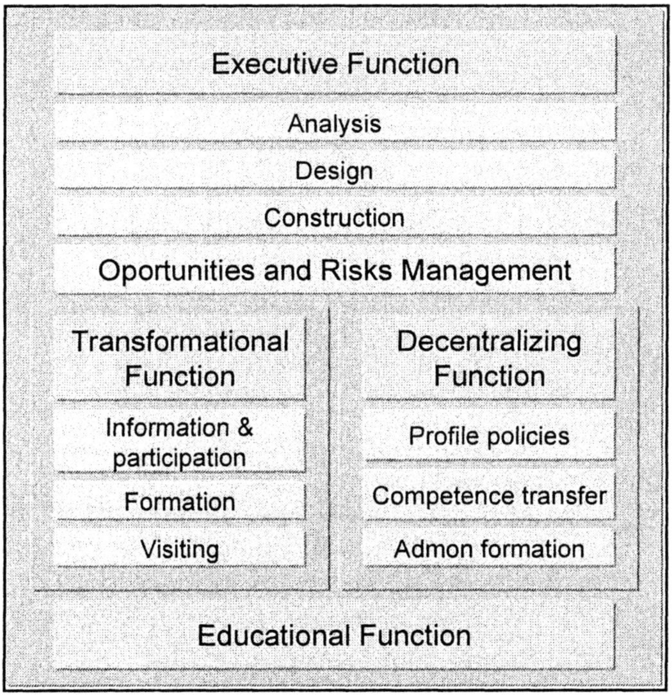

Figure 2. MEDUSA Office Functions

The mission of the executive function is to have a unique vision and to fulfill the objectives of the MEDUSA project. It manages and plans the MEDUSA project. In a project of these characteristics success will not only depend on good management of all technical tasks, but also to its capacity of adjusting to new situations. When dealing with a project of long duration, management of risks and opportunities is also carried out.

The mission of the transformational function is to manage the change and to eliminate the resistances of all type of people in the educational system. It fulfils the transformation characteristics. Change management has identified three types of functions: leadership, commitment and knowledge (Huber & Glick, 1993). These functions have been developed in the MEDUSA project through a complete management method that integrates the deployment of the infrastructures in schools with schemes of presentations, visits and courses. The experience in the MEDUSA project has evidenced that change management is indissolubly together with installation of ICT infrastructure. When the deployment of the technological architecture goes with actions of change management a larger increment of the demand of ICT formative and more personalized ICT solutions or services have taken place. This has led to redefine the formative planning and to develop in Phase II a service with a more individualized support from MEDUSA office.

The mission of the decentralizing function is to facilitate autonomy of the school in execution of its educational project. It reinforces the educational autonomy. Schools that want more autonomy in administration of their ICT resources and whose teachers have advanced knowledge can have delegated a great part of the work of computer system administration. As a result, when a school acquires bigger abilities in the administration of computer systems, a procedure has been enabled so that the school can receive bigger technical powers. The educational function propitiates the popularization, extension and support to a wide group of educational applications. This function favours the use of corporate applications with independence that each school can select other different ones.

7.2 ICT Centre

ICT Centre manages and administers the whole ICT infrastructure, as well as a level of attention and service to all users. ICT Centre is the most technical level in the Management System. All servers and computers of the schools can be managed and administrated from ICT Centre. Computer environments of the schools are monitored so that actions to prevent the systems becoming unstable or saturated can be carried out.

From this centre all users are assisted. ICT Centre has been endowed with an organizational structure and technological tools to carry out the centralized administration of ICT resources. ICT Centre gives support to the systems and users of the Individualized Schools Networks and those of the IBN. It has a group of tools and functions to provide a wide range of services (figure 3). ICT Centre provides support to the users of all the schools and administrative centres. All kind of inquires, problems, petitions or mishaps are managed until their complete resolution. It is constituted as a unique point of direct attention available 24 hours a day, 7 days a week and 365 days a year. In an environment, where schools are dispersed, monitoring of all their components is absolutely necessary as well as remote assistance, with the purpose of avoiding long time waiting for answers. Remote control is made through the distribution of agents to all computers and servers.

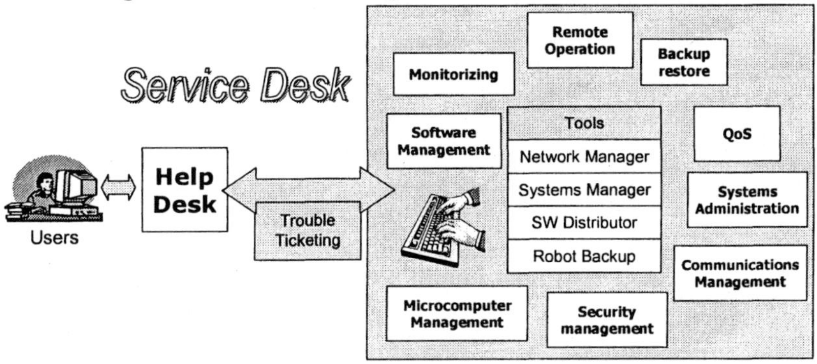

Figure 3. Tools and functions of ICT Centre

ICT Centre also gives quick answers to new necessities or upgrades of educational applications, office applications and operating systems. Software distribution services allow the centralized definition of software packages and centralized planning and pursuing of its distribution. Personalized distribution is necessary for groups of computers, servers, users or locations. ICT Centre performs quality control prior to software distribution in schools.

An improvement in levels of QoS has occurred during Phase I. This has led to upgrade ICT Centre. The demand of more QoS has been increasing for two reasons: first, the educational community makes bigger use of the central services and, second, the demand for quicker answers to user inquires has increased. In Phase II ICT Centre is going to be improved with special attention to the improvement of the software distribution service.

8 CONCLUSION

The basic technological architecture has been designed starting from definition of the characteristics that should complete ICT integration with the educational system. This architecture has been materialized in three clearly differentiated evolutionary projects: The Individualized Networks of the Schools, Integrated Broadband Network and Management System. With these three evolutionary projects all the characteristics would be fulfilling the basic ICT necessities of schools and the corporate environment.

At the present time, the current solution completes a great part of the characteristics of the environment of the school and corporate environment. Nevertheless, the demand of the educational community makes still necessary to keep on improving the service. Thus, in Phase II of THE MEDUSA project the mobility concept inside the school will be improved through the incorporation of wireless technologies. Currently, it is not being considered high-priority to enlarge the mobility concept to the 'mobile' users or to improve the integration concept with the incorporation of VoIP.

Finally, it is necessary to increase levels of school autonomy. This will be carried out in Phase II through two actions: competences transferring of Management System to schools and developing other functionalities that allow accounts creation for pupils and a bigger flexibility in creation of work groups. In Phase II levels of QoS will be increased to improve characteristics of friendliness and intelligence through upgrading ICT Centre.

9 REFERENCES

Boar, B.H. (1993). The Art of Strategic Planning for Information Technology. John Wiley.

Cabrera, J. M. & Afonso, J. M (2002). El sistema educativo en Canarias. Una perspectiva socioeconómica. Consejo Económico y Social. http://www.cescanarias.org/

CECD, (2003). Consejería de Educación, Cultura y Deportes del Gobierno de Canarias. http://www.educa.rcanaria.es/

CIDE (Centro de Investigación y Documentación Educativa). (2002). Spanish Education System. Ministerio de Educación, Cultura y Deporte: Dirección General de Educación, Formación Profesional e Innovación Educa. www.mec.es/cide/publicaciones/pub_cide.htm

Davis, W. & Yen, D. (1999). The Information System Consultant's Handbook: Systems, Analysis and Design. CRC Press LLC.

Dubendorf, V. A. (2003). Wireless Data Technologies. John Wiley & Sons Ltd.

Fowler, D. (1999). Virtual private networks. Morgan Kaufmann Publishers.

GC (Gobierno de Canarias). (2003). Plan para el desarrollo de la Sociedad de la Información de Canarias (PDSIC). http://www.gobiernodecanarias.org/dgtsi/pdsic.pdf

Goncalves, M. & Niles, K. (1998). IPv6 Networks. McGraw-Hill.

Harney, J. (2002). Application Service Providers (ASPs): A Manager's Guide. Ad. Wesley.

Huber, G.P. & Glick W.H., (1993). Organizational Change and Redesign. Ideas and Insights for Improving Performance. Oxford University Press.

ISTAC, (2003). Instituto Canario de Estadística. http://www.gobiernodecanarias.org/istac/

Maxwell, K. (1999). *Residencial Broadband.* Wiley.

Pelgrum, W. J. (2001). Obstacles to the integration of ICT in education: results from a worldwide educational assessment. Computer & Education, 37 (2), 163-178.

Saunders, S. (1996). The McGraw-Hill High-Speed LANs Handbook. McGraw-Hill.

Wisely, D., Eardley, P. & Burness, L. (2002). IP for 3G—Networking Technologies for Mobile Communications. John Wiley & Sons.

Zamir, S. (Ed.) (2000). Handbook of Emerging Communications Technologies: The Next Decade. CRC Press LLC.

To Adopt or Not to Adopt Computer-Based School Management Systems?
An ITEM Research Agenda

Arthur Tatnall
Graduate School of Business, Victoria University, Australia.
Arthur.Tatnall@vu.edu.au

Abstract: While information systems are used in educational management by many schools in many countries, some schools in some countries use them more effectively than others. This paper questions the reasons for this. The introduction of new computer-based educational management systems in schools should be thought of in terms of innovation. Although a large amount of research has been done on the process of technological innovation some of it is not well grounded in innovation theory, and not much ITEM research relates to this topic. Of the ITEM research that does investigation innovation most is concerned with the management of change in schools and how to best implement these systems, rather than a consideration of why some schools choose to adopt some or all aspects of an ITEM system while others choose not to adopt. This paper outlines two theories of technological innovation and advocates the advantages of the theory of innovation translation in investigations in this area.

Key words: Innovation, innovation diffusion, innovation translation, technology adoption, centralised/ decentralised education systems, ITEM research.

1 INTRODUCTION

A large number of schools in many countries around the world make good use of information systems to assist them in aspects of their educational management. Some, however, make better use of this technology than others. One simplistic explanation of this has to do with the quality of the software used. Proponents of the educational management software used in a school system in one country may claim that they have a greater adoption rate and better use of information technology in educational management (ITEM) because their software is better than that used in another school system in another country. By 'better' they may mean that it is easier to use, cheaper, has more features, or is better suited to the sort of administrative tasks schools perform. While it may well be true on one level that the quality of the educational management software available is an important factor in the implementation and use of ITEM systems, I will argue that it is not the only factor and not even the most important factor.

In this paper I will contend that the use of information technology in educational management in schools should be regarded in terms of innovation, and investigated through the lens of innovation theory. I will question the extent to which the popular theory of innovation diffusion (Rogers 1995) can be gainfully applied to researching the adoption of ITEM by schools around the world, and advocate instead the advantages of the alternative approach offered by innovation translation (Callon 1986; Latour 1986; Law 1991; Latour 1996) informed by actor-network theory.

2 INNOVATION

The dictionary defines innovation as "the alteration of what is established; something newly introduced" (Oxford 1973) and "introducing new things or methods". The word 'innovation' is used synonymously with 'newness' and 'change' (Dutch 1962), and an innovation can be described as an idea that is *perceived* to be new to a particular person or group of people (Rogers 1995). As the introduction or improvement of an information system in an organisation *necessarily* involves change of some sort (Tatnall 2002; Tatnall and Lepa 2003), in this paper I will advocate that the introduction of ITEM systems into schools should be considered as an innovation, and that theories of innovation should be given due consideration in any study of the success, or otherwise, of this undertaking. The features and quality of the management software available to schools may well be one factor in determining whether or not they will adopt ITEM systems but, as I will show, innovation is a highly political process and many more factors also influence its success. All this, however, depends upon schools having some choice in the matter.

I will digress here to distinguish between *invention* and *innovation*. Invention can be seen in the discovery of new ideas, while innovation involves putting these ideas into commercial or organisational practice (Maguire, Kazlauskas and Weir 1994). Invention does not necessarily invoke innovation and it a fallacious to think that invention is necessary and sufficient for innovation to occur. For a formal definition of innovation I will accept that of Maquire et. al. (1994 :5): "Innovation is the application in any organisation of ideas new to it, whether they are embodied in products, processes, services, or in the systems of management and marketing through which the organisation operates".

3 DEGREE OF CHOICE SCHOOLS HAVE IN ADOPTING ITEM

The application of innovation theory to the adoption of a technological innovation assumes that the potential adopter had some choice in whether or not to make the adoption. In some highly centralised school systems this is not the case and schools have no choice but to adopt (Tatnall and Pitman 2003). Even in these situations, however, the school system itself had some choice, and I will question the extent to which this can be investigated through innovation theory. On the other hand, in more decentralised systems the decision of whether to adopt a particular management approach or to make use of specific educational management software may be left up to individual schools. There are also, of course, many situations in between these extremes.

3.1 Centralised school systems that have adopted ITEM

In centralised school systems I will assume that the central education authority, whether it be national or regional, will have determined whether or not schools should make use of computer-based educational management systems and have specified the particular software packages to be used. If this central authority has decreed that a specific educational management system should be used then it is likely that it will also require schools to submit financial and other reports in a format determined by this system. Taking this approach will effectively force schools to adopt and use the system, but to what degree? There is an old English saying to the effect that "you can lead a horse to water, but you cannot make it drink" (Wilson 1970), and it is almost impossible to force any organisation to make effective use of a piece of software or specific management approach.

The notion of *IT infusion* (Linderoth 1997) can be used to characterise situations where the full potential of an IT innovation is being used with beneficial effects by an organisation. In studies of the use of information systems in business it is common to find an organisation that is making some use of IT, but is not getting as much out of this use as they could because they have not taken the trouble to integrate it into their management structures and let it change the way they operate. In situations where schools are forced into the use of educational management systems an interesting research question involves the degree to which these systems are infused into the schools' management structures.

3.2 Decentralised school systems

In some cases central education authorities in decentralised school systems may suggest, or recommend to schools the use of educational management software, while in other cases it may be silent on this matter. Mostly in educational systems of this type the choice to adopt of not to adopt ITEM systems is left to the individual school (or school cluster). This presents the classic situation in which innovation theory can be applied to investigate adoption, by considering the factors and interactions in each school that led to adoption (Tatnall 2002).

4 THEORIES OF INNOVATION: INNOVATION DIFFUSION

The dominant paradigm in innovation research is that of *innovation diffusion*. In diffusion theory the existence of an innovation is seen to cause uncertainty in the minds of potential adopters (Berlyne 1962), implying a lack of predictability and of information. Diffusion is considered to be an information exchange process amongst members of a communicating social network driven by the need to reduce uncertainty (Rogers 1995). Diffusion theory contends that a technological innovation embodies information, and so its adoption acts to reduce uncertainty. The new ideas upon which an innovation is based are communicated over time, through various types of communication channels, among the members of a social system. Rogers (1995) argues that there are four main elements to innovation diffusion:

- **Characteristics of the innovation itself.** Rogers argues that attributes and characteristics of the innovation itself are important in determining the manner of its diffusion and the rate of its adoption. He outlines five characteristics of an innovation which, he argues, affect its diffusion:
  - **Relative advantage**. This is the degree to which an innovation is perceived as better than the idea it supersedes. Rogers contends that an innovation's relative advantage is positively correlated with its rate of adoption.
  - **Compatibility** – the degree to which an innovation is perceived by potential adopters as being consistent with their existing values and

past experiences. Rogers claims that perceived compatibility of an innovation assists adoption.
  - **Complexity** – or the degree to which an innovation is perceived as difficult to understand and use. Rogers claims that the more complex the innovation, the less likely it is to be quickly adopted.
  - **Trialability** – the degree to which an innovation may be subjected to limited experimentation. Rogers' research suggests that if a potential adopter is able to 'play' with the innovation then adoption is more likely.
  - **Observability**. The more the results of an innovation are visible to others, the more likely the innovation is to be adopted.
- **Nature of the communications channels**. To reach a potential adopter the innovation must diffuse through a communications channel and Rogers shows that channels involving mass media are the most rapid means of spreading awareness, but interpersonal channels are generally more effective in persuading someone to accept a new idea.
- **The passage of time**. Rogers argues that time is involved in three aspects of innovation diffusion: the innovation-decision process, the degree of innovativeness, and an innovation's rate of adoption. He outlines the following sequential steps in the innovation-decision process: knowledge, persuasion, decision, implementation, and confirmation.
- **The social system**. Diffusion occurs within a social system in which the social structure constitutes a boundary. Rogers argues that the system's structure affects diffusion through the action of social norms, the roles taken by opinion leaders and change agents, the types of innovation decisions that are taken, and the social consequences of the innovation.

Innovation diffusion has had considerable success in describing how innovations move, or diffuse, through large populations. It has, however not so often been used as successfully in investigating small scale implementations by single individuals or small organisations (Tatnall 2002). Also, there are occasions when diffusion does not occur at all despite the excellence of the idea or the supposed quality of the innovation, and the diffusion model finds these instances difficult to explain.

5 THEORIES OF INNOVATION: INNOVATION TRANSLATION

An alternative view of innovation is that of *innovation translation* proposed in actor-network theory (ANT). The core of this approach is translation, which can be defined as: "... the means by which one entity gives a role to others." (Singleton and Michael 1993 :229). While many approaches to research in technological areas treat the social and the technical in entirely different ways, ANT proposes instead a socio-technical account in which neither social nor technical positions are privileged. In actor-network theory an actor is a human or non-human entity that is able to make its presence *individually felt* by the other actors. An actor can, however, in many ways also be thought of as a 'black box' (Callon 1987), the contents of which we can chose not to worry about. We can consider this entity just as an actor, but when doing so it must be remembered that behind each actor there hide other actors that it has, more of less effectively, drawn together, or 'black-boxed' (Callon 1987). When the time comes to open the lid of the black box and look inside, it will be seen to constitute a whole network of other, perhaps complex, associations.

It is often the case that an organisation which is considering some technological innovation is interested in only some aspects of this innovation and not others (Tatnall 2002). In actor-network terms it needs to *translate* (Callon 1986) this piece of technology into a form where it can be adopted. This may mean choosing some elements of the technology and leaving out others, resulting in what is finally adopted not being the innovation in its original form, but a translation of it into a form that is suitable for use by the recipient (Tatnall 2002). When considering the implementation of an ITEM system in a school, in actor-network terms the ITEM system needs to negotiate with each individual school to determine how it could best be implemented by them.

5.1 Problematisation, Interessement, Enrolment, Mobilisation

Callon (1986) outlines the process of translation as having four 'moments' the first of which he calls *problematisation*, in which one or more key actors attempts to define the nature of the problem and the roles of other actors to fit the solution proposed. The problem is re-defined in terms of solutions offered by these actors who then attempt to establish themselves as an 'obligatory passage point' (Callon 1986) which must be negotiated as part of its solution. In implementing an ITEM system the problematisation proposed by its designer is that school administration is best performed with the assistance of a computer. For the project to be successful its instigators must convince the school to see the ITEM system as an obligatory passage point to good educational administration.

The second moment is called *interessement* and is a series of processes that attempt to impose the identities and roles defined in the problematisation onto other actors. It means interesting and attracting an actor by coming between it and some other actor (Law 1986). In the case of the ITEM system, schools need to be convinced that this technology is more worthwhile and offers them better prospects of good administration than the approaches they now use. It must convince them to stop using manual administrative systems and instead use the ITEM system.

The third moment: *enrolment* then leads to the establishment of a stable network of alliances. For enrolment to be successful however, it requires more than just one set of actors imposing their will on others; it also requires these others to yield (Singleton et al. 1993). It is not enough for those promoting the ITEM system to eloquently espouse its benefits, the schools must also give up their old methods of administration. Finally, *mobilisation* occurs as the proposed solution gains wider acceptance (McMaster, Vidgen and Wastell 1997) and an even larger network of absent entities is created (Grint and Woolgar 1997) through some actors acting as spokespersons for others. The ITEM system can be judged to be truly successful when school principals are advocating its advantages to each other. When looked at in this way the process of adopting, or choosing not to adopt some technology begins to be seen in its true complexity, not just as a yes/no decision, but as a complex set of negotiations between a number of human and non-human actors.

6 ITEM INNOVATION RESEARCH QUESTIONS

As Smith and Wild (2001) point out, a great deal of research has been done on how technological innovation occurs. Fung (1997) notes that there is more to ITEM innovation than hardware and software, and that a process of change management is an essential factor in getting these systems accepted. It appears to me, however, that most of the research on ITEM innovation (Fung 1997; Telem and Barta 1997) does not attempt to relate this back to the established models and theories that are applied to innovation in business, but I believe that there may be value in doing so.

In an attempt to explore the usefulness of innovation theory to ITEM implementation I suggest an attempt at its application to the following research agenda:

- Why do national or local education authorities adopt (or chose not to adopt) ITEM?
    - Does the initiative come from national or regional governments wanting to make schools more accountable? (Tatnall 1995).
    - Is the situation in other countries taken into account?
    - Is what is happening in business organisations taken into account?
    - To what extent does innovation theory explain the spread of ITEM in school systems around the world? Which theory best explains this?

- In a centralised system, if an education authority has adopted ITEM (and forced its schools to adopt) to what extent is this infused into individual schools?
    - What variation occurs in levels of use and infusion?
    - Does innovation theory help to explain this? Which theory explains this best?
- In a decentralised system, why do individual schools choose to adopt or not to adopt?
    - What variation occurs in levels of use and infusion?
    - To what extent does innovation theory provide a plausible explanation?
    - Which theory offers the best explanation?

7 CONCLUSION

While some schools are forced by central education authorities to implement ITEM systems, many have to make a choice in either adopting or not adopting these systems. In this paper I have outlined two theories of technological innovation, and suggested some research questions that should be investigated.

In a research project such as an investigation of the adoption of ITEM in schools, a researcher who concentrated on the technology as the driving force, or one who ignored the affects of the technology and focus only on the human and social interactions involved would, in my view, produce a very unbalanced account. In socio-technical situations like this where the contributions of both human and non-human actors are equally important, an approach like that offered by innovation translation from actor-network theory has, I contend, much to offer. I would like to see ITEM researchers adopt a research agenda to investigate why some schools implement and infuse ITEM systems more effectively than others, and whether this differs in countries around the world.

8 REFERENCES

Berlyne, D. E. (1962). "Uncertainty and Epistemic Curiosity." *British Journal of Psychology* 53: 27-34.

Callon, M. (1986). Some Elements of a Sociology of Translation: Domestication of the Scallops and the Fishermen of St Brieuc Bay. *Power, Action & Belief. A New Sociology of Knowledge?* Law, J. London, Routledge & Kegan Paul: 196-229.

Callon, M. (1987). Society in the Making: The Study of Technology as a Tool for Sociological Analysis. *The Social Construction of Technological Systems*. Bijker, W. E., Hughes T. P. and Pinch T. P. Cambridge, Ma., The MIT Press: 85-103.

Dutch, R. A., Ed. (1962). *Roget's Thesaurus*. London, Longman.

Fung, A. C. W. (1997). Managing Change in 'ITEM'. *Information Technology in Educational Management for the Schools of the Future*. Fung, A. C. W., Visscher A. J., Barta B. Z. and Teather D. C. B. London, Chapman & Hall: 37-45.

Grint, K. and Woolgar, S. (1997). *The Machine at Work - Technology, Work and Organisation*. Cambridge, Polity Press.

Latour, B. (1986). The Powers of Association. *Power, Action and Belief. A new sociology of knowledge? Sociological Review monograph 32*. Law, J. London, Routledge & Kegan Paul: 264-280.

Latour, B. (1996). *Aramis or the Love of Technology*. Cambridge, Ma, Harvard Uni Press.

Law, J. (1986). The Heterogeneity of Texts. *Mapping the Dynamics of Science and Technology*. Callon, M., Law J. and Rip A. UK, Macmillan Press: 67-83.

Law, J., Ed. (1991). *A Sociology of Monsters. Essays on power, technology and domination*. London, Routledge.

Linderoth, H. C. J. (1997). *Information Technology Infusion - Beyond Information Technology Implementation?!* Information Systems Research in Scandinavia, IRIS20 Conference, Hanko, Norway, University of Oslo.

Maguire, C., Kazlauskas, E. J. and Weir, A. D. (1994). *Information Services for Innovative Organizations*. Sandiego, CA., Academic Press.

McMaster, T., Vidgen, R. T. and Wastell, D. G. (1997). *Towards an Understanding of Technology in Transition. Two Conflicting Theories*. Information Systems Research in Scandinavia, IRIS20 Conference, Hanko, Norway, University of Oslo.

Oxford (1973). *The Shorter Oxford English Dictionary*. Oxford, Clarendon Press.

Rogers, E. M. (1995). *Diffusion of Innovations*. New York, The Free Press.

Singleton, V. and Michael, M. (1993). "Actor-Networks and Ambivalence: General Practitioners in the UK Cervical Screening Programme." *Social Studies of Science* 23: 227-264.

Smith, D. and Wild, P. (2001). The Future of School Information Systems. *Information Technology in Educational Management*. Visscher, A. J., Wild P. and Fung A. C. W. Dordrecht, The Netherlands, Kluwer Academic Publishers: 137-160.

Tatnall, A. (1995). Information Technology and the Management of Victorian Schools - Providing Flexibility or Enabling Better Central Control? *Information Technology in Educational Management*. Barta, B. Z., Telem M. and Gev Y. London, Chapman & Hall: 99-108.

Tatnall, A. (2002). Modelling Technological Change in Small Business: Two Approaches to Theorising Innovation. *Managing Information Technology in Small Business: Challenges and Solutions*. Burgess, S. Hershey, PA, Idea Group Publishing: 83-97.

Tatnall, A. and Lepa, J. (2003). "The Internet, E-Commerce and Older People: an Actor-Network Approach to Researching Reasons for Adoption and Use." *Logistics Information Management* 16(1): 56-63.

Tatnall, A. and Pitman, A. (2003). Information Technology and Control in Educational Management. *Management of Education in the Information Age: The Role of ICT*. Selwood, I., Fung A. C. W. and O'Mahony C. D. Assinippi Park, Massachusetts, Kluwer Academic Publishers / IFIP: 73-82.

Telem, M. and Barta, B. Z. (1997). Information Technology Assimilation in Schools: A Theoretical and Practical Framework. *Information Technology in Educational Management for the Schools of the Future*. Fung, A. C. W., Visscher A. J., Barta B. Z. and Teather D. C. B. London, Chapman & Hall: 9-14.

Wilson, W. G., Ed. (1970). *The Oxford Dictionary of English Proverbs*. Newton Abbot, UK, Oxford University Press.

Future Directions in ITEM Research

Arthur Tatnall and Bill Davey
with Omponoye Kereteletse, Javier Osorio, Tuulikki Paturi and Adrie Visscher

Abstract: A good deal of ITEM research has been undertaken and reported over the ten years since IFIP WG 3.7 first met. It now appears that use of ICT is becoming mature in educational management in developed countries. The same is not yet true, however, of developing countries and further research is needed to identify problems faced by these countries. Much past research in school implementations of ITEM systems has made use of the Visscher model, but the group thought that this model now needed some updating. This paper outlines these issues and points to several future directions for ITEM research.

Key words: Educational management, information technology, research.

1 INTRODUCTION

Over the ten years that the ITEM working group has been meeting since the Jerusalem conference a good deal of ITEM research has been undertaken and reported. This paper outlines what the above focus group saw as useful future directions for ITEM research. It begins with an outline of recently reported ITEM research, and research directions identified in this.

It appears that the use of information and communications technologies (ICT) is becoming mature in educational management, and that what is now required is the identification of what is 'good management in education': case studies of lighthouse schools and educational managers. Another area of interest identified by the group was the implementation of ITEM systems in developing countries, and whether cross-cultural factors are of significance. ITEM systems have been implemented in educational institutions of all types, and research can usefully be undertaken for each of the following:

- Government primary schools.
- Government secondary schools.

- Non-government (independent) schools.
- Universities and other institutes of higher education.
- Central education systems vs. decentralized education systems.
- Developing vs. developed countries.

Visscher's model (1995) for the implementation of ITEM systems in schools has been referenced by a number of papers over the years, but the group felt that it was now time to attempt an explanation of these results in an attempt to move towards cause and effect. Another identified avenue of future research relates to the adoption of ITEM systems: to what degree are they actually used and infused into individual schools? Also, what can we learn from business management practice in the use of computers? The remainder of this paper explores these issues and outlines an ITEM research agenda for the future.

2 PREVIOUS ITEM RESEARCH

A good deal of ITEM research has already been done, particularly as related to the use of ITEM systems in schools. Application of the Visscher model (Visscher 1995) to ITEM implementations in schools has been an important direction here. Recent research in use of ICT in educational management includes a number of strong themes. These include:

- Use of models to determine the factors of successful use of information systems (Fung 1995), (Fung and Visscher 2001), (Visscher 2001), (Visscher, Wild, Smith and Newton 2003), (O'Mahony 2000), (Stevenson 1997), (Visscher and Bloeman 1999).
- The factors involved in ICT in schools in developing countries (Aguti 2002), (Bisaso 2003), (Kereteletswe and Selwood 2003), (Riggs 1964).
- The ICT support needs of school managers (Haughey 2003), (Fulmer and Frank 1997), (Tatnall and Davey 1995).
- Change management strategies for implementing ICT in school management (O'Mahony 2002), (Selwood, Smith and Wisehart 2000).
- Applications of adoption models to uptake of ICT in school management (Cox, Preston and Cox 1999), (Mumtaz 2000), (Fung 1997).
- Strategies for developing and extending information systems in educational management (Lawrence Shah and Golder 1997), (Tatnall 2001), (Kirkman 2000), (Smith and Wild 2001)

- Evaluation of the effects of ICT system use by managers (Newton and Visscher 2003), (Visscher 1995), (Tatnall 1995), (Tatnall and Pitman 2003), (Telem and Barta 1997).
- Interactions between web based educational delivery systems and new management requirements (Baker 2003), (Alavi 1994), (Althaus 1997), (Webster and Hackley 1997), (Song Singleton and Hill 2004), (Okamoto 2001), (Okamoto, Cristea and Kayama 2000), (Kayama and Okamoto 2002).
- Quality requirements for the use of ICT in educational management (Roffe 2002).
- Issues relating to primary schools.
- Issues relating to teacher education.
- Special issues relating to Universities (Bates 2000), (Davey and Tatnall 2003), (Lieblein 2000), (McGorry 2003), (Pond 2001).

3 DEVELOPING NATIONS: IMPLEMENTATION AND USE OF ITEM SYSTEMS IN SCHOOLS

Most developed countries now have in place some form of ITEM system for use in school education, and there was discussion on how developing countries might be able to benefit from the collected experience of these countries. The basic research question asked was: "What should an educational administrator in a developing country be advised to do next in relation to implementation of ITEM systems?"

One important issue that should be researched, for each country, concerns the alignment of information and communications technologies with the business directions determined by the Ministry of Education, and what processes are available for determining this alignment. This could be informed by research into what is best practice in determining ITEM priorities in other countries, and what are the methods best suited to avoiding producing systems that will not meet the needs of *all* their potential users. The hope is that this research will point towards a determination of implementation strategies that are best suited to developing countries.

Another interesting research question identified was: how does government structure influence the direction of ITEM development? Related to this are issues of centralized versus decentralized education systems and how these structures affect the development and implementation of ITEM systems for schools. In recent years most developed countries studied have moved towards, or are moving towards, decentralized education systems. As many developing countries have at present retained more centralized systems we might question how decisions get made in such highly centralized government structures. A research question might then be framed in relation to the degree of centralization and how this affects implementation of ITEM systems.

4 UNIVERSITY VS SCHOOL ITEM SYSTEMS

Although much ITEM research in the past has related to school education, an increasing amount of research on university (and other higher and further education) ITEM systems has now been embarked on by members of the ITEM working group. To link research in these areas, the first research question we should ask is: how do university and school ITEM systems differ? The answer to this question might seem obvious, and some aspects of it are, but the important issue is one of identifying how, or whether, ITEM research on school-based systems can be related to ITEM research on university systems. Are there any common issues relating to both types of ITEM system? Are there any common problems? If the answer to these questions is found to be 'no', then these will have to proceed as two related but independent lines of research. On the other hand if the answer is 'yes' then the challenge will be to make use of some of the school-based research in investigating university ITEM systems.

Little has been written in case study form about university ITEM systems either. A first step in researching these systems will be to ask questions like: what is the experience? Are these systems typically developed on-site by the university? How many are vendor supplied? Are vendor solutions inevitably flawed? How much do the administrative processes of an individual institution affect their ITEM needs?

Another research question that some of the group members have been recently researching is: are any of these ITEM systems designed to assist teaching and learning as well as providing administrative data? Preliminary research suggests that mainly they are designed only for administrative use, and it seems that there is a missed opportunity here to make better use of data that has been already collected. Further research is needed on this topic.

5 IMPROVEMENTS TO THE VISSCHER MODEL

The group noted that the Visscher model (1995) has been used by a number of researchers as a starting point for conceptualizing the design and implementation of ITEM systems. Members of the group, however, thought that further development of the model was needed to improve its usefulness. The model has identified correlations between factors and use, and these can be used as starting points to investigate more detail for further developing the model. Other suggested improvements to the model include:

- Training qualities: how can the model be improved to consider the effectiveness of different strategies for training?
- What change management strategies are best suited to the education environments?
- What are the components needed to provide local support of ITEM systems?
- A number of support strategies are available: central call centre, local support, etc. Which of these is the most effective?

6 ADOPTION AND INFUSION OF ITEM SYSTEMS

Purchasing and installing an ITEM system is of little value to an educational institution if this system is not used to the full. This raises the issue of *infusion* or level of use. If an information system has become an indispensable part of an organization's operations then it is said to be highly infused into that organization. Research is needed to find out in which countries ITEM systems are highly infused into schools, and in which they are merely peripheral to daily operations.

Adoption of an ICT into any organisation implies not just its purchase and installation, but also its use. The best way to frame research on ITEM adoption appears to be by making use of innovation theory as these systems must be seen as innovations. One interesting line of research could involve seeing how different groups make use of their ITEM systems, and the factors that influenced them to choose these uses.

7 OTHER ITEM RESEARCH QUESTIONS

A number of other ITEM research questions were also identified from across a range of topics. Firstly, in relation to cross-cultural issues:

- What methods are available to tackle cross-cultural research in ITEM systems?
- How do we identify cultural vs. global factors in ITEM adoption?
- Comparison of geographically similar societies.

Comments were made on the issue of IT managers in schools, and their backgrounds – some are teachers with some time-release for doing this job while others are ICT professionals who bring quite a different outlook. One question here is: are school ICT managers going to be taken from the pool of teachers in the future? What steps should be taken by management to provide the best support? How should we assess the performance of educational management? Along similar lines, is there a change in the nature of ICT support staff to handle ITEM systems?

Another set of question are: do ITEM systems add value and how do we measure their value and quality? Do we use measures of return on investment (ROI), efficiency and effectiveness, the school being better able to meet its aims, or resulting in better decision making? What are the uses for information at a high level of educational management? In some countries, educational managers use system information to rank teachers and to provide rewards for staff. A framework to set out these measures needs to be developed.

Regarding ITEM development, research could be undertaken to find out if development size matters and the best ways of evaluating the potential of vendor ITEM systems (particularly for university-level ITEM). Are the needs of users being sufficiently considered? Are these systems achieving all that is possible, and what is going to make them better? It was noted that in many cases, more important than money and culture is the political will to implement these systems.

8 CONCLUSIONS: THE NEXT STEP

In summary, we need to look at previous ITEM research to see how we can make use of this for planning future research. The Visscher model has been useful in the past but now needs to be adapted to meet changing requirements. Cross-cultural factors will be a fruitful area of future research as will the implementation of ITEM systems in developing countries. Seeing ITEM systems as innovations, and investigating their adoption and use using innovation theory is another important research direction.

We still, however, do not know enough about what is actually being done in relation to use of ITEM in educational institutions. What is best practice? What constitutes good use of ITEM systems? What are the flagship uses of computers in educational management at the school principal level? A combination of qualitative and quantitative research approaches is called for. We need to identify lighthouse examples of the use of computers in educational management and also example of good managers who use this technology.

9 REFERENCES

Aguti, J.N. (2002). Facing up the challenge of UPE in Uganda through Distance Teacher Education programmes. Paper presented at Pan Commonwealth Forum on Open Learning: Open Learning: Transforming Education for development. Durban, South Africa.

Alavi, M. (1994). Computer–mediated collaborative learning: An empirical evaluation. *MIS Quarterly, 18(2),* 159 – 174.

Althaus, S. (1997). Computer-mediated communication in the university classroom: An experiment in on-line discussions. *Communication Education, 46,* 158 – 174.

Baker, R. (2003), A Framework for Design and Evaluation of Internet-Based Distance learning Courses: Phase One – Framework Justification, Design and Evaluation, *Online Journal of Distance Learning Administration, VI*(11). Retrieved September 15, 2003 from http://www.westga.edu/%7Edistance/ojdla/summer62/summer62.html

Bates, A. W. (2000). *Managing technological change: Strategies for college and university leaders*. San Francisco: Jossey-Bass.

Bisaso, R. (2003). Computerised School Information Systems Usage in the Administration and Management of Secondary Schools in Uganda: An Exploratory Study, University of Twente, Faculty of Behavioural Sciences, The Netherlands.

Cox, M., Preston, C. and Cox, K (1999*), What factors support or prevent teachers from using ICT in their classrooms?* Paper presented at the British Educational Research Association Annual Conference, University of Sussex, Brighton, November 1999.

Davey, B. and Tatnall, A. (2003). Involving the Academic: A Test for Effective University ITEM Systems. Management of Education in the Information Age: The Role of ICT. Selwood, I., Fung, A. C. W. and O'Mahony, C. D. Assinippi Park, Massachusetts, Kluwer Academic Publishers / IFIP: 83-92.

Fulmer, C. L. and Frank, F. P. (1997). Developing Information Systems for Schools of the Future. Information Technology in Educational Management for the Schools of the Future. Fung, A. C. W., Visscher, A. J., Barta, B. Z. and Teather, D. C. B. London, Chapman & Hall / IFIP: 122-130.

Fung, A. C. W. (1997). Managing Change in 'ITEM'. *Information Technology in Educational Management for the Schools of the Future*. Fung, A. C. W., Visscher A. J., Barta B. Z. and Teather D. C. B. London, Chapman & Hall: 37-45.

Fung, A.C.W. (1995). Managing change in "ITEM". In Barta, B.Z., Telem, M., & Gev, Y. (Eds.)(1995). Information technology in educational management (pp. 37-46). London: Chapman & Hall.

Fung, A. C. W. and Visscher, A. J. (2001). A Holistic View of SISs as an Innovation, and the Factors Determining Success. Information Technology in Educational Management. Visscher, A. J., Wild, P. and Fung, A. C. W. Dordrecht, The Netherlands, Kluwer Academic Publishers: 79-95.

Haughey, M. (2003). The Impact of ICT on the work of the principal. In Selwood, I.D, Fung, A.C.W., & O'Mahoney C.D. (Eds.) Management of Education in the Information Age. The Role of ICT. (Pp 63-81). London: Chapman & Hall

Kayama M. & Okamoto T. (2002) "Collaborative learning support in the internet learning space: a platform for a learning environment and knowledge management in the educational context", International Journal of Industry and Higher Education, Vol.16, No.4, pp.249-pp.259.

Kereteletswe O.C. and Selwood I.D. (2003). The Implementation of Information Technology in Educational Management in Botswana in Selwood, I.D., Fung, A.C.W., & O'Mahony C. (Eds) *Management of Education in the Information Age - The Role of ICT.* Boston: Kluwer.

Kirkman, C., (2000), "A model for the effective management of information and communications technology development in schools derived from six contrasting case studies", *Journal of IT for Teacher Education* (JITTE), V 9, No 1, 2000.

Lawrence, D. R., Shah, H. U. and Golder, P. A. (1997). Business Users and the Information Systems Development Process. *The Place of Information Technology in Management and Business Education*. Barta, B. Z., Tatnall A. and Juliff P. London, IFIP / Chapman & Hall: 118-127.

Lieblein, E. (2000). Critical factors for successful delivery of online programs. The Internet and Higher Education, 3 (3), 161-174.

McGorry, S. Y. (2003). Measuring quality in online programs. The Internet and Higher Education, 6 (2), 159-177.

Mumtaz, S (2000), "Factors affecting teachers use of information and communications technology: a review of the literature", *Journal of Information Technology for Teacher Education*, 9, 3, 2000.

Newton, L R and Visscher (2003) 'Management Systems in the Classroom.' In Selwood, I.D., Fung, A.C.W. and O'Mahony, C. D. Management of Education in the Information Age-The Role of ICT. Dordrecht: Kluwer Academic Publishers.

O'Mahony, C.D. (2002), *Managing ICT Access and Training for Educators: A Case Study*, Proceedings: Information Technology for Educational Management (ITEM2002 conference), Helsinki (Forthcoming).

O'Mahony, C.D., (2000), *The evolution and evaluation of information systems in NSW Secondary schools in the 1990s: the impact of values on information systems.* PhD Thesis (unpublished): Sydney: Macquarie University.

Okamoto, T. (2001). The Distance Ecological Model to Support Self/Collaborative Learning in the Internet Environment. Institutional Improvement through Information Technology in Educational Management. Nolan, P. Dordrecht, The Netherlands, Kluwer Academic Publishers: 21-30.

Okamoto, T., Cristea, A.I. and Kayama, M. (2000) "Towards Intelligent Media-Oriented Distance Learning and Education Environments", Proceedings of ICCE2000.

Pond, W. K. (2001). Twenty-first century education and training. Implications for quality assurance. The Internet and Higher Education, 4 (3-4), 185-192.

Riggs Fred, W. (1964) *Administration in Developing Countries: The Theory of Prismatic Society.* Boston: Houghton

Roffe, I. (2002). E-learning: engagement, enhancement and execution. Quality Assurance in Education, 10 (1), 40-50.

Selwood, I., Smith, D., Wishart, J., (2001). Supporting UK teachers through the National Grid for Learning in Nolan, P., Fung, A.C.W., & Brown, M.A. (Eds), *Pathways to Institutional Improvement with Information Technology in Educational Management.* p 159-171. Boston: Kluwer.

Smith, D. and Wild, P. (2001). The Future of School Information Systems. *Information Technology in Educational Management.* Visscher, A. J., Wild P. and Fung A. C. W. Dordrecht, The Netherlands, Kluwer Academic Publishers: 137-160.

Song, L., Singleton, E. S., Hill, J. R. & Koh, M. H. (2004). Improving online learning: student perceptions of useful and challenging characteristics. The Internet and Higher Education, 7 (1), 59-70.

Stevenson, R., (1997), *Information and Communications Technology in UK Schools: an independent inquiry* (The Stevenson Report).

Telem, M. and Barta, B. Z. (1997). Information Technology Assimilation in Schools: A Theoretical and Practical Framework. *Information Technology in Educational*

Management for the Schools of the Future. Fung, A. C. W., Visscher A. J., Barta B. Z. and Teather D. C. B. London, Chapman & Hall: 9-14.

Tatnall, A. (1995). Information Technology and the Management of Victorian Schools - Providing Flexibility or Enabling Better Central Control? Information Technology in Educational Management. Barta, B. Z., Telem, M. and Gev, Y. London, Chapman & Hall: 99-108.

Tatnall, A. (2001). Design Strategies. Information Technology in Educational Management: Synthesis of Experience, Research and Future Perspectives on Computer-Assisted School Information Systems. Visscher, A. J., Wild, P. and Fung, A. C. W. Dordrecht, The Netherlands, Kluwer Academic Publishers: 97-113.

Tatnall, A. and Davey, B. (1995). Executive Information Systems in School Management: a Research Perspective. World Conference on Computers in Education VI. WCCE'95. Liberating the Learner. Tinsley, J. D. and van Weert, T. J. London, IFIP / Chapman & Hall: 579-588.

Tatnall, A. and Pitman, A. (2003). Information Technology and Control in Educational Management. Management of Education in the Information Age: The Role of ICT. Selwood, I., Fung, A. C. W. and O'Mahony, C. D. Assinippi Park, Massachusetts, Kluwer Academic Publishers / IFIP: 73-82.

Visscher, A. J. (1995). Computer Assisted School Administration and Management: Where Are We and Where Should We Go? Information Technology in Educational Management. Barta, B.-Z., Telem, M. and Gev, Y. London, Chapman & Hall: 15-26.

Visscher A., Wild P., Smith D. and Newton L. (2003) Evaluation of the implementation, use and effects of a computerised management information system in English secondary schools. British Journal of Educational Technology, June, vol. 34, no. 3, pp. 357-366(10)

Visscher, A.J. & Bloemen, P.P.M. (1999). Evaluation and use of computer-assisted management information systems in Dutch schools. Journal of Research on Computing in Education, 32(1), 172-188

Visscher, A.J. (1995). Computer assisted school administration and management: where are we and where are we going? In Barta, B.Z., Telem, M. & Gev, Y. (Eds.) (1995). Information technology in educational management. London: Chapman & Hall.

Visscher, A.J. (2001). Computer-Assisted School Information Systems: the concepts, intended benefits, and stages of development. In Visscher, A.J., Wild, P. and Fung, A.C.W. (Eds.)(2001). Information Technology in Educational Management: Synthesis of Experience, Research and Future Perspectives on Computer-Assisted School Information Systems. Dordrecht: Kluwer.

Webster, J., & Hackley, P. (1997). Teaching effectiveness in technology-mediated distance learning. *Academy of Management Journal, 40(5),* 1282 – 1309.

Managing Distance and Lifelong Learning

Connie L. Fulmer
with Alex Fung, Ragton Mazhani, Jorge Rodriguez, Toshio Okamoto, Brian Samways, Geoff Sandy and Barbara Tatnall.

1 INTRODUCTION

The Managing Distance and Lifelong Learning Working Group focused first on how to tackle our task. The group discussed possible strategies for working on the topic and possible outcomes of each. We spent some time debating the meaning of the terms included in our charge. As we interacted with each other about our topic the following four questions emerged and guided the remainder of our conversation.

1. Who do we think will *manage* distance and lifelong learning?
2. What do we mean by the terms *distance* and *lifelong* learning and how are they related?
3. Is there a *model* or *framework* that would guide or support our discussion?
4. What *contribution* can our discussion group make to this topic?

2 WHO WILL MANAGE?

The working group quickly agreed that the management of distance and lifelong learning would depend on the conceptual perspective in play. Is the view one of the lone ranger (Bates, 2000) or that of the thousand flowers (Collis, 1999). Van Der Klink and Jochems (2004) talk about three levels of management: organizational, curricular, and individual course. However, our working group took a wider perspective. In one instance, an individual would be the best choice for managing his or her distance or lifelong learning activities. In another, while a department or working group might select an individual to manage the design, implementation, and delivery of distance or lifelong learning, the task is conducted on behalf of a small collection of individuals. The organizational level would include more than one working group and require a more complex management strategy. Those who write about this at a public administration level, managing distance and lifelong learning would need to be constructed at the community level, quite possibly linking public and private sectors. At a much larger level, a society or a country would need to plan how this management function would best be conceptualized. Therefore, the answer to the question, who will do the managing depends on the perspective of those asking the question.

3 WHAT DO WE MEAN BY 'DISTANCE' AND 'LIFELONG' LEARNING AND ARE THEY RELATED?

As the working group moved to the task of defining the terms of our charge, we struggled with the term distance learning and quite naturally wanted to change it to e-learning. We immediately tried to distinguish between face-to-face, synchronous and asynchronous, and online learning, only to realize that online learning could actually be face-to-face but at a distance.

As for lifelong learning, the working group discussed the issue that the term was like a *slogan*, a frame of mind about learning, its context, and duration for human beings. For leaders of many countries, the term lifelong learning represents a kind of cultural strategy for improving the human condition. Lifelong learning is a much broader term than distance learning and could quite possibly be an umbrella term. Some members of the working group made excellent arguments for changing the term to lifelong education (LLE). To be sure, the integration of the terms 'distance' and 'lifelong learning' illustrate the mediating effect to be experienced by both. Distance learning enhances the process of lifelong learning or education while lifelong learning readily embraces the opportunities for distance or online learning opportunities.

4 IS THERE A 'MODEL' OR 'FRAMEWORK' THAT WOULD GUIDE OR SUPPORT OUR DISCUSSION?

The working group discussed several models that might guide our work. Some focused on instructional design while others focused on assessment. However, the charge to our working group was about management, not necessarily about design or assessment. So a model of leadership might be more productive to guide our work. As the group continued to work, we found that the distributed leadership framework (Spillane, Diamond, & Halverson, 2002; Gronn, 2002) was most useful in organizing our work. The model can be simplified and conceptualized in the following terms: Actors, tools or artifacts, goals, rules, and both micro and macro tasks. Taken together and operating in an integrated fashion they create or exist within a community of practice. Each component is described below:

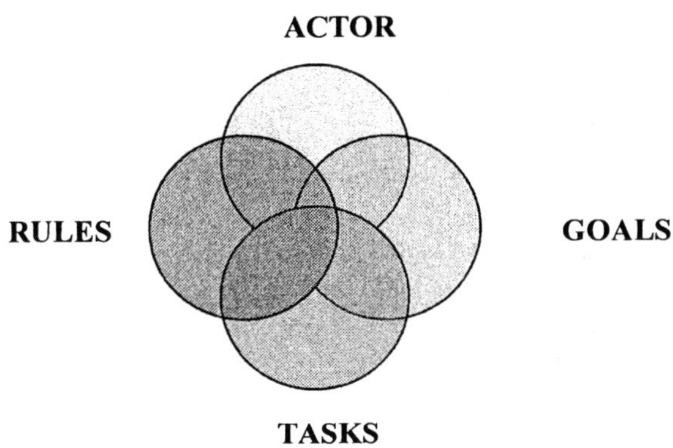

Figure 1.Distributed leadership for managing distance and lifelong learning.

ACTORS: Leadership is often distributed across multiple leaders: principals, assistant principals, curriculum specialists, reading or Title I teachers, and classroom teachers, ICT specialists, and others. Jochems, Van Merriënboer, and Koper (2004 p.xii) include additional players: Instructional designers developers of course materials, educational technologists, consultants, training department managers, faculty managers, course directors, and teachers and trainers at the post, and students in educational sciences interested in including distance or lifelong learning into the materials.

TOOLS & ARTIFACTS: Rather than treating material artifacts, tools, (e.g. curricular frameworks, teacher observation protocols) and organizational structures as backdrop for leaders' practice, we see them as defining components of that practice. The structure of the technology and the design of the learning environments do indeed impact the levels of efficiency and effectiveness of learning outcomes. In their work, Van Merrienboër, Bastiaens, and Hoogveld (2004) argue that leaders should always ask if current and technological developments enable innovative instructional methods necessary to make learning more effective, efficient and appealing.

GOALS: Goals represent the intentions of the individual or learning group and as such become the focus of purposeful activity and learning.

Krischner, Strijbnos, and Kreijns (2004) outline six design principles as well as guidelines for task ownership, task character, and task control as goals for well designed online learning environments. Their underlying assumption is that goals should view learners as self-sufficient and in control of their own learning. Other authors provide different goals. Van Der Klink and Jochems (2004) describe three types of goals. The first is substitution where the new way replaces the traditional. The second is innovation where the current pedagogical and managerial perspective is rethought. Their final type is transformation, where radical change describes the outcome. The point we are making is that no matter the goal or the quest to achieve it, the goal should be distributed through the system.

RULES: These are criteria under which the community of practice tend to operate or the cultural view of the work of the group. They are created, modified, and policed by the group.

TASKS (Macro & Micro): A task perspective provides a framework for analyzing practice that enables us to attend to the daily work of school leadership without losing sight of the big picture. Macro tasks, or large scale organizational tasks involve constructing and selling an instructional vision of distance and life-long learning; building norms of trust, collaboration, supporting teacher (and others) development and training; monitoring instruction and innovation. Micro tasks or the day-to-day work involves creating opportunities for teachers to work together; creating in-service opportunities for teachers; completing classroom observations; distinguishing formative from summative observations.

In a community of practice focused on distance and lifelong learning, the work related to the managing of such can be mediated and informed by each element of the distributed model described above.

5 RECOMMENDATIONS FROM WORKING GROUP

In the end, our working group generated the following list of recommendations from our work on managing distance and lifelong learning. Listed below is our collective contribution.

- Create and foster learning environments in which people feel motivated to learn.
- Guard against decisions based on economy at the cost of better learning systems.
- Distribute the management of distance and life long learning.
- Expect learning to take many different paths.
- Provide multiple options, strategies, venues, and opportunities for learning.

- Create entrance options for any consumer to enter learning opportunities at appropriate levels for optimal learning.
- Ensure that technology helps to individualize instruction for learners and to provide personal preference.
- Provide opportunities for self-assessment of learning or diagnostics for helping consumers select appropriate learning activities.
- The new goal is to manage learning (coach) and not just to provide content.
- Avoid being trapped in the old paradigm of one teacher to a group of students but rather seek to help individuals or groups search for information or new content to be learned. Many times traditional learning modes crush a student's spirit of learning.
- Foster students taking responsibility for their own learning.
- Create activities, policies, practices that empower parents to play a stronger role in the education of their own children.
- Focus on the ICT side and track, record, and enhance the quality of learning activities.
- Base all decisions and activities on a strong ethical foundation.

6 REFERENCES

Bates, A. W. (2000). *Managing technological change: Strategies for college and university leaders*. San Francisco: Jossey-Bass.

Collis, B. A. (1999). Implementing ICT in the faculty: Letting a 1000 flowers bloom or managing change? In M. Mirande, J. Riemersma, & W. Venn (Eds.) *De Digiatale Leeromgeving* [The electronic learning environment] (pp. 121-1260). Groningen, Netherlands: Wolters-Noordhoff.

Gronn, P. (2002). Distributed leadership. In. K. Leithwood, and P.Hallinger (Eds.), *Second International Handbook of Educational Leadership and Administration* (pp. 653-696). Dordrecht: Kluwer Academic Publishers.

Jochems, W., Van Merriënboer, J., & Koper, R. (Eds.) (2004). *Integrated e-learning: Implications for pedagogy, technology and organization*. New York: RoutledgeFalmer.

Krischner, P., Strijbnos, J-W, & Kreijns, K. (2004). Designing integrated collaborative e-learning. In W. Jochems, J. Van Merriënboer, & R. Koper (Eds.), *Integrated e-learning: Implications for pedagogy, technology and organization* (pp. 24-38). New York: Routledge Falmer.

Spillane, J. P., Halverson, R., & Diamond, J. B. (2001, April). Investigating school leadership practice: A distributed practice. *Educational Researcher, 30*(3), 23-28.

Van Der Klink, M., Jochems, W. (2004). Management and organization of integrated e-learning. In W. Jochems, J. Van Merriënboer, & R. Koper (Eds.), *Integrated e-learning:*

Implications for pedagogy, technology and organization (pp. 151-163). New York: RoutledgeFalmer.

Van Merrienboër, J., Bastiaens, T., & Hoogveld, A. (2004). Instructional design for integrated e-learning. In W. Jochems, J. Van Merriënboer, & R. Koper (Eds.), *Integrated e-learning: Implications for pedagogy, technology and organization* (pp. 13-23). New York: Routledge Falmer.